BARBARA BUSH

ALSO BY PAMELA KILIAN

Ellis Island: Gateway to the American Dream
(as Pamela Reeves)

What Was Watergate?

PAMELA KILIAN

BARBARA BUSH

MATRIARCH OF A DYNASTY

THOMAS DUNNE BOOKS
ST. MARTIN'S PRESS
NEW YORK

THOMAS DUNNE BOOKS.
An imprint of St. Martin's Press.

www.stmartins.com

Design by Kathryn Parise

Library of Congress Cataloging-in-Publication Data

Kilian, Pamela.
    Barbara Bush : matriach of a dynasty / Pamela Kilian.—1st ed.
        p. cm.
    Includes index.
    ISBN 0-312-28659-7
    1. Bush, Barbara, 1925– 2. Presidents' spouses—United States—
Biography. 3. Bush, George, 1924—Family. 4. Bush family. I. Title.

E883.B87 K56 2002
973.931'092—dc21
[B]

                                                                2001058584

First Edition: September 2002

10 9 8 7 6 5 4 3 2 1

CONTENTS

ACKNOWLEDGMENTS

Many thanks to the people who talked with me to make this book possible.

Mrs. Bush's staff and friends were quite helpful, including her White House press secretary, Anna Perez, and her post-White House aide, Brooke Sheldon.

Historians Gil Troy of McGill University in Montreal, Lewis L. Gould of the University of Texas at Austin, Ruth Mandel of Rutgers University in New Jersey, Robert Watson, a presidential scholar and author, and Myra Gutin of Rider University in New Jersey provided much insight into the Bush presidency and Barbara Bush's role in it.

Mrs. Bush's childhood companions—June Biedler, Rosanne Morgan Clarke, and Kate Siedle—provided details about her younger years while Ashley Hall friends Cordelia Stites, Shavaun Robinson Towers, Marjorie Macnutt Thurstone, Susan Estes Edgerly, Frances Baker Turnage, Miriam House, and Jane Thornhill filled me in on her later school adventures.

Thanks to Otha Taylor for her story about traveling cross-country with Mrs. Bush during the era of segregation.

Three of Mrs. Bush's close friends—Mary Ann (Andy) Stewart, Shirley Pettis Roberson, and Betsy Heminway—were very helpful, as was Becky Beach, Mrs. Bush's traveling companion during the 1980 campaign.

Thanks also to Janet Steiger, Jessica Catto, Patsy Caulkins, Pete Teeley, Edward Derwinski, and W. Tapley Bennett.

And finally, thanks to my husband, Michael Kilian, for all his help and understanding.

BARBARA BUSH

AN AMERICAN ICON

On a day of mourning, September 14, 2001, three days after terrorists destroyed the World Trade Center in New York City, Barbara Bush was among those paying their respects at the National Cathedral in Washington. Cameras caught her looking on proudly as her husband, the forty-first president of the United States, reached out to comfort their son, the forty-third.

Because of these two men and her relationship to them Barbara Bush is assured of a prominent place in history. Her four years as first lady were not especially notable, but her dual role as both mother and wife of a president is.

The only other first lady to achieve this status in America was Abigail Adams almost two centuries earlier. And as Barbara noted somewhat dryly during the 2000 Republican presidential convention, where her firstborn won nomination, there is a key difference: "I don't think she was living," she said. "I plan to be living."[1]

Abigail Adams was the wife of John Adams, the second president, and mother of John Quincy Adams, the sixth. She died at age seventy-four, seven years before her son became president. Barbara Bush was seventy-five when George W. Bush moved into the White House and was able, when he took the oath of office, to brush his cheek with a kiss, and murmur, "I am so proud of you."

These two first ladies nevertheless have much in common. Both were married at age nineteen to upper-class men of uncommon abilities and ambitions. Each spent most of her early marriage at home caring for children and both lost a child to illness.

Like John Adams, George Bush was a diplomat, congressman, and two-term vice president before winning the White House, and both men were defeated when they tried for a second term. Each suffered in the shadow of an extremely popular president—George Washington and Ronald Reagan. Adams wrote to Abigail that at his inaugural, the outgoing president still seemed triumphant, and "Methought I heard him say, 'Aye. I am fairly out, and you fairly in. See which one of us will be happiest.'"

Similarly, George Bush was so accustomed to living in Reagan's shadow that he had to be reminded—by Barbara—to respond at his inauguration when "the president" was called to speak.

John Adams lost in his bid for a second presidential term. The victor was Thomas Jefferson, a man whom Abigail Adams disliked so intensely she could hardly be civil to him. Barbara had similar feelings about Bill Clinton.

Barbara's son became president without winning the popular vote and he locked up the electoral vote only after interference by the U.S. Supreme Court. Abigail Adams's son won the presidency over Andrew Jackson without the popular vote or the needed number in the electoral college and only after interference by the U.S. House of Representatives.

Still, the Adams family legacy is outstanding in American history. John Adams was a key figure in the American Revolution. John Quincy Adams was considered intellectually ahead of his time and was the only president to serve in Congress after his term in the White House. In the House of Representatives he was known as Old Man Eloquent.

The Bush family legacy is still in the making, with George W. in the White House, his younger brother Jeb serving as governor of Florida, and Jeb's charismatic young son George P. just barely offstage. Dynasty is an idea that the family shies from, at least in public. "I don't like dynasty and legacy and all that stuff," George Bush told reporters. "The history part of it does not affect me. Nobody believes that, but it doesn't."

Ditto George W. Bush. The day his father was inaugurated in 1989, *The Washington Post* asked if he and other members of the family were feeling a sense of history. "History?" he said. "I don't think so. I didn't feel it."[2]

Barbara Bush, whose ancestors include another president—Franklin Pierce—says she has no interest in dynasty building either. But her attitudes tell another story. She grew up at a time and place—Westchester County, New York, in the 1940s—where class and good breeding often led to success and a degree of prominence in society. She had every reason to think that she would have a place in this tradition, and a fortuitous marriage put her into the history books.

It's too soon to tell how history will judge her performance during her four years as first lady. She may suffer by comparison to both her immediate predecessor and her successor, each of whom had eight years on center stage at the White House and both of whom were compelling and controversial figures on their own.

Nancy Reagan was an actress who brought a lot of Hollywood glamour along with her to Washington. While she had many critics, the nation was fascinated with her clothes, her spending, her friends, her personality, and her husband, Mrs. Reagan ranks at the bottom of current-day polls among historians, who judge first ladies on their effectiveness, primarily because she broke one of the golden rules of first ladydom—don't cause controversies that reflect badly on the White House. But some historians now say that Mrs. Reagan will rise in the polls since it is becoming clear she had a major influence on her husband's decisions on nuclear disarmament.

Hillary Clinton set a new standard for presidential wives. Better educated than any previous first lady—and most presidents—she held a law degree from Yale and already had substantial experience in politics when she married Bill Clinton. Her desire to take part in decision making along with the president challenged tradition and led to a lot of criticism. But she left the White House on a triumphant note, winning a place for herself in the United States Senate while she was still first lady. Even though she caused trouble for the president, historians admire her because she was so actively involved in policy.

Barbara was more popular with the American public than either Nancy Reagan or Hillary Clinton. That was in large part because she carefully avoided controversy, taking few public positions on the issues of her time while she was in the White House. Her witty manner, white hair, and rounded figure made her seem more approachable than any other recent first lady. Women could imagine having a cup of coffee with Barbara Bush or living next door to her in a comfortable suburban community. Not so Nancy Reagan or Hillary Clinton.

This performance was all the more remarkable because, while Barbara Bush is warm and funny, she also is frosty, imperious, and snobbish, and she carries a grudge. She has said somewhat archly that while she could sit down and have coffee with just about anyone, she is comfortable dining with the Queen of England as well. She will freeze out anyone who does damage to her husband or sons. She remembers who offered early support and who didn't. She has a streak of bitterness that came rampaging to the fore during the unsuccessful 1992 campaign.

"I actually think that Barbara Bush pulled off a bit of a feat because my sense is that her personality is a lot less warm and cuddly and grand-motherly than her image," said presidential historian Gil Troy, a professor of American history at McGill University in Montreal and author of *Mr. and Mrs. President*. "The image that she transmitted to the American peo-ple was exactly what the American people wanted, especially after Nancy Reagan. Especially after the glitzy eighties and the decadent seventies and the rebellious sixties, they wanted a kind of a reassuring, upbeat traditional presence in the White House and Barbara Bush gave them that.

"And the fact that there's a gap between who she appeared to be and who she was is almost more of a compliment to her skills than what she did. She helped the American people look to the White House as a source of stability, as a bastion of tradition . . . and I think that was quite an ac-complishment."

Troy thinks, however, that history will not rank Barbara Bush as high as the public does today because historians "often look for a kind of ac-tivist agenda," which Mrs. Bush did not have.

Eleanor Roosevelt, a partner with FDR in much that he did, is almost always at the top of first-lady lists, ranking first or second in the Gallup poll of Most Admired Women every year from 1948 to 1961, and also topping surveys among historians. She was an upper-class activist who befriended the poor and brought working-class women home for dinner.

Some of them, her mother-in-law noted acidly, drank from the finger bowls.

Barbara Bush was sometimes measured against Eleanor Roosevelt but objected to comparisons because she grew up in a Republican household where the outspoken Eleanor was much disliked. During the 1992 campaign, Barbara was asked where she would put herself between Bess Truman on one side and Eleanor Roosevelt on the other. "I always thought Bess Truman was terrific," she said. "I got ridiculed for that once, but she was a great wife. So was Eleanor Roosevelt. . . . I think I'm half Eleanor, half Bess. I think I go out and do a lot of things. I do lots of traveling and a lot of programs. . . . I really stay out of government business if I possibly can."[3]

In reality, though, Barbara was not much like either Bess Truman, who withdrew from Washington and left Harry in the White House alone during the darkest days of World War II, or Eleanor Roosevelt, who spoke comfortingly to the public before Franklin did after the Japanese attacked Pearl Harbor. Against the Roosevelt model, Barbara Bush's accomplishments pale, in the view of most historians.

"I don't think she left a legacy of leadership in her own right," said Ruth Mandel, director of the Eagleton Institute of Politics at Rutgers University in New Jersey. "She will be remembered as someone who had a certain kind of wit, a sense of humor, was nobody's fool, would let her feelings be known in a way that people found witty or sometimes endearing. So I think she'll be known more as a personality than as a leader . . . Barbara Bush did not use the role to do anything new."

Troy agrees with that assessment but thinks that many historians and the media have the wrong ideas about what a first lady should be.

"A first lady like Barbara Bush who was universally beloved by the American people, who did not embarrass her husband, who reached out not only to proper white-gloved, blue-haired Republican ladies but also in her famous Wellesley speech, to a new generation—someone like that is going to get less high marks and less kudos because it's the 'wrong model,' " Troy said. "But sometimes I think that academics are focused on the wrong model and not on looking at what the American people say they want."

Robert Watson, presidential scholar and author of *The Presidents'* *s, thinks Barbara will be ranked among the top ten on first-lady lists far into the future, primarily because she was so popular. His own poll of presidential and first-lady scholars, taken in 1996 and 1997, put Barbara nineteenth on a list of thirty-nine first ladies. A poll by Siena College of New York, taken in 1993, ranked Barbara eighth.

"I think she'll be remembered for these wonderful quips, so straight-talking, so witty and so straightforward," Watson said. "In a day and age when politicians and their spouses are holding their fingers to the wind of public opinion, Barbara Bush was a breath of fresh air. She was straight-talking, she was herself, she was comfortable in her own skin."

Historians differ on whether Barbara will be pulled down in the historical rankings by her husband, a one-term president whose time in office was notable for little more than the Gulf War.

"In some ways, the reputation of the first lady tracks the reputation of the president," says Lewis Gould, retired history professor at the University of Texas and editor of *American First Ladies.*

"I think being wedged between Reagan and Clinton it's a high probability that this is going to be one of those administrations that will be seen as a transitional one, which is the kiss of death. That will probably mean that Barbara Bush will not be seen [to be] as interesting as she might have been. In fact it may be that her real historical significance will be seen as more the mother of George W. Bush than as the wife."

Mandel noted that sometimes a legacy depends on "the moment in history" when a first lady is in the spotlight. Laura Bush, for example, came into office determined to stay in the background and that's what she did for the first six months in the White House. But after the terrorist attacks on September 11, 2001, she became far more active and took on the role of national comforter. "The times have created a situation in which she has begun to play a role that could very well end up making her a very important first lady, who found a way to be a voice of influence and even leadership that we don't know yet," Mandel said. "It's been fascinating to see her emerge and develop a public persona that was contrary to the expectations that she herself had set up for the public."

Both Barbara and George Bush have carefully avoided detracting attention from George W. and Laura since he won election. While father and son talk often by phone, the advice is always private. Whatever Barbara may say to her son and daughter-in-law is also behind closed doors. And Laura has developed a style in office distinctly different from Barbara's. "One senses between Laura and Barbara Bush, these two very strong personalities have learned how to deal with each other and how to create zones of their own competence," Troy say. "One senses Barbara Bush's presence as a matriarch but also one doesn't really sense her presence in the White House."

Laura had a shorter and easier path to the White House than Barbara, going through just one losing campaign and spending two terms as the first lady of Texas. She married George W. Bush after he was already well established.

The path to the White House for Barbara started when she was nineteen and in love with a handsome and very ambitious young man who took her from the comforts of suburban New York City to the flat, unattractive plains of Texas and often left her at home alone for days at a time with a house full of young children while he was out in the oil fields seeking his fortune. But there were many young families in a similar situation and they fell into an informal camaraderie that Barbara still recalls fondly.

When the oil business improved, the Bushes moved to Houston and their political life began. First, George won at the county level and later became a congressman, which entailed a move to Washington. Barbara made a lot of friends in the capital but also suffered a serious six-month depression while George was head of the CIA.

"I think when you go back to her breakdown, her crisis moment, I think that comes from her feeling neglected by her husband or by his career," historian Gil Troy says. "I think some of the things she talks about in her memoirs, the peppery little stories she would often tell about George Bush and his career, it was very clear that she was in the role of the caretaker. That put her subordinate to George Bush and there were definitely frustrations there."

An unsuccessful run for the presidency in 1980 nevertheless left George and Barbara with a win of sorts—he became vice president, a job he held for eight years. Barbara was in the shadows during that time, not unhappily but definitely kept out of the limelight most of the time by Nancy Reagan. When Nancy drew up a guest list for a dinner honoring Prince Charles and Princess Diana, George and Barbara Bush were not among those invited. An aide protested, saying that would be a breach of protocol. "Just watch me," Nancy replied.[4]

By the time she got to the White House, Barbara was ready for the spotlight, and somewhat surprised by how much she enjoyed it. "Part of the fun of the White House was that she came into her own," Troy said. "You take the eight years when Bush was vice president and she was not only playing second fiddle to George Bush's career but also watching her and her husband get often shunted aside and then quite dramatically dissed by Nancy Reagan. I think those four years in the sun where she really came into her own were quite wonderful and quite empowering for her."

Once she got to the White House, Barbara became a symbol for the millions of women who put home and family first, whether or not they held jobs in the paid workforce. Her easy relationship with her five children and fourteen grandchildren delighted a nation that had become accustomed over eight years to the sad alienation between Ronald and Nancy Reagan and their children.

Despite an upper-middle-class childhood, Barbara managed to convey a down-to-earth image, much in contrast to the Beverly Hills style that Nancy Reagan cultivated. After the Bushes had been in the White House a little more than a year, the Ikea furniture store, makers of inexpensive do-it-yourself Scandinavian styles, ran an advertisement on the sides of buses in Washington: "Nancy Reagan style at Barbara Bush prices."

Despite her grandmotherly image—"I always say she was Mrs. Santa Claus. She even looked like her," says historian Robert Watson—Barbara has her hair styled regularly and wears designer clothes. But when she was in the White House, she didn't dwell on fashion. She said early on that she was a size 14, had a tendency to gain weight, and wore fake pearls to cover up the wrinkles in her neck. She said she had no plans to dye her white hair or to get a facelift. "I'm so old now that I don't have to pretend to be something I'm not," she said shortly after becoming first lady when she was sixty-four years old.

During inauguration week, the Kennedy Center held a salute to her and she appeared on stage looking great—hair nicely styled, perfect makeup, and wearing a blouse that matched the jacket lining of her periwinkle suit. She turned around slowly, model style, and told the audience,

"Please notice: hairdo, makeup, designer dress. Look at me good this week because it's the only week of my life you're ever going to see it."

When she was invited to speak at the Alfred E. Smith fund-raising dinner in New York that year, she used the occasion to poke fun at herself. "It's not easy being the wife of the president," she said. "Last Sunday a reader of *Parade* magazine wrote in with one of those burning questions. . . . She wrote, 'I would like to know how much Barbara Bush weighs,' and they answered it. *Parade* magazine says I weigh between one hundred and thirty-five and one hundred and forty pounds. George said, 'The press never gets anything right.' Just for starters, I was born weighing one hundred and thirty-five pounds."

Half the women in America identified with this kind of humorous self-put-down—"My mail tells me a lot of fat, white-haired, wrinkled ladies are tickled pink"—and Barbara's looks and wardrobe ceased to be a primary topic of conversation.

Like many people, Barbara grew in the White House. She became more skilled in public speaking, in deflecting questions she didn't want to answer, and in using her high profile to showcase people and causes she cared about.

During the Persian Gulf War when the threat of terrorists kept many Americans from flying, she took a commercial jet to visit military families in Indianapolis. She said she wanted to show people that the skies were safe. Public officials did the same thing in 2001 after the air attack on the World Trade Center.

Shortly after Barbara became first lady, she visited Grandma's House, a home for abandoned babies with AIDS. When she picked up one of the infants and cuddled it, the picture ran in newspapers across the country. The message was clear. It's okay to get close to someone with AIDS; the disease isn't easily spread. The effect on Grandma's House was overwhelming. Money and volunteers came pouring in. A later visit to a hospital in Harlem got similar results.

When Washington malls decided to end a long-standing tradition and ban the Salvation Army bell ringers at Christmas, Barbara made a point of going to a mall and dropping in money, telling the startled bell ringer, "I'm a great fan of the Salvation Army." Some malls relented after that, allowing the bell ringers back in.

Her best-known work has been on behalf of literacy, a subject she was drawn to because one of her four sons, Neil, has dyslexia, a disorder that makes reading difficult. "Both George and I were brought up to feel that we were very lucky and we ought to give back to society," she said. "And knowing that George was going to run for national office, I spent a whole summer thinking about what would help the most people possible. And it suddenly occurred to me that every single thing I worry about—things like teenage pregnancies, the breakup of families, drugs, AIDS, the homeless— everything would be better if people could read, write, and understand."

Barbara also did a lot of volunteer work during the eight years George Bush was vice president, and she sought out people whose work she admired, and told them so. In the fall of 1988, shortly before the presidential election, she telephoned Calvin Woodland, who worked with troubled youths in Washington. She had read about his work in the newspaper and invited him to lunch to discuss it. Woodland was surprised to learn that he was one of only two guests at the lunch, the other being George Kettle, active in an organization that provided scholarships to needy students.

"The things we talked about weren't some questions she thought she should ask me because I was a black person," Woodland said. "She had read about the things I had been doing with kids and youth in the community. She told me not to give up, that people do know what is going on and they care about people like me."[5]

Despite all her years in the public eye and the cutting wit she often directs at others, Barbara herself is thin-skinned and can't stand it when criticism is directed at her husband or sons. During campaigns, she often stops reading newspapers and watching television because they make her too angry. When George Bush lost to Clinton in 1992, she lashed out at the press, at people in the White House who gave anonymous quotes— "those cheapskates"—and at longtime Bush aide James Baker, blaming him in part for the campaign loss.

She also became more political that year in an effort to salvage a failing campaign, a posture that cast her in a less positive light.

"I think she didn't really put a foot wrong in terms of flaps or controversy almost until the Republican convention of 1992," said historian Lewis Gould. "She began to be seen as more of a partisan and I think that took some of the edge off of the grandmotherly reputation she had so carefully cultivated. But before it could do real damage to her reputation, the presidency was over.

"If he had pulled it out, I think it would have been a much more difficult period for her because she wouldn't have been simply the grandmotherly successor of Nancy Reagan but would have faced questions from the press about, 'Is literacy all there is,' that kind of thing. She didn't want her husband to lose, but for her reputation, she kind of escaped unscathed."

Troy thinks the fact that Barbara remained popular even during the 1992 recession and "the terrible campaign," is a tribute to her skills. "The fact that years later she remains very popular is a real tribute to her emergence into the sunlight after also many years of being upstaged and pushed aside by her husband, or feeling pushed aside by her husband," he said.

Barbara could have taken some satisfaction at that point in the knowledge that she was helping the campaign with her popularity, and indeed was more popular by far than the president. "The public doesn't vote for a first lady but the first lady can help prop up a president's popularity. It can help firm up support and I think that was the case with Barbara," historian Watson says. "What goodwill he had in the end, a lot of it came from Barbara. Barbara was more popular than him."

Barbara said over and over during the campaign that it wasn't fair to compare her popularity with the president's because he had to make all the hard decisions, which gained him enemies. Years later, when she analyzed the election, she said one reason Bush lost was that the press told Americans the economy was bad "when it really wasn't." Also, Bush was at a disadvantage generationally with Clinton, she said, and the world had changed: since communism was no longer a big threat, Bush's greatest strength—foreign policy—became less valuable.[6]

Barbara also touts her own success but in an indirect way. When her memoirs were published in 1994 she was asked how she saw herself compared with the more activist Hillary Clinton. "I think you don't get the report card . . . until the four years are over and I'd be interested to know who accomplishes the most," she said. "I feel very good about the Literacy Act of 1991, which was my major interest and the different things . . . having to do with education, which I don't take credit for but I worked hard on."

She said she sees the role of first lady much as Lady Bird Johnson did and quoted from Johnson's memoirs: "If your project is useful and people notice it and that reflects well on your husband . . . heavens, that's one of your biggest roles in life."[7]

Such a role, says historian Troy, is just what most Americans want from their first lady.

"I look at the role of the first lady as part of a joint image-making project with the president in the modern world," he says. "What Americans want to see is the wife of the president involved in tone setting, in setting an example involved in reassuring the nation when necessary and more broadly kind of helping to set a kind of vision. . . . That's not necessarily my reading of what the ideal role of what the first lady should be, but my sense of what the American people have said to public opinion polls.

"They want the first lady there as a kind of reinforcer of the president's image and message but not someone going off the reservation and marching to the beat of her own drum."

Barbara Bush never did wander off the reservation. She was taught from an early age to play a proper role and neither the revolutionary changes in the 1960s nor her years in the public spotlight have changed that. She still takes great pride in being George Bush's wife and the mother of five children.

On the other hand, she herself has become an American icon, one of the most popular first ladies of the twentieth century, and she is the force behind a growing political dynasty. This is her story.

2

RYE BEGINNINGS

Barbara Pierce grew up in the comfortable upper-middle-class New York City suburbs. She lived in Rye, a fashionable town in Westchester County, the third of four children.

June Biedler, a childhood friend of Barbara's, described the suburb in those years: "Rye was a small town and although it was certainly a snobby town, it was not one of big estates. People lived in a relatively modest sort of way."

Barbara's father, Marvin, had been a big man on campus at Miami University in Ohio. He was captain of the football team, a top tennis player and an excellent all-around sportsman. He graduated summa cum laude, then went on to earn degrees in architectural engineering from Harvard and the Massachusetts Institute of Technology. When Barbara was born—June 8, 1925—Marvin was working his way up the ladder at McCall Publishing Company. Twenty years later, in 1946, he became president of the firm and eventually was named publisher.

Marvin Pierce was a descendent of the fourteenth president of the United States, Franklin Pierce, but Barbara said her family did not dwell on its famous relative. "The only thing I remember about him was years ago as a child, reading that he was one of our weakest presidents," she said. "I was humiliated."

Marvin's family owned an iron foundry in Sharpsville, Pennsylvania, and had been wealthy. But in 1893, the year he was born, there was a crash in the iron market and the family never recovered financially. Marvin met Pauline Robinson, three years his junior, when she was a student at Oxford College in Ohio. She was a campus beauty and the daughter of an Ohio supreme court justice. They married in 1918. Their first child, Martha, was born in 1920, and their second, James, nineteen months later. Barbara came along three and a half years later and remained the baby of the family for five years until Scott was born in 1930.

The Pierces lived in a three-story, five-bedroom brick house with a garage, set among large trees on a quarter-acre lot. It was luxurious for the times but the family of six and their live-in servants, a Chinese husband and wife, filled the space to capacity.

Barbara looked up to her pretty older sister, squabbled with James, and doted on young Scott, who was in and out of hospitals for years, suffering from a cyst in the bone marrow of his shoulder. Years later Barbara can still recall how unhappy she was when her mother devoted more attention to her sick son than to her younger daughter.

"My mother, I'm sure, was tired and irritable and I didn't understand at the time," she said. "But I guess I felt neglected that she didn't spend as much time on me. She had this enormous responsibility, which I was never sympathetic about. Now, as a mother and a grandmother, I realize what she was going through."[1]

Even after Scott recovered, though, Barbara remained much closer to her father than to her mother. She remembers Pauline as a beautiful but humorless woman, a joiner of clubs and a top-notch gardener—she was conservation chairman of the Garden Clubs of America.

Kate Siedle, a childhood friend of Barbara's, recalls Pauline being much involved with her own interests. "She spent more time in the garden than in the kitchen," Ms. Siedle said. "A lot of the mothers weren't all that motherly, let's put it that way. They had household help and they were social. They had their own little social world."

June Biedler remembered Mrs. Pierce as "very sweet but very austere. One was always afraid of her." She fondly recalled, however, that at Barbara's birthday parties, Pauline "would always have either chocolate souffle or lemon souffle."

Barbara herself also had some fond memories of her mother, especially the holiday joys she created. "My mother was a big Christmas person," she said. "In my house, on Christmas Eve we hung our stockings by the chimney with care and my daddy read a story to us. We went to bed and awoke to a wonderland."

Of course, her parents were up all night creating it, and Barbara said her mother advised her years later, "Don't you ever do that. Your father and I were irritable all Christmas Day."[2]

Pauline passed on to Barbara her love of gardening, the hands-on, in-the-dirt type, and also of needlepoint. But Barbara ran a different kind of household. She recalled that her childhood home was full of fine antiques and crystal so that "every time you turned around you knocked a piece of Chinese export off the table." Her own houses have been designed to accommodate five rambunctious children and a slew of grandchildren. Pauline and her daughter also shared a love of dogs. Pauline's dog often had puppies, which were kept in the parental bathroom, a fact that delighted the children but not the husband.

Barbara had her own dog, Sandy, who appeared with her in a picture that Mrs. Pierce sent to the young George Bush during her daughter's courtship.

Barbara Bush's fondness for animals is well-known and has been a big boon to charity. When George Bush was vice president, she wrote a book about the family's cocker spaniel, *C. Fred's Story*. It sold fifteen thousand copies, and the profits went to two national literacy groups, Laubach Literacy Action and Literacy Volunteers of America. When C. Fred died, he was replaced by Millie, who went on to become First Dog. Barbara wrote her story as well and *Millie's Book* was on the national best-seller list for months.

From her father Barbara inherited a sense of fun, a sharp wit, and love of sports. She romped in her brothers' tree house and learned to swim and play competitive tennis at the Manursing Island Club on Long Island Sound.

As she recalled it, her father always took her side. "I think because Mother never took my side." Her girlhood friends remember Marvin Pierce being warm and welcoming to children while his wife was cold and unapproachable.

Barbara credits her father with the philosophy she used to raise her own children. "He used to say that children should be given lots of love and be shown good examples, in addition to being taught honesty and to follow the work ethic."

A fond memory of childhood involved an unusual aspect of her father's job. "My dad commuted to New York and he didn't bring his business home with him," Barbara said. "I knew nothing about the publishing business, but I grew up with McCall's pattern books because we waited for the outdated one. He brought it home and we cut out new dolls every year. All my little friends made dresses for them. We'd put them on cardboard and we had our little families and put clothes on them. With that big McCall's pattern book, I was the envy of the neighborhood."[3]

Barbara had several close friends throughout childhood, all about the same age and living within two blocks of one another—June Biedler, Rosanne "Posy" Morgan Clarke, Kate Siedle, Lucille Schoolfield, and Joan Herman. They liked to play make-believe—Lucille enjoyed being Lady Rosanne—and they spent a lot of time playing dress-up in their parents' clothes.

"We acted through the Louisa May Alcott books," said June Biedler, who eventually went on to earn a Ph.D., "and we did a lot of reading." Among their favorites was Hugh Walpole and his "Rogue Harry" series and the love poetry of both Rupert Brooke and Lawrence Hope, a woman who published under a man's name.

"We were around seven, when the poetry reading started," Dr. Biedler said. "We didn't understand it, but we knew it was a somewhat kind of dirty adult sort of thing."

The girls also climbed trees and played football with the neighborhood boys and got into "mean" games of croquet. "We played with partners and we had a lot of fun playing it," Ms. Siedle said.

"We were a very close-knit group because we all lived on the same block or parallel streets," Dr. Biedler said. She described Lucille as "the gang leader," a girl who was a year or two older than the others and who had boy cousins besides. It was Lucille who told the others that there was no Santa Claus and, when the time came, about "birds-and-bees type things."

But it was Barbara who caused mischief among the friends, especially during the fourth and fifth grade. June Biedler and Posy Morgan Clarke both remember the sting when Barbara decided that she and the others would not speak to someone in the group that day.

"She would determine who was speaking to whom when we got on the bus together," Dr. Biedler said. "It would be all planned, nobody's going to talk to June this morning. You'd sit there on the bus with your friends and no one spoke to you. Dreadful feeling."

"She'd call ahead and say, 'We're not going to speak to June this morning,'" Posy Clarke said. "Or she'd call June, and say, 'We're not going to speak to Posy.'"

Barbara also zeroed in on weakness. "She could make fun of you and, since I stammered, that was one of her delights," Dr. Biedler said. "She was sort of the leader bully. We were all pretty afraid of her because she could be sarcastic and mean. She was clever, never at a loss for what to say—or what not to say."

Posy Clarke remembered "just absolutely being aghast; 'What have I done?'" when the freeze treatment was turned on her. "She was a very strong personality as you can plainly see, and I think she was practicing her skills on us."

The hurt from those early humiliations lingered long enough that Dr. Biedler mentioned them to Barbara Bush years later when they had lunch together. Barbara confessed that she had been pretty nasty and "she was sweet about it," Dr. Biedler said. She remains friends with Barbara to this day, as does Posy Clarke.

Barbara wouldn't let her own children be as mean as she was. They recall being reprimanded when they made fun of someone's weakness. Barbara herself eventually learned to control her tongue in public pretty well but the sarcasm and searing criticism are still part of her personality.

Barbara's girlhood friends all remember her brother James as a terror. "He was a demon," Ms. Siedle said. "He was sort of the bad boy of the neighborhood. He was a bit wild. He scared us all, he was just that much older." Once he accidentally shot Barbara in the leg with a BB gun and warned he would kill her if she told their mother. "For a week I wore high woolen socks and feared death," she said years later.

June Biedler recalled Halloweens where James would ring a doorbell and run "and we would stand there with a raw egg to throw into some-body's house if we didn't like them."

The girls also soaped windows. "That's what we were put up to" by James and his friends, Dr. Biedler said. "We were glad to have all these boys paying attention to us."

One time, she said, she and Barbara and the others "set fire to the vacant lot next to the Pierces' in order to get the fire company coming," which at the time seemed very exciting. "We were punished."

The Pierce children did not want for anything but the family was not as rich as many in the neighborhood. When the girls were older, Lucille Schoolfield brought filet mignon for picnics with her friends and charged it to her parents' account.

Pauline Pierce was something of a spendthrift. Barbara recalls that her mother was always behind on her charge account bills and after she died in a freak accident in 1949, Marvin was surprised to find that his wife had made deposits on antique furniture at a number of places around the country. "I mean, she bought on the installment plan all over America," Barbara Bush said disapprovingly. "And nobody dared say, 'Well, Mrs. Pierce never would have done that' because the truth was, she would have."[4]

Barbara was tall as a child and somewhat overweight. At age twelve she weighed 148 pounds. She remembers family meals fondly. "We had won-derful food at our house," she said. "We always had real cream on our cereal and mashed potatoes made from the real McCoy. Posy Clarke recalls walking back and forth for lunch with Barbara to the Rye Country Day School in the junior high years, eating jelly rolls along the way.

Although Barbara wasn't concerned about her weight, her mother was. "I spent all my life with my mother saying, 'Eat up, Martha' to my older sister, and 'Not you, Barbara.' "

Barbara attended dance class on Friday nights and found that boys, often not as tall as she, chose shorter girls as partners. So Barbara danced with her girlfriends, usually taking the part of the boy. "I didn't want to be left. Not me. I was five foot eight at the age of twelve."

The dancing lessons were formal. Both boys and girls wore white gloves. Boys bowed when they asked a girl to dance. "Miss Covington (the dance instructor) was a rather large-bosomed lady who would wear black lace and glide up the floor," demonstrating the "lead foot" and the "copycat foot" Kate Siedle recalled. "We were told never to put our weight on the arms of the boy," she said. "The elbow was to be pointing out so you didn't make the job too hard for him. It wasn't the jitterbug or anything. It was the waltz and the fox-trot. When we left, we curtsied and shook hands with Miss Covington. This was in the Episcopal church."

The dancing lessons were put to good use later at country club parties arranged by parents. Millie Dent, who grew up in the area at the same time Barbara Pierce did, recalled that mothers "worked like dogs to get extra boys" so that girls would not be left standing on the sidelines. During the teen years, "No girls danced with girls," she said. "You'd rather be caught dead."

At the beginning of a dance, Mrs. Dent said, a large crowd of boys would gather on one side of the room in a stag line. When one of them spotted an attractive girl, he would ask her to dance. But first he would arrange for several buddies to cut in on him. That way he wouldn't get stuck if he didn't like the girl. This arrangement also worked wonderfully for the girls because they were always getting new partners, even if not for the reasons they might have wished. "You felt popular whether you were or not," Mrs. Dent said. "We felt like we were butterflies. It was fun. You met a lot of people that way. It was just a wonderful solution."

Barbara's friends said she never had to worry about standing on the sidelines by the time she reached her teen years. While she had been plumpish as a child, "she became so pretty, the boys were wild about her," June Biedler said.

"She had more beaus than anybody," Posy Clarke said. "She was just extremely popular. She was just awfully good with people. She was like her father, who was a delightful man. She was confident. Very confident."

Mrs. Dent was friendly with Barbara's brother James at the time and years later in Washington she became a friend of Barbara Bush's. She recalled the Pierce family as a standout because all four children were friendly and welcoming.

As a young girl, Mrs. Dent spent summers in Bedford Hills, a neighboring suburb to Rye. Since Manursing was the nearest country club, she and her friends were taken there by their parents to swim and play tennis. Coming from another town, they felt unsure of themselves at first but soon found that "there were about three big families that were a lot of fun (one of them being the Pierce family). They were outgoing, that was the thing," Mrs. Dent said. "We were sort of shy and they just made us feel at home and we enjoyed them."

Barbara went to the local public school through the sixth grade. She still recalls, with mixed feelings, her first day there. "At age six, in 1931, my mother led me by the hand into the public school at Rye, New York," she said. "We met the teacher and then my mother was gone. She disappeared with no good-byes. I felt abandoned. But I truly loved school so much I forgave her by the time I got home."

Along with most of her friends, Barbara transferred to the private Rye Country Day School after elementary school. For her junior and senior years, she was sent away to a finishing school—Ashley Hall in Charleston, South Carolina—just as her sister Martha had been. "My mother thought my sister and I should be exposed to different parts of the country," Barbara said. "She thought we should be exposed to the South."

June Biedler said many students went away for junior and senior year because the Rye school "was just not that good. And in those days, in some cases, those schools (out of town) were meant to be sort of finishing up. But in any case, the schools were good—high educational standards."

By the time Martha graduated from Ashley Hall, she had become a beauty, just like her mother. In August 1940 while she was at Smith College, Martha was chosen for the cover of a college issue of *Vogue* magazine. She was posed in an above-the-knee skirt with shirt and blazer, loafer and bobby socks, and leg warmers. An antique big-wheeled bicycle was used as the backdrop.

Friends from both Rye and Ashley Hall described Martha as a knockout and Barbara as quite pretty. But when Barbara gathered with future classmates at New York's Grand Central Station for the trip south in September 1941, her self-image was low. "There were a lot of fat, squatty girls there, leaving for Ashley Hall," she said years later. "I felt miserable." All through the trip, she thought about the good times she was leaving behind. Her mood was not improved by the time she reached Charleston. "I distinctly remember walking up the long flight of stairs to the third floor," she said. "I felt miserable for about four minutes—until I got to know some of the other girls."[5]

During her junior year, Barbara Pierce shared a room with three other girls. "The room was very ample," said roommate Cordelia Lambert Stites. "We had a fireplace and nice big windows looking out over the oak, dripping with Spanish moss." The closets and the community bath were in the hall, leaving space in the room for sprawling, studying, and daydreaming.

Ashley Hall had only a hundred fifty students at the time. The education was classical and the atmosphere proper and straight-laced. "Boarding students like Barbara Pierce couldn't go outside school unless they were wearing a hat, gloves, and no lipstick," said Jane Lucas Thornhill, a classmate at the time. "Anyone could recognize a group of Ashley girls coming down the street a block away."

Classmate Miriam House, who lived in Charleston, recalled arriving at school one Monday morning with her nail polish still on. "I had to go into the library and have it removed," she said.

Barbara recalls being confined to campus most of the time. "We hardly went out at all," she said. "It was right in the middle of the war and the navy men were in town. I don't think it was until my senior year that we could go to church on Sunday without a chaperon."

On mixed social occasions, the chaperons were especially vigilant. Barbara remembers attending a dance at The Citadel, a military academy in Charleston, and being accompanied by an attentive chaperon. "That lady never let me out of her sight."

Mrs. Thornhill, who lived in Charleston, said she frequently invited classmates to her house—her mother had to sign them out—and they were eager to come "because they wanted to see boys." But she said that Barbara—called Barbi by her classmates—"didn't go out as much as the others and wasn't really looking around at the Charleston boys."

Mrs. Stites said Barbara did have several casual dates with a young man at The Citadel who had gone out with her older sister, Martha, earlier. While there were not serious romances, Barbara and Cordelia worked together to thwart one especially onerous rule at Ashley Hall. Girls were allowed to invite dates into the parlor for two hours on Sunday afternoons with no chaperon in the room. "But you couldn't have the same boy two weekends in a row. So Barbara and I traded off a couple of times," each one signing up for the other's date.

Another roommate, Susan Estey Edgerly, was president of the student government at Ashley Hall and got the best grades in the class. She remembers Barbara as attractive and self-confident. "She was just the prettiest thing and very outgoing and athletic at Ashley Hall," Mrs. Edgerly said. "I envied her. She was slender and I was fat. In recent years, I've gotten slender and she's gotten a little heavier."

Despite all the restrictions at Ashley Hall, Barbara was happy at the school. She even has fond memories of the headmistress, Mary Vardrine McBee. "I rather liked her, which wasn't a very popular thing to do," Barbara said.

The educational program was rigorous and Barbara was a good student. "She loved history and English and she was quite good in French," Mrs. Stites said.

There were two study halls every day, one in the afternoon and one in the evening. When the girls weren't studying they were kept busy with sports and extracurricular activities. Barbara was a member of both the student council and the drama club and she kept up her swimming and tennis. As a junior she played Beatrice in the Shakespearean comedy *Much Ado About Nothing*. During her senior year, she and Cordelia Lambert played the twin roles in *Twelfth Night*.

"During one of my two years, I was an angel with a speaking role in the Christmas play," Barbara recalled. "And, I think I'm right, I was the underwater swimming champion of the class of '43. I swam something like two and one half times across the pool."

The girls at Ashley Hall were acutely aware of the war. The dining room was sandbagged and used as an air raid shelter as well as for meals. The class of 1943 decided to give up its yearbook to help the troops. "That was the only year Ashley Hall didn't have an annual," said classmate Frances Baker Turnage. "It was during the war and we contributed the paper to the cause. Instead, we exchanged pictures."

Mrs. Turnage said that Barbara wrote on the back of hers, "Please let me know when something important happens to you. I know I'll hear from you first. Love, Barbi." Barbara wrote that affectionate message even though she and Frances were not close friends. "We knew each other mostly in sports and classroom activities," Mrs. Turnage said. "I remember her being quiet and ladylike, not loud. A good girl."

Other classmates and teachers must have agreed with that assessment. When she graduated, Barbara was awarded the Rosalie McCabe Cup for general sportsmanship at Ashley Hall.

Barbara kept in touch with Ashley Hall and some of her classmates over the years. For the fortieth reunion of the class of '43, she invited all members to Washington. And during the years the Bushes lived in the vice presidential mansion in Washington, several groups of young Ashley Hall students were taken on special tours.

While having fun at Ashley Hall, Barbara Pierce retained strong social ties with her friends back home. It was during an outing with them over the Christmas holidays of her junior year that she came upon a real romance.

3

LOVE AT FIRST SIGHT

G eorge Bush was rich, smart, friendly, and a big man on campus. But none of those qualities come to mind when Barbara Bush recalls what first attracted her. "He was the handsomest-looking man you ever laid your eyes on, bar none," she says. "I mean, my boys don't even come close to him, nor did his own brothers."

They met at a dance at the Round Hill Country Club in Greenwich, Connecticut, during the Christmas holidays in 1941. In his autobiography, *Looking Forward*, George Bush remembers the occasion in detail.

"I'm not much at recalling what people wear but that particular occasion stands out in my memory," he said. "The band was playing Glenn Miller tunes when I approached a friend from Rye, New York, Jack Wozencraft, to ask if he knew a girl across the dance floor, the one wearing the green and red holiday dress.

"He said she was Barbara Pierce, that she lived in Rye and went to school in South Carolina. Would I like an introduction? I told him that was the general idea and he introduced us just about the time the bandleader decided to change tempos, from fox-trot to waltz. Since I didn't waltz, we sat the dance out. And several more after that, talking and getting to know each other."[1]

Barbara recalls the evening more romantically. She was so taken with this good-looking, self-assured, outgoing boy that, "I could hardly breathe when he was in the room."

The Bushes have obviously repeated this story fondly for their children, each of whom adds his own spin.

"It seems that my dad was zonked over the head by this outgoing, charming woman," says number four son Marvin. "And just like everything else he's done in his life, he decided that she was the one he was going to marry and so he did."

"I'm told it was love at first sight," said George W. Bush. "I think Mother had heard of George Bush's reputation from a nearby city and Dad saw Mother at a party and fell in love with her."

George Bush, known as Poppy during his childhood and teen years, grew up in Greenwich, Connecticut, a monied New York City suburb. His family was rich. Even during the Great Depression there were three full-time maids and a chauffeur who took the Bush boys to the Greenwich Country Day School.

Prescott and Dorothy Bush hewed to the Protestant ethic. They believed in hard work, temperate living, and daily Bible readings. Prescott used a belt for discipline and the boys were required to wear jackets and ties and to speak only when spoken to at the dinner table. Prescott Bush was a Wall Street investment banker, a U.S. Senator, a graduate of Phillips Academy in Andover, Massachusetts, and of Yale. He was a strict man who expected a lot of his children and young George was much in awe of him. He still recalls his father with great respect but also as "pretty scary."

George's mother, Dorothy Walker Bush, was more fun. She had a cheerful personality and, like her husband, a love of competitive sports. Her father, George Herbert Walker, had been a highly successful investor with a strong interest in golf—he donated money for the Walker Cup, which still bears his name. George Walker also built the family summer house at Kennebunkport, Maine.

The Bush children spent their spare time playing tennis, golf, baseball, and card games. They swam and hunted and learned early on that winning was important. Bush has recalled returning home from tennis when he was about eight years old and telling his mother he had been off his game. "You don't have a game," she replied. "Get out and work harder and maybe someday you will."

Prescott Junior and George were the two oldest boys, born just twenty-one months apart, and they were very close. Dorothy Bush said the boys were given their own rooms when the family moved to a bigger house. "That was in September. Then along in November the two boys came to their father and me and said, 'Do you know what we want for Christmas? It won't cost you anything but we would like to tell you now.' What they wanted was to go back to sharing the same room. And that's the way it was until they grew up and left home to get married."

George started school a year early so he could be with Prescott during the day instead of being left home without a playmate. That meant he was a year ahead when he entered prep school at Andover, which was fortunate because he developed a respiratory infection during his junior year that put him behind in his studies. Between his early entry and his illness, he spent five years at the school, graduating in 1942. He was a senior at Andover when he went home for Christmas break in 1941. It was a busy social season and the dance at the Round Hill Club was one of several that teens in the area attended during the holidays. They were formal affairs with boys in tuxedos and girls in long dresses. An orchestra provided live music, the punch was nonalcoholic, and there were plenty of chaperons.

After George and Barbara were introduced, they sat and talked through several dances, then each returned home with friends, George to Greenwich, Barbara to Rye. Barbara told her mother that night she had met someone she liked. By the time she woke up the next morning, late, her mother had already been on the telephone investigating and had discovered he came from a proper family.

Barbara was miffed, but memories of the handsome young man from Greenwich took the edge off her anger. That night they saw each other again at a dance at the Apawamis Club in Rye. George cut in on Barbara and asked her for a date. Just at that moment, however, Barbara's brother James cut in on George, hoping to get his sister out of the way so he could convince George to take part in a basketball game. George, showing early diplomatic skills, agreed to play in the game and asked Barbara to be there too. The date was set.

To Barbara's dismay, her whole family turned out for the game, the better to get a look at the boy who had captured her attention. George borrowed a family car, choosing the one with a radio in case there were awkward silences. He needn't have worried. He and Barbara went out for ice cream sodas and fell into easy conversation.

After Christmas vacation George returned to Andover and Barbara to Ashley Hall. They were bursting with excitement about each other.

"She came back from vacation full of news about a new boyfriend by the name of Poppy Bush," Susan Edgerly recalls. "She was pretty much in love, I guess, and then he started writing and she shared his love with us. He was certainly wooing her."

Mrs. Edgerly said many of the girls shared their letters, reading parts aloud to their roommates. But the precious letters never actually changed hands. Barbara "was a kind of shy person in the love department and I can remember her shyness and kind of almost blushing when she read those letters. She would be almost embarrassed but loved every word of it."

Another roommate, Shavaun Robinson Towers, had a mailbox right next to Barbara's and remembered with amusement how she kept a close and jealous eye on the Pierce mailbox. "She got a letter from George Bush every damned day, and once a week I got a letter from my mother," Mrs. Towers said.

When Barbara met George she already had a boyfriend—a nonkissing relationship, as she describes it—but quickly lost all interest in him. It was, she said, a fortunate turn of events. "I had a beau at the time and to show how lucky life can be, he now has had four wives," she said. "It's true, and all twenty years younger. I would have been gone long ago."

As it was, George banished all thoughts of other boys. In her spare time, "she used to knit argyle socks for George," Cordelia Stites said.

George and Barbara saw each other again at spring break on the single day that their vacations overlapped. They went on a double date to see *Citizen Kane*, and to her delight, he invited her to his senior prom that spring, held in the school gymnasium. After the dance, he kissed her good night—on the cheek. It was the spring of 1942 and she had just turned seventeen years old. He was the first boy she had ever kissed.

Their romance developed more fully during the summer that followed but the shadow of war loomed over their plans. George had decided right after the Japanese bombed Pearl Harbor—December 1941, the same

month he met Barbara—that he would not go straight on to Yale after
graduation, even though he had been accepted. He wanted to join the
navy and take part in the war.

So in June 1942, as soon as he turned eighteen, George Bush signed
up as a seaman second class. Two months later, on August 6, he reported
for duty at the navy's preflight training center in Chapel Hill, North Carolina. He took a train from New York City and wrote later that he felt
frightened and alone, much as Barbara had a year earlier when she made
her first journey to Ashley Hall.

But just as she quickly learned to fit in with her schoolmates, George
made friends at Chapel Hill. As the youngest in the group of trainees,
however, he was conscious of both his age and a face that made him look
even younger. He had been in training only a few weeks when Barbara,
who worked in a department store over the summer, agreed to stop by and
see him on her way back to school. The self-conscious Bush asked her to
tell everyone she was eighteen, even though she had only turned seventeen
a few months earlier.

They held hands as they walked around the grounds and George introduced Barbara to his friends. And, of course, she said not a soul asked
how old she was.

During her senior year, Barbara saw little of her boyfriend but they
kept in close touch by letter. "She was a one-man woman as I recall and
writing letters constantly, not like the telephoning that young people do
today," said Marjorie Macnutt Thurstone, Barbara's lone roommate during
senior year. Mrs. Thurstone said she and Barbara were both active in
student government and "we became good friends . . . we'd sit in our room
and talk." She also remembered Barbara as a good student during her
final year of high school. "I think we both studied hard. Her getting into
Smith proved that."

Meanwhile, George finished his initial training at Chapel Hill, got further training in Minneapolis from November to February, and completed
the ten-month basic flight-training course at Corpus Christi, Texas, in
June. He received his ensign's bars on June 9, 1943, and was exultant at
becoming a real navy pilot.

Barbara graduated from high school that same month along with her
twenty-nine classmates. When she returned to Ashley Hall forty-one years

later as commencement speaker, she thanked the school for "allowing me to relive some of the happiest years of my life."[2]

She spent the summer at home in Rye, working at a factory, thinking about George Bush but also preparing for college. She was going to Smith, just as her sister Martha had a few years earlier. A number of her class-mates from Ashley Hall were going there, too. Roommate Susan Edgerly said her mother sent her to Ashley Hall on the recommendation of a Smith counselor who said if Susan wanted to get into Smith, Ashley Hall was the best preparation she would find. Barbara's brother James went to Bowdoin in Brunswick, Maine. Scott graduated from his father's alma mater, Miami University in Ohio.

George spent most of the summer in advanced flight training, learning to land on an aircraft carrier, but in August he had time off and invited Barbara to Kennebunkport to meet his large family. It was an idyllic seventeen-day vacation for the young couple, the last extended time they would have together for a while. They sailed, played tennis, rode bicycles, went on picnics, and got secretly engaged. Barbara said George never pro-posed to her on bended knee or otherwise. They just talked about their future together and told their families they planned to marry.

Although Barbara was just eighteen and George nineteen and neither had yet spent a day in college, their parents did not object to the engage-ment. Barbara said her parents had put up a fight a short time earlier when her sister Martha married a Yale senior, and they weren't ready for another battle.

"Also, there was a war going on," she said. "One has to remember that when you got engaged at that time you weren't sure you would ever see that person again when they went overseas. I know my mother and father really liked George but I don't think they believed we would get married. I believe they were thinking they would take it one step at a time. George's parents probably felt the same way."[3]

At the end of that summer George reported for duty at the naval air base at Norfolk, Virginia, and joined a new squadron that was assigned to Chincoteague, a peninsula in Virginia, for his final training.

Barbara began her freshman year at Smith College in Northampton, Massachusetts. She had to make new friends because Smith had a policy of assigning girls from each prep school to different living quarters. That wasn't a problem for Barbara, who socialized easily. In fact, she spent much more time having fun, writing to George, and playing sports than studying. Her grades suffered. "I didn't like to study too much," she said in 1988 when a controversy erupted over vice presidential candidate Dan Quayle's college records. "I'd hate to have anybody go through my records from freshman year. I was all right in high school, but when it came to Smith, I was a cliff-hanger. The truth is, I just wasn't very interested. I was just interested in George."

She was active on campus, however. Always athletic, she was named captain of her eleven-member intramural soccer team, playing the position of center half.[4]

She also played lacrosse, went to movies on Saturday night, and kept up her spirits if not her grades. Her father sent her copies of *McCall's* magazine each month, to the displeasure of Smith's administrators.

"One day they came to me and they said, 'We notice you're getting pulp magazines in the mail. We don't allow pulp magazines,'" Barbara recalled. "I phoned my dad and said, 'Dad, I can't get those magazines.' He said, 'You tell that lady you're getting those magazines and you wouldn't be there if it wasn't for pulp magazines.'"

The high point of the school year came in December when George was in Philadelphia to attend a commissioning ceremony for the USS *San Jacinto*, a new carrier that was to become home to his squadron. He invited Barbara and his mother, Dorothy, to attend the festivities. The two women traveled to Philadelphia together on the train.

Barbara was nervous being alone with George's mother but she was savvy enough to hold her tongue when the question of an engagement ring came up. Dorothy Bush asked what kind of ring Barbara wanted. Barbara said she didn't care. "Does it have to be a diamond?" Dorothy Bush asked. Again, Barbara said she didn't care, unaware that Mrs. Bush was carrying in her purse a star sapphire ring that had belonged to George's aunt, Nancy Walker.

"Just before the commissioning ceremony started, George took the ring out of his pocket and gave it to me," Barbara said. "I was thrilled. I don't know to this day whether it's real and I don't care. It's my engagement ring and it hasn't been off my finger since the day George gave it to me."[5]

Three months later, in March 1944, George shipped out with his squadron for the South Pacific. Barbara finished her freshman year at Smith and also went to summer school, hoping to finish college in three years. But a short way into the fall semester, she dropped out. Her head was full of wedding plans and the thought of more Latin, history, and English left her cold. She and George planned to be married in December and she had a lot to do. It was the end of her formal education.

"I took a leave of absence from Smith to be married and never went back," she said later. "In those days there were not many coeducation colleges and when George got out of the navy, he went to Yale. I have to be absolutely frank. I could have gone to Connecticut College (near Yale) and George Bush would have killed himself to have gotten me there. If you want to do anything in life, you can do it. But the truth is, I didn't want to do it. Now I am sorry I don't have that in my background."

George began flying missions against the Japanese in May 1944 and had a number of harrowing experiences in the air during the summer. On September 2 his plane was hit by antiaircraft fire while he was on a bombing mission against one of the Bonin Islands, Chichi Jima. He bailed out, and, with help from a buddy in another plane, spotted a raft about fifty feet away. He was in the water for almost three hours before being rescued by a submarine. He remained on that craft for thirty days, out of touch with the world. When he was finally put ashore and flown to Pearl Harbor, he immediately sent a telegram to his parents.

George arrived home from the war on Christmas eve in 1944 ("What a Christmas present," Barbara said in her memoirs). In his autobiography, he described the scene like something out of the movies—a holiday setting, kisses and hugs, joy and laughter. He was home, his fiancée by his side, his family all around him.

He had missed his wedding day but that was no problem. Barbara was happy to reschedule. George and Barbara were married on January 6, 1945, in the First Presbyterian Church in Rye. She wore a long-sleeved white satin dress and a veil that had belonged to her mother-in-law. George was in his navy dress blues. The eight bridesmaids, including Ashley Hall roommate Shavaun Robinson Towers and childhood friend Posy Morgan Clarke, wore cap-sleeved, high-necked emerald green dresses "with green ostrich feathers that curled around in our hair," Mrs. Clarke said. They carried red and white carnations. George's older brother, Prescott, who had himself married just a week earlier, interrupted his honeymoon to be the best man. But most of the ushers, Mrs. Towers said, were "whoever was around" because so many of George's friends were fighting in the war.

"The wedding was lovely," Mrs. Clarke said. "The night before, there was a dinner in Greenwich, given by the groom's parents." She said Barbara later gave each of the bridesmaids a framed picture of the wedding party.

The reception, for more than 250 guests, was at the Apawamis Club in Rye where George and Barbara had made their first date. The bride and groom led off the dancing, much to George's displeasure. He whispered to his bride, "I hope you're having a good time. Enjoy it. It's the last time I'll ever dance in public."

For their honeymoon, the young couple set off in high spirits for a resort on Sea Island, Georgia. It was all too short, however. George was still in the navy and in line for special training that would prepare him to take part in a final assault on Japan planned for later in the year. He moved with his group from Florida to Michigan to Maine and then to Ocean Naval Air Station in Virginia. Barbara joined him when she could. In their one-room apartment in Wyandotte, Michigan, she discovered that she had much to learn as a housekeeper. "I ruined everything—and I mean everything," she said. "I shrank my whole trousseau. That was a weakness of my mother. She had a theory that if you could read, you could keep house."

George and Barbara were together in Virginia Beach in August that year when news came that Japan had surrendered. On August 14 they listened to a radio broadcast of President Truman's speech: "I have received this afternoon a message from the Japanese government in reply to the message forwarded to that government by the secretary of state on August 11. I deem this reply a full acceptance of the Potsdam Declaration, which specifies the unconditional surrender of Japan."

The Bushes, like all the young couples on base and elsewhere, were overjoyed. The end of the war meant they would lose no more friends in combat and that George would not have to ship out for a final assault on Japan. In Virginia Beach, the streets quickly filled with celebrants. The

Bushes joined their friends for the festivities but only after going to church to thank God that the war was at an end.

Because he had been in combat and received decorations, George was able to get a discharge from the navy just a month after the war ended. Two months later he was enrolled at Yale under a special program for veterans that would allow them to graduate in two and a half years. Five thousand of the eight thousand Yale freshmen that year were returning servicemen.

Housing was in short supply and George and Barbara had to move several times, but they finally settled into an apartment they liked not far from campus—one of thirteen carved out of an old house. That apartment became the first home of George W. Bush, born July 6, 1946, in the first year of the postwar baby boom. The other apartments in the building also were filled with young couples, most with a child. The Bushes had their own bathroom but shared a kitchen with two other families. It had two stoves, two refrigerators and orange crates mounted on the wall, which served as cabinets. Each family cooked in the kitchen, then used a tea cart to wheel food back to the apartment.

Even though the apartment was small, George and Barbara entertained frequently. Their nearby relatives often came for visits, along with friends. Barbara, already developing her excellent organizational skills, learned to cook food that could be made ahead of time.

George majored in economics and minored in sociology. He studied hard enough to earn Phi Beta Kappa, an academic honor, but also played baseball enthusiastically, becoming team captain his senior year. His first spring at Yale he played first base. Barbara, pregnant with young George, kept score and did it well, a fact that her husband remarked on proudly years later: "Not many people know how to score a baseball game."

Money was tight for everyone, including the Bushes. Before the baby came, Barbara worked at the Yale Coop to help bolster the family finances. But they also had money George had saved during the war from his military pay, and his tuition was covered by the GI bill.

Like other young couples, the Bushes were planning for the future. Bush, in his autobiography, said that after reading *The Farm* by Louis Bromfield, he and Barbara imagined themselves settling in the Midwest and raising a family among wide pastures and fields of grain. When they looked into the costs, however, they realized they didn't have enough money to get started.

"If I'd really believed there was a solid business prospect to discuss, I wouldn't have hesitated to go to Dad," he said. "No matter how we looked at it, though, George and Barbara Farms came off as a high-risk, no-yield investment."[6]

What the Bushes finally settled on was just as exotic as farming to city-bred easterners. A friend of the senior Bushes, Neil Mallon, suggested the young couple head for Texas to learn the oil business. Mallon, an oil man himself, was head of Dresser Industries and he offered George a job at the International Derrick and Equipment Co.—Ideco—which was one of Dresser's subsidiaries. George would start as an equipment clerk.

George had saved $3,000 from his navy pay and his father gave him a 1947 red Studebaker when he graduated from Yale. It was all the young couple needed to start life in a different—very different—part of the country.

George was raring to go, having gotten a taste of the wider world outside Greenwich while he was in the navy. He wanted to be out from under his father's shadow so he could make his own mark on the world.

Barbara, however, had assumed that she and George would settle in familiar New England. She reacted to the idea of venturing to the wilds of Texas with a baby in the same way she initially viewed enrollment at Ashley Hall—with fear. But characteristically, she accepted with good humor the hand that fate had dealt her.

"I didn't want to go at the time," she said. "But a day after I got there, I thought it was really exciting. . . . If we had been bound by our past, we'd have stayed in Greenwich or Rye and done our thing like everybody else in our family did. But we ventured out."

Also, she said, "I've been brought up in a family where if your husband wanted to do something, you'd do it, and gladly. I still think there's nothing wrong with that. I would say the same if a wife wanted to do something very badly. Her husband should do the same."

In later years, Barbara realized that the shock of the move west took her out of the cocoon she had been in since childhood and helped her mature more quickly. "I remember I never bought a thing by myself," she said. "My mother and my sister bought everything and told me, 'This would be nice for you.' And after I was married . . . I went off and bought a tweed suit, brought it home to show my mother and Mrs. Bush, my first purchase. And they both said, 'Well, no hem, dear, and the color—so drab.' And whatever. 'It's cheap, dear.' Well, I think I kept it and hated it from then on. . . . I really was a late bloomer, in all honesty."[7]

Right after graduation from Yale, George took the Studebaker and drove across the country to find a place for his young family to settle. Barbara and baby George followed a week later by propeller plane—a flight of more than twelve hours. It was the start of a big adventure.

4

TEXAS

George and Barbara were both accustomed to comfortable homes, household help, lush green surroundings, and friends and neighbors schooled in eastern traditions. Life in Texas would be completely different.

George's first job was in Odessa, a strictly utilitarian town carved out of the harsh West Texas sagebrush. Its main business was oil and no attempt had been made to beautify the surroundings. The town consisted mostly of equipment yards.

George found a house on East Seventh Street, divided into two apartments. The Bushes had their own kitchen, a living room, and one bedroom with a rattling window fan. They shared a bath with the other tenants—a mother-daughter prostitute team, and the many male guests.

"Everything in life is relative," Barbara said. "We had the only house on the street with a bathroom and the only car."

Despite their odd surroundings, the young couple experienced a sense of exhilaration being on their own, far away from their powerful families. "It was the first time in our lives that we had lived in a place where nobody said, 'You're Marvin Pierce's daughter or Pres Bush's son," Barbara said. "It's pretty nice to be judged on your own."

Although they had little money, they had confidence in George's earning power, knew that family money would be available in an emergency, and never considered themselves poor. "We both knew that if we got into trouble someone would help us," Barbara said. "And so to say we knew what it was like to be poor is ridiculous. For us, it was a challenge and exciting and we'd rather have died than asked. But it's very easy to say when you know you've got a mother and father—in fact, two—who would help . . . that's very different."

Still, Barbara recalls with amusement that her mother used to send her Ivory soap, imagining that it wasn't available in the Wild West and "we were so poor, I let her." But there was no help available from home in learning the cultural mores of West Texas. The white-glove lessons of Ashley Hall and Smith and the bonhomie of Yale didn't apply here.

Neither of the Bushes were big drinkers but they kept one bottle of liquor for special occasions and guests. "We had one bottle, which was ruined for us the first time a man walked through the door," Barbara said. "George offered him a drink and he took our one bottle—and drank out of it."

George also had an unusual experience, getting dead drunk on Christmas Eve 1948 just months after he and Barbara had arrived in town. As he tells the story in his autobiography, he was a cohost at Ideco's office Christmas party, held in the company's supply store. Barbara and little George were waiting at home for him so they could decorate the tree together. But as the evening progressed, more and more guests came to the party and George kept filling drinks—and taking one for himself. He said he doesn't remember when the party ended, but Barbara tells him that a colleague eventually put him in the back of a pickup truck and took him home, depositing him gently on the front lawn.

Early on, the Bushes learned how much sports meant in Texas. "I had played baseball and soccer in college and knew how intense athletic competition can get," George said. "But Barbara and I had never experienced anything like the fever that took over Odessa during the football season. It was more than a game. It was a total experience. There were overflow crowds on Friday nights for high school games and whole towns would travel by caravan to neighboring towns to settle bragging rights for the coming year. . . .

"All this was different for Barbara and me. Like millions who had come West to start new lives before us, and like millions who have come since, d a lot to learn about the customs of our new home. But learn we did, because that, when you get right down to it, was what we had come to Texas to do—to shape our own lives and bring up our kids in a land of fresh challenge and opportunity."[1]

The Bushes lived in Odessa for less than a year. Dresser Industries had better things in mind for George and he was transferred to California, where he became a full-fledged salesman. The downside was that the family of three had to move five times in a single year—from Huntington Park to Bakersfield to Whittier to Ventura to Compton—and George traveled one thousand miles a week.

When their second child, Pauline Robinson Bush, was born in Compton in December 1949, Barbara met her doctor the day the baby was delivered. The Bushes had been in town such a short time they hardly had time to get to know their neighbors, much less develop the usual wider community contacts. The baby was named after Barbara's mother, Pauline, who had been killed in a freak car accident just two months earlier. Pauline had set a hot cup of coffee on the car seat next to her one morning while riding with her husband. Marvin saw the cup starting to slide toward her and reached over to get it. He lost control of the car on one of Westchester County's narrow country lanes and crashed into a stone wall. Pauline Pierce was killed instantly.

Barbara, seven months pregnant and living in California, did not go to the funeral. Her father, who suffered broken ribs in the accident, urged her not to, fearing the cross-country trip would be bad for the baby. Barbara agreed but later came to regret the decision. "I'll never forgive myself for not going to my mother's funeral or spending time with my father in the hospital," she said.[2]

Scott Pierce said that part of the conflict between Barbara and her mother at the time centered on Pauline's belief that Barbara was still a girl, not a woman out on her own. "My mother thought Barbara was still nineteen years old and living in the house and not a wife. So that might have been a conflict of sorts," he said. "But the truth of the matter is, my mother died so soon thereafter, that there was no resolution of that."[3]

Shortly after their daughter was born the Bushes moved back to Texas. This time Dresser Industries sent them to Midland, another scrub town but one filled with ambitious young couples from other places, families just like themselves, raising children and trying to make a killing in the oil business.

The Bushes bought a house for $7,500—847 square feet. It was part of a development, the first of its kind in Midland, and had a floor plan identical to all the other houses in the neighborhood. To compensate for this, the developer had painted each house a different pastel color. The area became known as Easter Egg Row.

Barbara and George settled comfortably into the neighborhood, finding many kindred souls. The women spent their day tending young children—three, four, and five children per family. The men worked long hours, many in the oil fields checking out problems and prospects.

"It was just the right time to live there," Barbara said. "I remember Dad visiting us in Midland and saying, 'I worry about you. What if something happened? Who would support you?' Well, we were all in the same situation. No one had any family. We were all newcomers and we came from all over the country. We formed really good friendships."[4]

Because Midland lacked cultural amenities, the young families had to make their own fun. Backyard barbecues, held after church on Sundays, were generally the week's big event. If there were enough people, a softball game might develop. It was all friendly and informal.

Martin Allday, a Midland lawyer, recalled the days when he was courting the girl he would later marry. She lived next to the Bushes. One day, he said, "I went over to pick her up and Bush and Barbara and the kids came walking across the street barefooted, sat down in the backyard to have a beer with my father-in-law."[5]

Bush had not been in Midland long before he decided to leave Dresser Industries and start his own oil firm. He went into business with one of his neighbors, John Overbey, who was already an independent operator, trading in oil leases and mineral rights. In late 1950 they formed the Bush-Overbey Oil Development Co., with financial help from Bush's uncle, Herbert Walker. Bush was twenty-six years old.

The company was profitable from the start. Bush was able to use his impressive contacts back East to raise the money needed to buy mineral rights and arrange for oil exploration. One of his investors was Eugene Meyer, owner of *The Washington Post*.

Despite his success, George worried more as his business grew, eventually developing bleeding ulcers. "I would worry a lot," he said. "I'd keep a lot inside me."

In 1953 Bush and John Overbey decided to merge their business with another independent oil company that had offices right next door. The partners were Bill and Hugh Liedtke, two lawyers who saw there was more money to be made in oil than at the courthouse. Each side put $500,000 into the new business. They named it Zapata Petroleum, after *Viva, Zapata*, a movie then playing in the Midland theater, about Emiliano Zapata, the Mexican rebel leader who fought for land reform in the early 1900s.

The Liedtkes were not the type of men who drank liquor straight from the bottle. Like Bush, they came from a privileged background. Their father was chief counsel for Gulf Oil, and they had attended private high schools and Amherst College. Johnny Hackney, who ran Johnny's Barbecue in Midland, remembered Bush, the Liedtkes, and others like them who hung out at his restaurant in the early 1950s.

"We had a bunch of Ivy Leaguers come to town then," he said. "They were all hardworking, aggressive, ambitious. Those Yankee boys were something else. I remember George Bush when he worked on the big oil rigs, worked in the warehouses, when he used to come in here dirty and sweaty."

The Bushes were also movers and shakers among the 25,000 residents of Midland. Allday said that George Bush "helped start the YMCA, establish three banks, worked in the cancer crusade, United Way, Community Chest." He became a director of one of the banks. He also coached Little League, and both the Bushes taught Sunday school at a Presbyterian church. By 1953, they had a second son, John Ellis Bush, called Jeb.

During those years George was gone much of the time, as were the other oilmen. Hugh Liedtke, who eventually became head of Pennzoil, recalls the Midland days as "hard on the girls" because they were left alone much of the time with houses full of young children. "We would sit up on an oil well all night, stay out in the field several days," Liedtke said. "Then we would come home, covered with grease."

Barbara has said many times since that while she enjoyed those years in Midland—typical of the lives of many young wives in that era—she also had resentments.

"I had moments where I was jealous of attractive young women out in a man's world," she said. "I would think, well, George is off on a trip doing all these exciting things and I'm sitting home with these absolutely brilliant children who say one thing a week of interest."

But she is not one to complain about her life for long and her strong belief that children need a mother nearby while they are young helped ease the boredom. "There's a time for babies, a time for growing," she said. "I just happened to lie dormant in rather important years and I might regret that. But I don't think so."

She was, by all accounts, a super-organized mother. She kept up the house by herself before George was earning enough money to hire household help. She went to the Little League games and kept score for her sons as she had done for her husband earlier. And she was the family disciplinarian.

"She may be a lot of people's grandmother, but she was our drill sergeant when we were growing up," said Jeb.

It was Barbara who dealt with the day-to-day problems. She recalls a time when young George was spanked with a board by the school principal. George senior was out of town at the time and when he learned of the incident he was furious. He sent his wife to the school to complain. Barbara said she told the principal, "My husband's going to kill you. He's out of town, but he's coming home to kill you immediately."

The principal defended his action, saying young George had disrupted the music class by painting a mustache on his face. He was sent to the principal's office as punishment but instead of being contrite, he "swaggered in as though he had been the most wonderful thing in the world." Fearing George would become the class clown, the principal swatted him on the bottom with a board.

"And before I left that school, I thought the principal was right," Barbara said. "First of all, he hadn't bruised him or he hadn't hurt him. He'd hurt his feelings. . . . You don't want the class clown, you want a kid who's going to do his best . . . and I backed the principal. And then I had to explain to George."

Such minor problems cropped up all the time, and like other parents, the Bushes learned to cope. But nothing in their experience prepared them for the heartache to come.

In the spring of 1953 young George was six years old. Pauline Robinson—called Robin—was three and a half and John Ellis—Jeb—was still an infant. Barbara, busy with the new baby, didn't notice the small bruises on her daughter's legs but became concerned when the normally active child became lethargic. Barbara took her to the family physician, Dr. Dorothy Wyvell, who examined Robin, took a blood test—and asked Barbara to come back that afternoon with her husband. Of course that set off alarm bells and Barbara quickly telephoned George. When they returned to the doctor's office, she met them with moist eyes.

"I'll never forget it," George said. "We walked in and the first thing, she pulled a Kleenex out of the box and just kind of wiped her eye. Then she said, 'I've got some bad news for you.' "[6]

Dr. Wyvell told the Bushes that Robin had an acute case of leukemia.

Neither George nor Barbara had a clear idea what leukemia was. They asked what the treatment would be. Dr. Wyvell told them there was nothing they could do—Robin's case was very advanced and she would not live much longer. The doctor advised the Bushes to take their little girl home, make her comfortable, and let her die.

"She said, 'Number one, don't tell anyone. Number two, don't treat her. You should take her home, make her life as easy as possible for her, and in three weeks' time, she'll be gone,' " Barbara said.

Reeling with shock, the Bushes went home and blurted out the tragic news so that shortly everyone in the neighborhood knew, except their young children. The next day they flew to New York to consult with George's uncle, Dr. John Walker, a cancer specialist. He urged them to try to save Robin's life.

Robin was admitted to Memorial Sloan-Kettering, a top New York research hospital, and was given a new cancer drug that helped.

For the next seven months, Robin was in and out of the hospital, her mother by her side. When Barbara and Robin were gone, neighbors helped George care for the two boys and eventually Dorothy Bush sent a nurse to fill in the gaps.

The drug Robin was taking worked well enough that she sometimes appeared to be a normal child—a hazel-eyed blond charmer.

"One day when she was in remission I took her down to the bank," George said. "We walked down there from the office ... And they said,

'Where's the little girl who was so sick?' And here she was, she looked so beautiful, just like she was at the peak of her life."

But Robin's leukemia never went into complete remission.

"I remember very clearly because she was one of those adorable children you can't forget," said Dr. Charlotte Tan, one of the doctors who treated Robin. "She always was a mature child. It takes a really big girl to tolerate an oxygen tent and all that when you're three years old."

During this period, George Bush began going to church by himself early in the morning to pray. "I can tell you that there was no one for us to turn to but God," he said. "And I really learned to pray. I would slip into our church sometimes when no one was there. I would ask God why? Why this little innocent girl?"[7]

Barbara said that when the church custodian discovered Bush was stopping in every morning around 6:00 A.M. before work, he told the church minister. From then on, Barbara said, "The minister then came every day. He didn't say anything. But he was there."

The Bushes' hopes were raised briefly when friends telephoned to say they had heard a radio report that a doctor in Kansas City had found a cure for leukemia. "Poor George got on the phone and called and called and he got the doctor," Barbara said. "George had gotten his hopes up so."

During the long days and nights at the hospital, the Bushes talked and prayed together and, in their typical fashion, tried to find the silver lining in a heartbreaking situation. They took comfort in their many blessings.

"We look around and nobody had what we had," Barbara said. "They either didn't believe in God, or they didn't love each other, or they didn't have other children or they didn't have brothers and sisters. In a way it was good for us because we realized we had much more than anybody else."

Robin died on October 11, 1953, about seven months after her leukemia was diagnosed. Her parents, both with her at death, can still see the bruises that covered an entire leg and the "hundred or so" ulcers she had on her stomach at the last. They donated her body to research. "First of all, I know there's a God, and secondly, I know Robin left," Barbara said. "We both had that feeling that she wasn't there. We combed her hair and she wasn't there."[8]

Barbara said that she was the strong one in the family while Robin was alive. George would cry—she wouldn't let him get teary-eyed around Robin—but she didn't. After Robin died, however, Barbara crumbled. "I hadn't cried at all when Robin was alive," she said. "But after she died, I felt I could cry forever."

Once back home in Texas, she wanted to retreat from the world. "I nearly fell apart," she said. "I couldn't put my right foot in front of my left."

In a speech at the Republican National Convention in 1988, Barbara recalled how her husband gave her strength during those dark days. "He held me in his arms and he made me share it and accept that his sorrow was as great as my own," she said. "He simply wouldn't allow my grief to divide us . . . push us apart, which is what happens so often where there is a loss like that. And for as long as I live, I will respect and appreciate my husband for the strength of his understanding."

Young George also helped his mother. After Robin's death, Barbara lavished attention on her two sons, almost fearful to let them out of her sight. Then one day she overheard George tell a friend that he couldn't come out to play because he had to be with his mother. At that point, Barbara said, she realized she had to pull herself together for the sake of her family. And gradually, she did.

Fifteen months after Robin's death, the Bushes had another child, Neil. Twenty-two months later, in October 1956, came a fourth, Marvin.

By this time the family fortunes had improved and Barbara had help taking care of her active brood. She had a full-time housekeeper, Julia Mae Jackson, and a part-time baby-sitter, twenty-four-year-old Otha Taylor.

Mrs. Taylor recalled that when she arrived at the Bush home for an interview, Julia Jackson warned her she probably would not get the job because Mrs. Bush already had interviewed many prospects and had rejected all of them.

"She called me in. We sat down and talked," Otha Taylor aid. "She wanted to know if I had any children. I said no, but my sister did and I spent most of my time baby-sitting."

During the interview, Mrs. Taylor said, she felt comfortable—"I liked her right away"—and she was hired. It turned out to be a good decision for both women. "She will really let you know about it if you've done something wrong, but it only lasts for a few minutes. She was good about that."

The year was 1957, almost four years after Robin's death, but, Otha Taylor said, "They were all still grieving." Every time the subject came up, she said, Mrs. Bush would say, " 'What I'm going to do, I'm going to keep trying until I get another girl.' "

Otha Taylor worked five hours a day for the Bushes. She came at two o'clock each afternoon, took the younger children to the park, bought them back to the house for supper and then gave them baths and got them ready for bed. At that point, she said, Mrs. Bush took over, reading bedtime stories until the children fell asleep.

Between six o'clock and seven, Mrs. Taylor said, she didn't have anything to do since her job was limited to child care. So, although she was paid to work until seven o'clock, Mrs. Bush told her she could leave after she finished with the daily baths.

"Mr. Bush came in one day and wanted to know where's Otha? She told him. He said, 'What? She can sit up and read a book or something. She's being paid until seven o'clock and she should stay until seven o'clock.' "

Mrs. Taylor said her first reaction to this decision was anger. "This made me mad at Mr. Bush, so I told my brother. I said, 'Mr. Bush is a real tight, stingy man.' I told him what happened." To her surprise, Mrs. Taylor said, her brother agreed with George Bush. "He explained to me that Mr. Bush was paying me and the money wasn't what he was concerned about. It was just doing the job."

Mrs. Taylor, who eventually became a quality control technician at Mobil Chemical in Temple, Texas, said she came to appreciate that point when she got into the work world. "Going through working life, I understood what was happening here," she said. "I learned a great lesson from Mr. Bush."

Mrs. Taylor said she spent most of her time at the Bushes with Jeb, who was four, and Neil, then two, while Mrs. Bush concentrated on her infant son, Marvin.

"Now Jebbie, I kind of enjoyed him," Mrs. Taylor said. "He was very observant. They were very, very easy to take care of. Their parents spent a lot of time with them. They were very mannerly kids even at that age."

She said the young Bushes had no idea about racial differences and Jeb tried to puzzle out the variations in skin color.

"Julia was a brown-skinned person, and I am black, and Julia's husband, Willie, was black," Mrs. Taylor said. "I can remember one day Jebbie and Neil were sitting at the table having a snack. Jeb said, 'Otha, me and Neil is the same color and you and Willie is the same color.' I said, 'What color is Julia?' " And that stumped him. "They didn't know the differences in races and color."

But questions of race loomed large in the rest of the country, brought into sharp focus by the school desegregation efforts and riots in Little Rock, Arkansas, that summer of 1957. Mrs. Bush, Otha Taylor, and Julia Jackson had firsthand experience with the racism still prevalent across the land when they drove from Texas to Maine with the three youngest Bush children.

"Mr. Bush didn't go for it at all," Mrs. Taylor said. "He didn't want her to drive that far. He wanted us all to fly."

But Otha Taylor and Julia Jackson were afraid to get on a plane, so George Bush bought a new station wagon for the six travelers—Mrs. Bush, the two helpers, Jeb, Neil, and baby Marvin. Young George was in a baseball tournament and planned to fly to Kennebunkport later with his father.

Mrs. Taylor recalled how excited she was when the trip began. It was to be an adventure for all of them. Their first stop was to be in Oklahoma City, where George Bush had made reservations at a hotel.

"When we arrived at the hotel, we went through the back to get unloaded," Otha Taylor said. "Mrs. Bush went in while we were sitting out with the kids. When she came back out she said, 'Girls, we're having a little problem.' She didn't say what it was. She said, 'I'm going to call Mr. Bush.' "

The problem was that the hotel did not allow African-Americans as guests. But after George Bush spoke with the hotel manager, he agreed that the family could stay as long as they kept out of sight.

"We went in and Mrs. Bush said, 'Girls, they're not going to let us eat in the restaurant. So all of us are going to eat up here. We're going to enjoy ourselves.' " As Otha Taylor remembers it, Barbara ordered a huge spread in an effort to make the occasion more cheerful.

"We had to leave early in the morning," Mrs. Taylor said. "The man could have lost a lot of business by letting us stay there. I don't know what Mr. Bush did (to convince the hotel owner). I guess he did the same thing he did over there in the Persian Gulf."

The next stop was Kansas, where Barbara planned to visit friends. They were able to find a motel and Barbara thought she had solved their problems by buying uniforms for Otha and Julia. 'She said someone had told her if you traveled in uniform, they wouldn't give us any trouble."

That didn't prove to be the case. At dinnertime, Julia and Otha took Jeb and Neil to the motel restaurant while Mrs. Bush was getting ready to visit friends. "We went in and sat down," Mrs. Taylor said. "And nobody paid us any attention for about ten minutes. Then a woman came over and said they didn't wait on colored."

With young Jeb full of questions, the party went back to the motel room. "Mrs. Bush was very upset and she called the manager, and she said, 'How's my girls and kids supposed to eat?' He said we could get room service. She told us to order big, to get anything we wanted."

Barbara still recalls that trip with anger. "I was just sick," she said. "We had those babies with us. You know Little Rock had happened in the middle of the trip so it polarized people. It was disgusting."

On the trip home, she recalled, "Howard Johnson's had that year . . . opened up to everybody. So they saved our lives."

Mrs. Taylor said the situation was not much better when the party arrived in Greenwich, Connecticut, to visit Dorothy and Prescott Bush. The Bushes suggested that Otha and Julia might enjoy seeing the sights of Greenwich and recommended a ferry ride. So they bought their tickets and got in line. When they reached the ticket taker, he told them they couldn't ride—no blacks allowed.

This time, however, Julia Jackson decided she wasn't going to be denied, and the magic of the Bush name came to her aid. She asked the man if he knew Senator Prescott Bush. "She said we are here with his daughter-in-law and they sent us down here to ride the ferry." The reaction was swift. "He let us ride that ferry all the evening. We didn't even have to pay."

Despite these ugly incidents, Mrs. Taylor said the trip was interesting. In Connecticut, she and Julia stayed at the home of the senior Bushes, observing the family and listening to the political talk. Prescott Bush made a strong impression, Mrs. Taylor said. "That's where I decided I wanted to be a Republican."

The group traveled on to the Bush home in Kennebunkport for summer festivities. There was the usual boating and sports and games, but Otha Taylor also recalled that the young children balked at spending time with their great-grandmother, an elderly woman who maintained a formal house not designed for active preschoolers.

However, George W., being the oldest, was required to go along to dinner at his great-grandmother's while the younger children got to stay behind and enjoy a deep-dish blueberry pie.

"His father said he had to come because he was a big boy. He and his father were always tussing about something," Mrs. Taylor said. "George didn't like to go there because Granny Bush had a very formal table. And she only served chicken salad sandwiches."

Otha Taylor worked for the Bushes for only six months. Shortly after the Maine trip she decided to get married. She said Mrs. Bush was not pleased at her departure but she accepted the decision.

During those years George Bush's oil business continued to prosper. In 1958, he moved the company headquarters to Houston. A year later the Bushes had their last child—the much-wanted girl. They named her Dorothy Walker Bush.

The family was complete now. And Barbara was immersed in her life as wife and mother.

5

THE BUSH CHILDREN

When George Bush is asked what he is most proud of, he says it is the fact that his five children still come home. Everyone in the family appears to like everyone else and they go to bat for each other fiercely—as in the 2000 presidential election when Florida Governor Jeb Bush did everything in his power to deliver the state to his brother.

The fabric of these relationships is Barbara Bush's finest accomplishment. While the children were growing up, George was often away working, either at his job or in community or political affairs. "Dad was the chief executive officer, but Mother was the chief operating officer," said Jeb.

It was left to Barbara to set the tone for the family, impose the day-to-day order and discipline, and provide the hugs, encouragement, and sympathetic ear.

"I think what made for a great family experience was that there was always a feeling of warmth," Marvin Bush said. "When I came into the house, I felt that. I knew I was surrounded by people who loved me. At first I really wasn't that aware of it; I thought everyone else had the same situation. But when I started bringing friends home, I realized that we had something special."[1]

Barbara recalled with some pride that the neighborhood children often drifted to her house and played in the Bush backyard, where a pool helped to draw a crowd. She devoted all her energies to her husband, her children, and her household. Never one to say she has regrets, she nevertheless remembers those years with mixed feelings.

"It was a period for me of long days and short years," she said in a 1985 speech, "of diapers, runny noses, earaches, more Little League games than you could believe possible, tonsils, and those unscheduled races to the hospital emergency room; Sunday school and church, of hours of urging homework, short chubby arms around your neck and sticky kisses and experiencing bumpy moments—not many, but a few, of feeling that I'd never, ever be able to have fun again, and coping with the feeling that George Bush, in his excitement of starting a small company and traveling around the world, was having a lot of fun."

When she was left alone with a house full of small, active children, she said, "There were days I thought I would scream if the children didn't say something intelligent."

When George Bush was home, he played with the children, caught up on their lives, and added a lively presence to the family unit. But when he was away, Barbara was left to deal with the problems.

"When Jebbie was twelve he walked peculiarly; the doctor thought it might be a rare bone disease," she said. "George was away, so my friends held my hand. But it turned out to be only an infection in his heel. Neil had an eye emergency and I had to rush him from Midland, Texas, to Houston, but it turned out to be nothing."[2]

When the children needed discipline, Barbara said, she was "the enforcer," even spanking them occasionally. "I didn't spank hard, but I spanked," she said. "I would scream and carry on."

Marvin recalled how she managed to keep order in the car with her large brood. "She had something that we referred to as the claw," he said. "She had an amazing ability. She had a rubber arm. So she could reach back in the backseat and it didn't matter if you were two rows back, she had the ability to grab you with those red fingernails of hers and dig right into your arm. It got your attention."[3]

George W. put it succinctly: "I've been reprimanded by Barbara Bush as a child and I've been reprimanded as an adult. And in both circumstances, it's not very much fun."

George Bush didn't get into these frays because he often was away at the moment the misdeed occurred. But the children still feared his anger, which he expressed psychologically rather than physically.

"Mom was always there," Neil said. "My father was the ultimate authority whenever there was a conflict which couldn't be resolved at the mom level."

"I don't remember him punishing us," Jeb said. "But just knowing he was disappointed in me was enough. I couldn't stand it."

Added Barbara, "The way George scolded was by silence or by saying, 'I'm disappointed in you.' And they would almost faint."

George W., the oldest son, was especially vulnerable to his father's disapproval. He still remembers a time when, as a young man, he walked out on a summer job on an offshore oil rig a week early to be with his girlfriend, thus failing to fulfill a commitment.

"Well, my father found out about it," he said. "Follow-through and commitment were among the things he strongly believed in. So I was called into his office in Houston. He looked at me, and said, "Son, you agreed to work a certain amount of time and you didn't. I just want you to know that you have disappointed me."

Young George said that was about the harshest his father got—no yelling but a lot of moral suasion. So he left the office feeling guilty and rotten. But, typically, George Bush did not stay angry for long. About two hours after the office confrontation, he telephoned his son and invited him—and the girlfriend—to a Houston Astros game.

The two men had a more serious confrontation when George W. was twenty-six. By then the family had moved to Washington and George W. was on his own. When he came for a visit one afternoon, he took his fifteen-year-old brother Marvin to a friend's house, where they both had too much to drink. On the trip home, George W. ran into a neighbor's garbage can while turning into the Bush driveway.

"It wasn't long before the father asked his son to step into the den. George W. recalls being drunk and having a belligerent attitude as he entered the study. "I hear you're looking for me," he said to his father. "You want to go mano a mano right here?"

The boys are quick to admit they had rough edges when they were young, despite the Father Knows Best image the Bush family projects. "I think we were all rebellious when we were in the rebellious stage," Jeb said.

"We weren't all Goody Two-shoes," Neil said, referring to his high school years in the early 1970s. "I don't think we were hippies but we weren't unaffected by the times we were raised in. I remember being in Washington for high school when the city was on fire and those were troubling times, the Vietnam War, the protests. No one [in the family] was actively protesting, but when you're in a school environment you can't help be affected by what goes on around you."[4]

He said he and his brothers also engaged in a lot of competition, friendly but intense. "We played basketball and we'd throw elbows at each other and duke it out. After it was over, we'd always be friends." But, he added, "No one in our family likes to lose."

Doro, the youngest child and the only girl, wasn't so much involved in the fray and she had an easier time with her father than her brothers did. "I hate to say this but Dad let me do anything I wanted," she said. "Mom was the one who had all the rules. Dad always gave in. My friends were always jealous. They'd say, 'God, you've got the greatest dad.'"

The children don't remember their parents fighting over discipline methods or money or any of the other things that typically cause family squabbles. Barbara Bush said they did argue in their early years together, but George also used quiet disapproval as a weapon in these match-ups, which put his wife at a disadvantage. "What's the point?" she said with some of the exasperation she must have felt years ago. "He would just let you flail and flaunt. . . . I mean, it's no fun to argue in a one-sided argument. He knows what he thinks and he's perfectly willing to let you scream and yell, but I just gave that up. That was a waste of our energy."

She also sometimes despaired of getting George to take the children's misbehavior seriously, as she illustrated in a speech at the 1988 GOP presidential convention. "I called George one day when the boys were small, and said, 'Your son just hit a ball through the neighbor's upstairs window.' And he said, 'My gosh, what a great hit.' And then he said, 'Did you get the ball back?'"

George W. said he realized when he was growing up that his mother "put her relationship with her husband above her relationship with us."

But, he said, that didn't cause resentment because she was generous with her time with everyone.

"I played a lot of Little League, and I still have vivid memories of seeing her sitting at our games, keeping score," he said. "She bent over backwards for me and my brothers, especially in our love of sports."

When the boys got older, she was nice to their girlfriends, too, although she recalled that some of them were "real dogs." But remembering the warm reception she got from Dorothy Bush even before her engagement, Barbara said, "I treated them all like they were neat, nice people."

Barbara has an easy relationship with her oldest son, who has a feisty nature similar to her own. "We fight all the time," she said. "We're so alike in that way. He does things to needle me, always."

George W. is the only Bush child born on the East Coast, but he is the most confirmed Texan of the bunch. He lived in Midland from the time he was two until eighth grade, a small-town boyhood full of baseball, bicycling, swimming, and neighborhood buddies. And like his mother, he was a bit of a bully, according to a longtime baby-sitter.[5]

He was almost grown by the time his father started out in politics. And he was the child most affected by Robin's death, a fact that he had to face up to at age seven. He still recalls the day he realized his three-year-old sister had died.

"I was at school that day in the second grade and I can still see in my mind's eye my parents pulling up in the parking lot. I was carrying a Victrola back to the principal's office with a kid named Bill Sallee. My parents had been in New York City at the Sloan-Kettering clinic with Robin and they had just returned. I remember looking in the car and thinking I saw Robin in the back. I thought I saw her, but she wasn't there."[6]

By the time the family moved to Houston, George W. was ready for high school and he followed the family pattern, going first to Andover, then to Yale. But his experience was far different from his father's.

Where George Bush had grown up with chauffeurs who deposited him each day at Greenwich Country Day School, George W. had gone, on his own power, to San Jacinto Junior High in Midland, Texas. Thus, Andover, whose upper-class students were mostly from east of the Mississippi, came as a culture shock; it was where George W. first discovered his distaste for the effete East.

At Yale, George Bush was Phi Beta Kappa but George W. got mediocre grades. "I was never a great intellectual," he said. The campus in the late 1940s was full of World War II veterans, some of them, like Bush, war heroes. George W. was at Yale during the Vietnam War, when campuses across the country were alienated from government and bogged down in protests. Many young college men sought to avoid the draft; few were willing to volunteer for the front in such an unpopular war.

George W. didn't join the protests of his era; he signed up for military service, learning to fly fighter planes just as his father had done. But he chose the Texas Air National Guard instead of the navy, and although he was in a program that rotated National Guard planes to Vietnam, he was not called.

During George W.'s time at Yale, his father ran for the Senate and lost to the incumbent, populist Democrat Ralph Yarborough. "I ran into William Sloane Coffin, who was the preacher at Yale, supposedly the guy that was there to comfort students," Bush said years later. "I introduced myself and he said, 'Yeah, I know your father, and your father lost to a better man.'" Such rudeness, Bush said, was one reason he couldn't wait to leave Yale and get back to Texas. "Texas people are more polite. I don't think a Texan would do that to a son."[7]

In his late twenties—after the "mano a mano" incident with his father—George W. decided to get a master's degree in business and he was accepted at Harvard. He got the degree but didn't have an easy time. It was the height of Watergate and his father was part of the Republican establishment. Nancy Ellis, George W's aunt, living across the river in Boston, recalls the period as a rough one for her nephew. "You know Harvard Square and how they felt about Nixon," she said. "But here was Georgie, his father head of the Republican National Committee. So he came out a lot with us just to get out of there."

Like his father, George W. had no desire to work on Wall Street, and he was even more eager to leave the East Coast. After college, he repeated the journey his parents had made, driving home to Texas to test his entrepreneurial skills. He started out researching mineral and land records and eventually went into business for himself.

Young George did not have the same success in oil that his father had—he later complained, "I'm all name and no money"—and he is teased by his friends and relatives for his skinflint ways. But he was always solvent and able to attract investors with the Bush name. He put together a group that bought the Texas Rangers baseball team in 1988 and he started out in politics earlier than his father. He ran unsuccessfully for Congress in 1978 and was considering entering the race for Texas governor in 1990. With George Bush in the White House, however, Barbara publicly urged her son not to run, fearing "a filthy campaign. I thought the hurt would be enormous."

He didn't run then, waiting to launch his successful runs for governor and president until his father was voted out of public office.

George W. didn't marry until he was thirty years old. Barbara called it a red-letter day when he finally announced his intention to marry the daughter of a Texas contractor, Laura Welch, a librarian he had met just three months earlier. Said Laura of the brief courtship. "We were both thirty and had had a lot of single years. We were glad to find each other."

Jeb, the second-born son, is seven years younger than George. He considers himself "the serious one" of the Bush siblings, maybe because he spent scarcely any time as the family baby. His brother Neil was born when Jeb was just two years old and Marvin came along a year after that. Neil said—long before George W. became president—that "although George might dispute this, Jeb and Marvin are probably the brightest of the boys."

Jeb, Neil, and Marvin, so close in age, sometimes hung out together. Jeb recalls a weekly neighborhood newspaper they put together and sold for a nickel a copy. The family lived in Houston during most of Jeb's childhood, years in which George Bush was prospering in the oil business.

Jeb followed his father and older brother to Andover for prep school, but his experience there was not a happy one. It was the late 1960s and the political disaffection that had afflicted college campuses was also alive at Andover. "The school was rebelling against itself," Jeb says. "Our class particularly. I think the school hit bottom with us."

By his senior year, though, Jeb had found an interest that would last a lifetime—Mexico. Taking part in a work-study course titled "Man and Society," he worked in a Mexican village and helped build a schoolhouse. One evening, he was invited to the home of a Mexican girl who was dating another Andover student. Jeb sat down next to the girl's sister, Columba Garnica, and reacted to her much the way George Bush had responded to Barbara three decades earlier. "Boom, I was gone," Jeb said. "She was the first girl I ever loved and the last." He returned to Andover realizing his carpentry skills would never amount to much, but his respect for Mexico would be abiding.

Columba gave Jeb a goal in life. During his last semester, he made straight A's for the first time. And, like his father, he went through college in two and a half years. But his choice was the culturally comfortable University of Texas, not Yale. "I wanted to get it over, get on, get married," Jeb said. "She gave me a sense of purpose."

Jeb told his parents about Columba but was slow to let them know how serious the relationship was. It wasn't until Christmas vacation of 1974—Jeb was twenty-one by then and out of college—that he introduced her to the Bushes and informed them he planned to be married in Austin two months later. Whatever fears Jeb might have had about his parents' reactions dissolved. They didn't object to the marriage and Columba immediately found herself brought into the family circle.

Jeb and Columba sometimes speak Spanish at home and although Jeb was raised as an Episcopalian, their three children—George P., Noelle, and Jeb—were baptized as Catholics. The oldest of Jeb's children, George P., has an especially close relationship with his grandfather. George Bush was hurt and amazed during the 1988 presidential campaign at the outcry that developed when he affectionately referred to these three grandchildren as "the little brown ones." A decade later, the Latino heritage turned into a political plus for both Jeb and George W. And George P., handsome, articulate, and comfortable on the public stage, became something of a heartthrob during the 2000 presidential election.

Neil, the number three son, has had the most trouble of the five Bush siblings. As a child, he had a severe reading problem, which he managed to cover up until second grade. Barbara recalled sitting down with him one day when he was sick and trying to read. He didn't seem to know the words. She telephoned his teacher, who wasn't aware of any problem, so Barbara visited the classroom. She found that when Neil was called on to read, his classmates fed him the words. On his own, he couldn't do it.

Tests revealed that Neil had dyslexia, a disorder that makes it difficult for children to put letters together to form words and to sound out words from a group of letters. With great energy, Barbara went after solutions. She hired tutors, found books with large print, put together practice tapes and offered endless encouragement.

"Dyslexia, back in those days, was not well known," George W. said. "Mother worked hard with Neil, disciplining, training, encouraging. She was the one who really spent the time making sure that Neil could learn to read the basics."

Still, Neil had trouble in school and continued to dislike reading unless the subject was sports. He went along with his mother's program, but he said, "For years and years I hated it. I hated reading. The only thing more painful in my life than reading was once when I broke my front tooth."

He remains grateful to his mother, however, for bolstering his self-confidence, praising him for the things he did well instead of concentrating on his deficit in reading. "She loved gardening and I loved helping her because she made me feel I did it better than anyone else," he said. "She brought that out in me. To this day, I don't feel handicapped. I have all the confidence in the world because of her."

The Bushes were in Washington by the time Neil was ready for high school. He was enrolled in St. Albans, a good private school with many children from socially prominent families. Neil's teachers told Barbara that he might not be able to handle college but she refused to accept that negative message and so did Neil, who has a dogged and optimistic personality. He graduated from Tulane University in 1977 with a bachelor's degree in international relations and went on to earn a master's degree in business two years later.

Neil met his wife, Sharon, while he was campaigning for his father in New Hampshire in 1979. She was a schoolteacher at the time and a local Republican introduced them with the idea of generating a romance. They married less than a year later.

Sharon and Neil settled in Denver in the early 1980s and Neil planned to make his fortune in oil just as his father had. He and two friends started an oil and gas exploration firm with a $300,000 stake from two larger energy companies. But they drilled thirty-one holes without striking oil or gas.

Despite his lack of success in the oil business, Neil became a well-liked figure in Denver and was sought out by people attracted to the Bush name. In 1985 he joined the board of the local Silverado Banking, Savings and Loan Association at the invitation of its politically ambitious president, Michael Wise. Silverado failed and was taken over by federal regulators in 1988. Neil, as an outside director of the board that controlled Silverado, was caught up in a national scandal that involved sleazy dealings at dozens of savings and loans and failures that cost taxpayers billions of dollars.

The federal Office of Thrift Supervision, which regulated savings and loans, found in April 1991 that Neil had violated conflict-of-interest rules while serving as a Silverado director. The agency, in what amounted to a slap on the wrist, said that if Neil wanted to serve on a savings and loan board in the future, he would have to get advice from a lawyer about conflict-of-interest rules. It also said he would have to disclose all his financial and business interests to federal regulators for a year. Five Silverado officers were prohibited from working in the industry in the future.

Neil was accused of failing to tell the Silverado board of his relationship with two Colorado developers, Bill Walters and Kenneth Good. The men had invested in Neil's unsuccessful oil company, JNB, and later received approval for loans or lines of credit from Silverado, on which they defaulted.

The director of the Office of Thrift Supervision, which issued the sanctions against Neil, was Timothy Ryan, who had been a legal adviser to George Bush's presidential campaign. Even though the sanctions had been endorsed by a trusted friend, the Bush family felt that Neil had been singled out for prosecution because he was the president's son. George W. said his brother was "getting hosed because his father is president of the United States, period . . . there's not a devious bone in his body."

The president said, "It's tough on people in public life, to some degree. I've got three other sons and they all want to take to the barricades, every one of them, when they see some cartoon totally demeaning of the honor of their brother. I say, 'You calm down, now. We're in a different role. . . . You can't react like you would if your brother was picked on in a street fight.' "

Despite these measured words, the family was heartsick. "If he weren't my son or George's son, I don't think you would ever have heard his name," Barbara said. "I'm sorry for him because it's very costly for him. I think he feels this is hurting his father, which is ridiculous. One might think his father is hurting him . . . one of the prices children have to pay."

A week after the federal ruling against Neil, Barbara flew to Denver to speak to a local charity that he was supporting, her way of showing support.

Neil himself was angry and also hurt by the way federal prosecutors had pursued him. "I probably am guilty of not being the savviest political guy in the Bush family," he said. "I didn't do anything wrong. I acted properly as a director. I was as fit as any director to sit on the board."

During the controversy over Silverado, Neil also was investigated by a congressional committee for another business deal but the panel found no wrongdoing. The second investigation was launched because Neil and a colleague had invested $3,000 in a Denver oil company—Apex—in May 1989 and a federally subsidized small business fund had put up $2.3 million. Neil, as president of the company, was paid $160,000 a year although the company never made a profit. He resigned from Apex in April 1991, the same month the savings and loan ruling was issued against him.

Neil has led a mostly private life since then but a decade later his daughter, Lauren, stepped into the international spotlight as a model, doing photo shoots for *W*, a fashion magazine, as well as *Vogue, George, Texas Monthly* and a number of catalogues.

Marvin, the youngest of the Bush sons, has stayed away from both oil and politics. He is credited by his siblings with the best sense of humor and is considered by many people to be the most personable of the Bush children. Like his father, he has hundreds of friends and easygoing charm. His business is finance and investment, which is just fine with his parents. "Never once growing up did I feel pressure from either of my parents to be something I'm not," he said. "That to me is one of their greatest accomplishments. All their children are extremely different and they appreciate us for who we are."

Just twenty-one months younger than Neil, Marvin keenly felt the presence of three older brothers during his childhood. "We never sat around our house discussing issues," George W. said. "We talked about what the Astros did that day or whether Marvin had finished his peas yet."[8]

Being so much younger, Marvin tried hard to keep up with his brothers. "I remember one afternoon up in Maine," he said. "My brother George and I were playing tennis when things got a little tight on the tennis court. I was about ten years younger than he was and it got to an especially tense point in the match. I think I was fairly brash and was making sure he knew exactly what the score was. The next thing I knew he was chasing me up a fence."

Perhaps because of his struggles to compete with so many older siblings, Marvin eventually improved his tennis game to the point where he is the acknowledged family champ. "I guess you could say I was the classic little brother, always trying to emulate my brothers, always trying to hang around," Marvin said. "Sometimes, in a particularly feisty mood, I'd accuse my parents of adopting me, just to get their attention. It never worked."

He also recalled being upset as a child at the amount of time his mother devoted to charity—time he thought could have been better spent on him. "I remember being jealous when my mom would run off to the Washington Home," Marvin said. "I thought she spent an inordinate amount of her time there. It wasn't until I was older that I appreciated what she told me, that to live a complete life, you need to help other people."

Marvin went to college at the University of Virginia in Charlottesville, just two hours from Washington, D.C. When he fell in love with a fellow student, Margaret Molster, he talked with Mom and Dad before deciding to marry her.

"I was fairly young, twenty-four, and I wanted to feel comfortable and get some reassurance with what I was planning to do," he said. "They said I'd better marry Margaret because the chances were slim I'd find someone as special again. That turned out to be excellent advice."[9]

Because she had ovarian cancer, Margaret, who is trained as a teacher, cannot bear children. But she and Marvin adopted two infants, Marshall in 1986 and Charles in 1990.

Marvin said the strength Margaret drew from overcoming her childhood illness helped him cope when he developed life-threatening ulcerative colitis in 1986 and had to have his colon removed. In May that year Marvin had a colostomy, an operation that creates an opening in the abdomen for the passage of waste. The waste goes into a pouch attached to the body at the opening.

George Bush was vice president when Marvin had the operation and both he and Barbara spent a lot of time at the hospital praying for their son, an ordeal that reminded them of the loss of Robin more than two decades earlier.

"I can't help but think that while my mother was with me during that period she might have had some flashbacks to twenty-five years ago when she was with my sister," Marvin said.[10]

For a long time after Marvin's illness, Barbara still got teary-eyed when discussing it. "Since then we've put things in perspective," she said. "We've realized there are worse things than losing an election. Marvin's very valuable to us. We knew it, but we didn't know how valuable. I just think that our fresh perspective had something to do with Marvin."

Marvin himself felt depressed after the operation. He was only twenty-nine years old and feared the bag at his waist would mean an end to sports and perhaps affect his relationship with Margaret. But, cheerful by nature, Marvin turned his thinking around before long. "I thought of the alternative, the unbearable pain, the increased risk of colon cancer associated with long-standing colitis, and possibly death. Wearing a pouch seemed a small price to pay for the privilege of leading a normal, productive life."[11]

He said he was especially encouraged by a call from a man who had the same operation several years earlier, Rolf Benirschke, a former place kicker with the San Diego Chargers, who had gone on to a television career. Rolf assured Marvin he could still take part in sports, have a good relationship with his wife, and lead the same active life he led before. And he got Marvin interested in helping other people who have had the operation.

Marvin, like his mother, found that his high-profile name could be used to spotlight good works. "After a colostomy some people hide in their houses for years without coming out, thinking they're so unappealing or unattractive to others," he said. "I can show them that it doesn't matter at all."[12]

Marvin is three years older than his sister Dorothy, called Doro by the family, and admits he spent much of his childhood concocting ways to torture her. He is embarrassed about that today, but Doro seems to have survived intact. She has an especially strong relationship with her father, being the only surviving girl in the family, and she unabashedly adores him.

"My dad would just spoil me with love," she said. "There's something about our relationship I can't explain. He was just a soft touch with me."

The poignant memories of Robin may have been one reason. Doro says that when her father tucked her into bed at night during childhood, he would tell her about Robin "and we would both cry."

She recalled with amusement the time when she was ten or eleven and her father played a joke on her. "He called me from the office, and said, 'Hello, little girl. This is the telephone repairman. I'm testing your phone. Hold the phone away from your ear because there might be a loud noise.' I held the phone out for a real long time until finally Mom asked what on earth I was doing. She caught on right away."

Doro has fond memories of her childhood—the felt Christmas stockings decorated with sequins that Barbara Bush made for each child, the thrill of getting soaked in George's speedboat off the coast of Maine, the fun she had living with her parents at the Waldorf-Astoria in New York City—like Eloise at the Plaza—and being driven to school by a chauffeur to the U.N. School while George Bush was ambassador to the U.N.

But Doro was always shy and self-conscious. When the chauffeur drove her to school in New York, she asked to be dropped off a block away so no one would see her in the fancy car. When the Bushes first moved to Washington, she feared she wouldn't be dressed right, so her father took her across the street to ask a girl her age what the current fashion was. It turned out to be the right move; the short socks Doro wore in Texas looked nothing like the knee socks girls in Washington favored.

Like Barbara, Doro went to an exclusive girl's school, Miss Porter's in Farmington, Connecticut. She recalled how excited she was one day when her father, in New York for a speech, invited her out to dinner. "I thought I was really hot stuff going there to meet him," she recalled. "We were going to spend the night at the Waldorf, and after the speech, he took me to the 21 Club for dinner. I thought it was the neatest thing in the world. We were sitting there at dinner and all of a sudden Dad started to fall asleep because he was so tired. I was so excited and my dad was sleeping. It was funny."[13]

Doro had no great interest in a career but she did earn a degree in sociology from Boston College. While she was vacationing in Maine after her sophomore year in college, Doro met William LeBlond, and she said, it was "love at first sight." They married when she got out of college and had two children, Sam and Ellie.

Doro fondly recalls the birth of her first child and a special trip her father made to see her when he was busy running for reelection as vice president. "It was 1984, right in the middle of the campaign, and I was in the hospital having Sam," she said. "It was a big baby, ten pounds, and I was feeling pretty rough. The nurse looks out the window and says, 'Oh, there are police dogs and police and all these men in suits running around.' I said, 'Oh, my, it's my dad.' Then there was a knock on the door and there he was. I couldn't believe he came in the middle of the campaign. We walked down together to see Sam and it was the greatest day of my life."

Afterward, her father sent her this letter:

Dear Doro:

Monday was a very special day in my life. Sam is beautiful. He has two great parents who will give him love all his life. Seeing that little guy made many thoughts run through my head. Thank God he's strong and well. Thank God he's born to a family of love and kindness and caring. Then I must confess, I thought, I'm sixty—it doesn't feel old but it is pretty old, and here's Sam, one day old, just starting out in life, with much joy and happiness ahead of him and a mother who has given her own Dad nothing but happiness and love; and a father who will be at his side teaching him about decency and honor and the importance of family. Sleep on, fat little Sam—a lot of fun awaits you and when you hurt, your beautiful, wonderful mom will hug you.

Devotedly, Dad.

Doro overcame some of her shyness through a desire to help her father in his political campaigns. During his unsuccessful 1980 bid for the Republican presidential nomination, she took a course in typing and shorthand so she would have some skills to offer the campaign and she worked in his New England office. But, like her mother, she was initially shaky on the campaign trail. When Bush's aides persuaded her to speak at a tea for elderly women, she blanked out and sat down shaking. As the 1980 campaign progressed, however, she became more confident. She helped

organize caucuses in Maine early on, then began traveling. By the time
the Republican National Convention met in New Orleans, she was happily
speaking on her father's behalf every chance she got.

Early in her first marriage, Doro lived with her husband in Maine,
figuring her parents eventually would retire there and wanting to be near
them. Bill LeBlond ran a construction firm and Doro did bookkeeping for
him. The marriage was short-lived, however. In the spring of 1990, Doro
became the first—and only—Bush child to divorce. George and Barbara
were in the White House at the time and Doro moved to Washington where
she met Bobby Koch, an aide to the Democratic leader of the U.S. House
of Representatives, Richard Gephardt. The two married at Camp David in
June 1992 during Bush's second presidential campaign and Koch quit his
political job, probably to avoid a conflict with his very Republican in-laws.

Barbara is defensive about her children—admittedly so. She reacts like
a mother bear whenever they are criticized.

"My children have had only minor problems," she said. "They haven't
had any real problems. And don't forget. I'm right there with them every
step of the way. . . . They're all wonderful kids. We've always been very
conceited about how wonderful our family is."[14]

6

POLITICAL WIFE

George Bush won the first political race he ever entered. The year was 1962 and Republicans in Houston, hoping to end decades as the underdog party of Texas, saw the young eastern oil man as someone with a future. They asked him to run for chairman of the Harris County Republican party.

Bush was eager to get into politics, and he accepted right away, figuring the work he put in at the local level would pay off if he sought higher office later.

To Barbara's surprise, she enjoyed the campaign. After fifteen housebound years centered on children, with George away on business much of the time, she found it a pleasure to be at her husband's side in a fast-moving campaign.

The Bushes methodically visited all the precincts in Harris County. Barbara sat onstage while George gave his speech—the same one over and over. She did needlepoint to pass the time and found it also drew interest from women in the audience who wanted to know what she was working on and to tell her about their own projects.

But where she really became an asset was in the mix and mingle before and after the speeches. Her outgoing personality won the candidate friends and she was good at remembering names and faces and events connected with them, a much-valued skill in a world where who you know and what they think of you counts more than anything else except money.

Still, Barbara remembers her failures somewhat ruefully. Witty and opinionated, she was not accustomed to holding her tongue. "The first time I campaigned, I probably lost George hundreds of votes," she said. "I'm not only outspoken, I'm honest."

He won anyway, and young Jeb included the news in his hand-written neighborhood newsletter: "Mr. Bush wins unanimously as head of Harris County Republicans."[1]

By 1964, Bush decided to run for the U.S. Senate and went through an ugly primary fight before winning. The John Birch Society even dragged Barbara's father into the race. They noted that Marvin Pierce was publisher of *Redbook*. And *Redbook*, the John Birch Society said, was a communist magazine. Some voters in the far reaches of rural Texas who had never seen the popular women's magazine might even have believed it. Barbara was shocked to find hate mail shoved right under the door of her house.

Bush prevailed in the primary despite right-wing opposition. His opponent was a liberal Democrat, incumbent Senator Ralph Yarborough.

Barbara worked door-to-door in the Senate campaign, sometimes wearing a name tag that gave only her first name because she wanted to know what people really thought of George Bush. Too often, the answer was that he was just another upstart Republican, reason enough in Texas at the time to vote against him. Democrat Lyndon Johnson was elected president that year and Yarborough won reelection handily, defeating Bush 1.46 million votes to 1.13 million, or 56 percent to 43 percent.

George Bush took the defeat well, according to Barbara, but she didn't. "He was wonderful," she said. "He got right on the phone the next morning and thanked everybody who helped him, you know, cheering them up. I was terrible. I went out and played tennis and tears were flowing down my face."

Doro Bush, just five years old at the time, recalls breaking down in tears also when she learned her father had lost. "I said, 'Dad, I'll be the only one in school who has a father without a job,'" she said.

Not to worry. George Bush still had part ownership of a profitable offshore oil business and enough money to keep his large family comfortable.

It was during that campaign that Barbara gave up on attempts to dye her hair, which had turned white when she was only twenty-eight during Robin's illness. "I began coloring it myself, but it turned every color but the warm brown I wanted," she said. "So back when George was running for the Senate, I went to the beauty parlor and said how bad my hair looked. The beautician said, 'Let's try this rinse called Fabulous Fawn.' So we rinsed with Fabulous Fawn and off I flew to East Texas to campaign. . . . It was a hundred and five degrees in that plane. I asked the pilot to turn up the air-conditioning, but he told me it had just gone out. And my Fabulous Fawn began to run. It ran down my neck, my ears, my cheeks, and my forehead. I began to blot myself with Kleenex, used all that up, then started on toilet paper. I spent the whole flight mopping myself up."[2]

Despite his defeat in the Senate race, Bush was not ready to give up on politics. He ran for the House of Representatives from Harris County in 1966 and won—the first Republican ever elected in the district.

The victory meant another move for the Bush family. They had lived in Houston for seven years; now Washington would be their home. When they made the move, only three of the five children came along. George W. was at Yale and Jeb was getting ready for prep school at Andover. He spent ninth grade living with a friend in Houston rather than moving to a new city for his last year of middle school.

Barbara enrolled her three youngest in elite Washington schools. Doro, seven years old, went to the Cathedral School; both twelve-year-old Neil and ten-year-old Marvin were at St. Alban's, a prominent boy's school.

Marvin recalled that his mother was determined that her children would get to know Washington's famous sites, and quickly. "The first two weekends we were here, my mom got Neil, my sister Doro and myself, took us to the Washington Monument, took us to the Lincoln Memorial, the Jefferson Memorial. I finally told her, I said, Mom, it's a two-year term, relax."[3]

George had bought a house sight unseen from a retiring senator, and once the family settled in they discovered it had neither enough space nor enough light. It fell to Barbara to find something better. She had joined a study group organized by Shirley Pettis, the wife of another new Republican congressman, Jerry Pettis. The two women soon became friends, and one afternoon Barbara told Shirley she had found a house she liked.

"They were in a house and we were in a house and neither of us was happy," Shirley Pettis said. "She said she found one that interested her and she wondered if I could just hop in the car and look at it and so I did. I thought it was an absolutely superb house."

What Barbara had found was a pair of new houses at the end of a cul-de-sac in northwest Washington near the National Cathedral. The house she liked was a three-story brick townhouse with a small front yard and a patio in back. The second new house, a mirror image; was just across a courtyard, separated from the first house by a brick wall. Shirley urged Barbara to buy the house and Barbara in turn urged Shirley to buy the one next door.

The next day, Barbara got George to look at the house she liked and they signed a contract for it on the spot. Shirley and Jerry Pettis bought the one next door, but they took a little longer to make a decision. "I took my husband over and I took the children and they couldn't imagine why I couldn't make up my mind as fast at Mrs. Bush," Shirley Pettis said. "They let me know about it. But we did buy it a couple of months later."

Barbara set out immediately to fix up the house and the garden and to get to know her neighbors, among them Supreme Court Justice Potter Stewart and Franklin Roosevelt Jr.

"Bar was a very outgoing, neighborly type," Shirley Pettis said. "She soon knew everybody on our cul-de-sac. She walked the dog, C. Fred, so she would meet everybody."

Justice Stewart's wife, Mary Ann, had met George and Barbara earlier while Prescott Bush was in the Senate. Mrs. Stewart recalled George's mother, Dorothy, telling her, "You'll just love my daughter-in-law. I know you'll hit it off."

Dorothy Bush was right. Mary Ann, widely known as Andy, found herself attracted to Barbara immediately. The two shared an unusually high energy level and husbands with interesting and very public jobs. They became close friends.

Before the Bushes moved into the neighborhood, longtime residents had been looking unhappily at the two new houses at the end of their lane. "It was an area in our neighborhood where there had been an empty lot and somebody had built two houses facing each other," Mrs. Stewart said. "We were not at all pleased with the fact that the empty lot was gone."

Neither did the neighbors like the style of the new homes, which looked like town houses. "They seemed to be more modern," Mrs. Stewart said. "The rest of the houses were considerably older. They had been there and settled for a long time."

So it came as a pleasant surprise when the Bushes moved in, followed by the Pettis family. The new households added sparkle to the neighborhood. Barbara, in typical fashion, had her house organized in no time. "Within a week after she moved in she looked more settled than I had in four years," Mrs. Stewart said.

With a housekeeper to help inside, Barbara devoted a lot of time to the garden, mulching, mowing, weeding and even doing tasks that would daunt a lesser gardener. "As soon as the weather was propitious, the garden was planted," Shirley Pettis said. "She had hers in beautiful blooming order far before I did. She's extremely action oriented and she's so organized that I've always said she could easily run General Motors or the Pentagon."

Barbara also had a good eye for design, Mrs. Pettis said: "Her mental eye could just envision how each flowering bush was going to look. And furthermore, she would do a lot of the work herself. She had a wonderfully cooperative back. She'd bring in great loads of all the textured things that have to go into the soil."

"She's a prodigious do-it-herselfer," Mrs. Stewart said. "She thinks nothing of putting in a dogwood tree or moving bushes. She loves hands-on."

The Bushes, still lonesome for their Texas friends, began to entertain frequently once they got the house and garden in order, most often with the kind of informal barbecues they had been giving ever since Midland. Barbara made salads, soup, and casseroles. George cooked hamburgers on the grill—but Barbara got them ready beforehand. "She always had things masterfully organized," Shirley Pettis said, "it was always on paper plates and cups and napkins. There would be a big trash can immediately outside where we could dump everything."

"The dessert was always something very special, oftentimes meringues.

Paola (the Bushes' longtime housekeeper) made wonderful individual meringues and she would fill them with ice cream or berries."

The barbecues became a regular Sunday afternoon event, fondly recalled by guests even years later. "It was always great fun," Andy Stewart said. "They invited all kinds of people—people who worked for them or with them early in Texas, people they met around the world, relatives—thousands of relatives it seemed, they're a big family—their children and everybody else's children who were the same ages. It was just very nice, a buffet, and then we'd sit around and talk politics and interesting things around Washington.

"The thing that always interested me was not only their friends and all the people that came and went, but it was always very orderly. It was civilized."

Shirley Pettis said it was the talk that made the parties special, "all sorts of ideas exchanged, the bouncing of ideas one to another. It was really a fascinating sort of get-together."

At the same time, said Janet Steiger, whose husband was first elected to Congress the same year as George Bush, "There was never anything forced. It was very easy. There was always a football game going in the background."

George Bush was an immediate success on Capitol Hill. The thirty-nine other freshmen Republicans in the ninetieth Congress elected him to be their leader and thanks to his father's friendship with Democrat Wilbur Mills, George was appointed to a coveted spot on the House Ways and Means Committee. He was the first freshman of either party to serve on the powerful tax panel in sixty years.

Barbara was a success also, plunging into activities with wives like herself whose husbands were newly elected. "Barbara was a very sought-after member of the group of ninetieth club wives," Janet Steiger said. "She was then as she is now an extremely warm and outgoing person and she made friends instantly."

Mrs. Steiger recalled with amusement how Barbara took a liking to one of her ideas and improved on it. "I started the idea of a slide show of little-known places in Washington," she said. "It prompted some interest among some of the ninetieth wives and I showed it to them, being quite proud of it of course. Bar immediately took what I thought was quite an accomplishment and made mine look silly. Typically, she got into what I thought was most effective, the gardens of Washington. Then she got into the churches, making mine look at best like a raw beginning."

She laughed. "It's not surprising that nobody remembers I ever did it. Whatever anybody else does, Bar makes better."

The Washington slides, she said, made an effective campaign tool for the wives, who often were asked to speak in their home districts. "People are interested in Washington and most of them bring their youngsters. It was a nonpolitical piece, which meant the audience could be anything."

Barbara initially was fearful of showing her slides to an audience. "When she came to Washington she was positive that she could not do that," said Shirley Pettis. "Then one of the clubs in Texas asked her to show her pictures on Washington. I remember telling her that anybody who could preside over a dinner or a luncheon table with so much wit... you'll be a big hit."

In her memoirs, Barbara noted that a speaker can hide behind a slide show, much as she can hide behind a book written with her dog, an acknowledgment of her longtime fears of public speaking and a signal that she eventually overcame them.

Back in the '70s, though, Barbara worried a lot. Shirley Pettis said she would get up early and "five o'clock in the morning I'd see her light in her den." She was working on her speeches.

One reason Barbara was so popular with other congressional wives was that she made time for them when they were most in need, as Janet Steiger fondly remembers. The Steigers were from Wisconsin and while they were in Washington, Janet became pregnant. When she went to a local hospital to have the baby, the only relative she had in town was her husband, so she was surprised when a nurse told her a close relative had come for a visit and even more nonplused when Barbara came trotting in.

"Barbara was always a rock," Mrs. Steiger said, "somebody you'd want with you in a tight spot. She of course sent my husband away. She conferred with the medical types. It was obvious to her nothing was going to happen at that minute. She sent him back to his office [on Capitol Hill] and she then summoned him at the appropriate time."

Barbara could also be a demanding friend, not for her own needs but as a recruiter for her charity work. In the early 1970s when she was spending a lot of time at the Washington Home, a health-care center for the chronically ill, Janet got a phone call from her. "We're going to need a little help doing the Fourth of July picnic" for residents of the home, Barbara said. "You're home, so here are the directions."

Janet Steiger didn't argue. "This was a home for the incurably ill. I think it takes a very special person to dedicate themselves to that," she said. "Bar really adopted a couple of folks who were multiple sclerosis victims and she was just simply devoted. She's never been on a board that I can think of where she was just an honorary. Bar was a working member."

With that in mind, Janet Steiger responded readily to the holiday call. "It was the Fourth of July, they were short-handed. We went over to dish out the hot dogs and baked beans. You don't think about whether you're a volunteer . . . get with the program."

When Bill Steiger died of a heart attack in 1978, both George and Barbara flew to Wisconsin to be with Janet, who had to decide whether to run for her husband's congressional seat and what would be best for her young child. She said Barbara helped her put the questions into focus, and she ultimately decided she didn't want to be in Congress while her son was so young. "It put a focus when it's very difficult for you to focus," Janet Steiger said. "She's an extraordinarily sympathetic friend. Her tack is to see what she can do something about."

Old Texas friends also found Barbara a help when they came to town. Jessica Catto, whose husband, Henry, was appointed ambassador to the Organization of American States, came to Washington with four small children and was worried about finding good schools. "Barbara was the one who drove me around to get oriented," she said. "She was a congressman's wife at that point. She's just that way for her friends. She just was there."

George Bush was reelected to Congress in 1968 without opposition and probably could have gone on serving in the House for many years. But Texas Republican leaders and President Richard Nixon believed that Senator Yarborough was more vulnerable than ever by 1970 and they urged Bush to take him on again.

In his autobiography, *Looking Forward,* Bush said that among the people he consulted before making the decision was Lyndon Johnson. Although Johnson was a Democrat who never would have endorsed Bush, Johnson didn't like fellow-Democrat Yarborough.

Bush said he flew to Johnson's ranch for a talk about politics and got the advice he was seeking. He remembered the conversation this way: "Son, I've served in the House. And I've been privileged to serve in the Senate, too. And they're both good places to serve. So I wouldn't begin to advise you what to do, except to say this—that the difference between being a member of the Senate and a member of the House is the difference between chickenshit and chicken salad. Do I make myself clear?"[4]

Bush decided to make the Senate race, even though it meant giving up a safe House seat. To his surprise and chagrin, however, Yarborough was defeated in the Democratic primary that year by a conservative, Lloyd Bentsen. Years later, Bentsen would lose in a race to Bush—in 1988 he was the vice presidential candidate on a ticket with Michael Dukakis—but in 1970 Bentsen won the Senate race by a comfortable margin, 53.4 percent to 46.6 percent.

Barbara, at the end of an exhausting campaign, took defeat hard, as usual. "When I called her up after the loss of the Senate election, she couldn't stop crying," sister-in-law Nancy Ellis said years later.

The disappointment was short-lived. Nixon, having urged Bush to take a chance on the Senate race, was ready with a consolation prize. Would Bush like to be U.S. ambassador to the United Nations?

Yes, indeed.

The Bushes had spent four enjoyable years in Washington in a quiet, tree-filled, suburbanlike, neighborhood. But they were accustomed to moving and New York City was an attractive offer. Their new home was the elegant Waldorf Towers in the popular Waldorf-Astoria Hotel on the East Side in midtown. The U.S. government kept a suite in the Towers as the official residence for the ambassador.

At the time, all the boys were away at school and Doro was the only child at home, so a spacious hotel suite provided plenty of room for the family. With her customary zeal and organizational skills, Barbara set to work immediately making the government-issued apartment a home.

"Bar has a way of bringing fresh potted plants and flowers in, mostly flowers," said Shirley Pettis, who with her husband was a house guest of the Bushes in New York. "She's very feminine in that respect. She loves flowers and soft colors around her. She likes art that reflects the soft colors and flowers and children playing. She's really quite feminine in many of her artistic pursuits. Whatever home she's in, she's going to have blooming flowers. It's such a signature with her."

Tapley Bennett, a top aide to Bush at the United Nations, remembers the residence well. "She converted a rather drab hotel apartment into quite a sparkling residence," he said. "One room was all in greens and whites; that was entirely her decoration."

As visitors entered the residence through a foyer, they were greeted with examples of American artistry—displays of Steuben glass and American paintings borrowed from New York's top museums. American wines were served in the formal dining room.

"She added a touch of personal interior decorating; she put a little color and life into it," said Ed Derwinski, who was the congressional delegate to the United Nations at the time.

Barbara attended the U.N. sessions, bringing along her needlepoint, but stayed away from the government office where George worked. "She would come and sit in the delegates' gallery on the side," Bennett said. "She was very supportive of her husband."

With a busy social life, her husband always nearby, and interesting people coming and going, Barbara came to love the New York assignment. "I would pay to have this job," she said. "It was like being taken around the world to meet people from a hundred twenty-eight countries and yet never having to pack a bag or sleep in a strange bed."

She also made time for volunteer work, spending time at Memorial Sloan-Kettering Cancer Institute, where Robin had been treated.

And she accompanied George to the many diplomatic functions he was required to attend. She recalled one evening especially that turned out to be quite embarrassing: it was her husband's fault.

"To this day, he doesn't realize how sore I was at him," she said. "It was really horrible. We had a night where you charge from reception to reception. I'd worn a short, bright-red cocktail suit with gold threads. It could not have been redder, or louder. After three receptions, I said, 'Where to now? George said, 'Come on, I'll tell you about it later.' And we raced up some stairs. Next thing I knew, we were in a funeral parlor. The ambassador of a Central American country had died. All the ladies were properly dressed in black and I was there in bright red. We were thrust into the center of the lights as the television announcer said, 'And here comes the United States ambassador and Mrs. Bush,' I couldn't wait to get out of there."[5]

Bush liked the New York assignment as much as Barbara did and delved into it with his usual enthusiasm. By tradition, whenever a new ambassador arrives at the United Nations, he makes a call on the U.S. ambassador. Bennett said Bush used these occasions to learn more about the world, getting out history books and atlases to steep himself in information about the newcomer's country, in preparation for the meetings.

Bush had the United Nations job from March 1971 to January 1973, far too short a time to suit Barbara. But, as always, she was ready to move on when her husband's career was at stake. The change came shortly after Richard Nixon began his second term in the White House. He wanted someone he could trust to head the Republican National Committee in Washington, an important political post, and he offered the job to George.

Although investigations already were under way into the Watergate break-in, there was no indication in January of the revelations that would follow in the coming months. Bush agreed to take the job because it was what the president wanted him to do. He didn't feel that he had a choice.

The next two years were a dismal time for the Bushes and other Republicans in Washington. The Watergate scandal swept through the capital and dominated political and social life in the city. By the spring of 1973, just three months into the new job, Bush was put in the position of defending Nixon and the White House against increasingly serious charges. He stayed loyal right up to the end, joining the chorus calling for Nixon's resignation only after it became clear that the president would be impeached if he did not leave voluntarily.

Upon Nixon's resignation, Vice President Gerald Ford became president. Bush felt that with his hard-time duty as Republican National Committee chairman and his popularity within the GOP, he had earned the right to be named the vice presidential candidate. Ford chose Nelson Rockefeller instead.

As a consolation prize, Ford offered Bush an ambassadorship, mentioning both London and Paris, two plum assignments. Bush wasn't interested in either post since both England and France were firm allies and the job in either capital would be largely a social function. Instead he asked for something more challenging—Beijing.

Although the United States and China did not have formal diplomatic relations at that time, the two countries maintained "interest sections" in each other's capitals. Richard Nixon had "opened" China several years earlier, and the effort to establish a good relationship with the communist giant was still in the early stages.

Ford agreed to give Bush the job. He would be the first top-level diplomat stationed at the U.S. mission in Beijing.

George and Barbara left Washington eagerly. Almost two years of Watergate had soured them on life in the nation's capital for the moment; they both felt the need to get away for a while, and China proved to be a tonic. The children, all in their teens or beyond, stayed in the United States at schools and with relatives and friends.

It was Barbara's first extended time alone with her husband in many years and she loved it. It "was a whole new leaf in both our lives," she said. "Watergate was a terrible experience, so to go off to China and learn a whole new culture was beautiful. I loved the people. I loved the whole feeling."

They arrived in Beijing in October 1974. Their new home was an apartment in the Spanish-style compound reserved for foreigners. They had a household staff of six and enough room to entertain. But relations with the Chinese being what they were, it was hard going.

Early on, the Bushes decided to use their time to explore as much as they could. They gave up driving for the most part because few Chinese had cars. Instead they traveled by bicycle. They played tennis, read, and entertained visitors from the United States, including both Gerald Ford and Henry Kissinger, who considered China his personal fiefdom.

Barbara started a flowered needlepoint rug in China that would take her eight years to complete. She also studied the country's history and art and took pictures of everything she could, later organizing them into a slide show. China, she said in later years, was the place where she began to look at herself more closely, a time when she "deep delved."

"I don't mean to say that I didn't do a lot of things before," she said. "But I was always a nice little follower."

At Christmas that year George and Barbara were separated for the first time in their marriage. Barbara returned to the United States to be with the children. George remained in Beijing but his mother and an aunt arrived to keep him company.

During the summer of 1975, all the children except Jeb joined their parents in Beijing. Marvin, eighteen years old at the time, recalled later how bleak he found the Chinese city.

"My parents met us at the airport. All I remember about landing is how dusty it was," he said. "There was no grass . . . there was a lot of dirt in Beijing. It was a dirty city and I ended up getting a cough as soon as I got there. In fact, all of us did."[6]

There was a special purpose for the visit. Doro, who had not been baptized as an infant, celebrated her sixteenth birthday on August 18; she was to be baptized in Beijing, an unusual occurrence in communist China. The ceremony was held in the church used by the diplomatic community. Three Chinese Christian clergymen took part—an Episcopalian, a Baptist, and a Presbyterian. No other Chinese attended the ceremony, but representatives from the diplomatic community did.

Marvin, who stood in for absent godparents at the ceremony, described the church as plain and the organ as antiquated. But, he said, "It was moving to see people who had to make an effort to seek the place out. . . . It was so humble and yet so powerful to see this happening in the middle of the largest Marxist nation in the world."

During his stay, Bush met with both Mao Tse-tung and Mao's successor, Deng Xiaoping. He and Barbara both developed an abiding affection for the country and its people even though the appointment to Beijing lasted little more than a year. By December 1975 President Ford had asked Bush to return to Washington to become head of the Central Intelligence Agency.

Neither George nor Barbara was happy about this development. For one thing, it meant Ford did not want Bush on the 1976 presidential ticket. Vice President Nelson Rockefeller had announced he would not be on the ticket in 1976, so that left an opening. But Ford wanted a running mate who would satisfy the right-wing of the party since Ronald Reagan was prepared to make a challenge at the 1976 political convention. Ford gave the nod to Senator Robert Dole of Kansas.

Politics wasn't the only reason the CIA was unattractive. The agency had been involved in a number of questionable activities in the 1960s and the Vietnam War, leading Congress to launch several investigations that were still active in 1975. Whoever became director of the agency could expect to spent a lot of time on Capitol Hill answering questions and many hours at CIA headquarters across the Potomac River in Virginia trying to repair the agency's low morale.

Bush was aware of these drawbacks but he took the job anyway. He had always agreed to do what Presidents Nixon and Ford asked of him—and besides, he had nowhere else to go at the time, politically.

The move back to Washington was a hard one for Barbara. For the first time, all her children were off on their own, leaving a void that she hadn't felt in the excitement of China. When she got back to the United States, the women's movement was in full swing and even women who had been homemakers much of their lives were getting jobs. In Washington, it took courage to tell someone at a party that you were a housewife; chances were, they would move away quickly, figuring you would not have anything interesting to say.

"I think part of it was that the children were all gone and part of if it was women's lib which made that woman who stayed home feel that she had somehow or another been a failure," Barbara said.

Worse still, Barbara had become accustomed to talking regularly with George about the China job and spending a lot of time with him. When he became had of the CIA, there was little he could tell her about his work. And he worked long hours.

Barbara mentioned to Mary Ann Stewart that she felt left out of George's professional life for the first time. Mrs. Stewart, the wife of a U.S. Supreme Court justice, had long since learned there were subjects she could not discuss with her husband and had come to accept that fact.

"I said you just have to go with it," Mrs. Stewart recalled. "If you marry someone who's going to do interesting things, you just have to."

What Barbara did not tell Andy Stewart or Shirley Pettis or any of her other friends was just how depressed she was about her situation.

"About six months, maybe. I mean, we're talking major depressed," Barbara said years later. "And I didn't do anything about it except shake it off. . . . I think maybe I was at 'that age' whatever 'that age' is. But it makes you much more sympathetic for people who have depression. It is not something you can just say, 'Now pull yourself together and get up and go.'

"I would feel like crying a lot and I really, painfully hurt," she said. "And I would think bad thoughts. I will tell you, it was not nice."[7]

In retrospect, Barbara thought she probably should have talked with a doctor, but she didn't think about doing so at the time. "I gutted it out and poor George gutted it out. I told my doctor later, 'I came to see you once for a physical. You asked how I was and I sort of cried. That was very painful for me,' and he said, 'Well, you didn't say anything. I just thought you were tired.' I said, 'Well, I was tired, but tired of hurting.' "

Shirley Pettis said that although Barbara is an outgoing person, she is also by nature a private person and never one to discuss her problems. "I think politics definitely furthers that tendency to keep anything that might be negative, your family, your marriage, your general health, anything that's negative you don't talk about. I think it's hard because you keep everything within yourself. You just feel you can't say anything."

Unable to talk about the depression, Barbara decided to try work as therapy. She put in long hours at the Washington Home. "Boy, I just kept myself so busy though" which helped bring her out of the slough.

Although Barbara Bush is not an especially introspective person, she did a lot of thinking about her life during this time, about her role as wife and mother and whether she had missed out by not having a career. She concluded that the decision to stay home and raise five children had been the right one for her and her family. It had been the norm for women of her generation who married men capable of supporting them. She felt that the fact that the norm had changed in the 1970s did not mean she had made the wrong choice.

The CIA years were not all negative for Barbara. Once she got over her depression, she began to enjoy her friends once again.

In 1975, while the Bushes were in China, Jerry Pettis had been killed in a plane crash and Shirley had taken his seat in Congress. She recalled that by the time she started going out again, Bush was head of the CIA and the block on which they lived was the most secure in Washington— which complicated her dating. "I remember the very first time I had a date after my husband's death," Shirley said. "The Bushes had just come back from China and I hadn't seen Bar yet."

Still feeling shy and uncomfortable about dating, Shirley was chagrined when she drove up to her house with her date. "There was Bar sitting on the curb with Andy Stewart, like they were waiting with their tongues hanging out. I was just horrified."

Shirley got even. Years later, when she had remarried and moved back to her California district, she stayed active in Republican politics and sometimes had Barbara out to speak at political rallies.

"When I introduce her, I do a little tongue-in-cheek with some saucy reminiscences," she said. "I'd maybe tell that story about her waiting for me on my first date or irritating me to death by mowing the lawn when the gardener didn't come and she didn't like the way it looked. She did that a couple of times, which absolutely alarmed me."

Barbara filled her days in those years with friends, needlepoint work, and volunteer jobs. But by the late 1970s, this quiet life was coming to an end. George Bush, who stepped down as CIA chief when Democrat Jimmy Carter became president in January 1977, had decided to run for president in 1980. He and Barbara moved back to Houston and he started his campaign early at a low level, traveling to Iowa and New Hampshire with a couple of aides. But soon he had the entire family working on his behalf.

In 1979 and 1980, Barbara Bush was on the road almost every day for two years, campaigning for her husband—first for president and then for vice president. Much of the time, especially in 1979, she traveled with just one aide.

While she would have preferred campaigning with her husband, she knew that wasn't an efficient way to work. Although he had been in Congress for two terms and held several high-level jobs in Washington, George was not known outside Washington and Republicans circles. That meant campaign workers needed to fan out to reach as many people as possible, and to raise a lot of money early on.

Since Republicans thought correctly that President Jimmy Carter was vulnerable, there was a lot of competition for the GOP presidential nomination—Ronald Reagan, Senators Robert Dole and Howard Baker, and former Texas governor John Connally were among the candidates.

"It was pretty rough starting off with that field of candidates," said Andy Stewart. As the wife of a little-known contender, Barbara did not attract large crowds. Her audience generally consisted of a handful of Republican women meeting in someone's living room over tea and coffee.

Happily enough, she often ran into friends on the campaign trail and hooked up with them whenever she could. In Connecticut it was longtime friend Betsy Heminway, who remembers the early days of the campaign as a strictly informal affair. "Barbara would say, 'Let's run into Talbots. I need something to wear for next week.' It was that kind of thing. She never took herself too seriously. She would just be trying on things, saying, 'I've got four lunches and an afternoon thing,'" and she needed clothes for each event.

"She wasn't particularly comfortable at the beginning," Heminway said. "Her vehicle at the time was a slide show of China. Where she'd go, she would give a slide show and that's kind of what I think got her going. That was her original vehicle to get into the swing of making speeches. It was received very well."

Aside from being nervous about speaking in public, Barbara also had to contend with questions about her looks. Heminway recalled a fund-raiser in Rye, New York, Barbara's hometown, where George's mother, Dorothy, was present. One of the guests, wanting to introduce someone to the older Mrs. Bush, took him by mistake to Barbara, saying, "I'd like you to come over and meet George's mother."

"That had to be very tough," Heminway said, "and boy, she handled it well."

Such remarks prompted some of Bush's campaign aides to suggest that Barbara dye her white hair so she would look younger. Although she generally went along with the campaign strategies, she firmly resisted the idea of a makeover.

"When George was first going to run for president, a member of our family said, 'What are we going to do about Barbara?'" she recalled. "I said, 'Funny, it doesn't bother George Bush.'"

As it turned out, neither her hair nor her weight was a problem, especially among the women's groups she spoke to most of the time in the early days of the campaign. Her outgoing personality and well-honed social instincts helped her establish a quick rapport with audiences, and her confidence grew.

"She's a good speaker," said Pete Teeley, who was Bush's press secretary during the 1980 campaign. "She's very composed in terms of what she wants to say. She has a real presence. She worked hard and she was a first-class campaigner for George. She was a significant asset to him because, you have to remember, that nobody knew who the hell he was."

The Bush children also tried to remedy the "George Who?" problem. Teeley said that Neil was involved "to a considerable" degree, and Jeb, Doro, and Marvin to a lesser extent. George W., who would be a major player in later campaigns, "didn't do much" in 1980, Teeley said. "He was trying to make a living at that time."

Oddly enough, George Bush credited all his children with active parts in the campaign when he wrote his autobiography, but he made no mention of the long months that Barbara had put in.

Barbara saw both George and the children occasionally while she was campaigning but most of the time she was on her own with one aide, Becky Brady. Becky was the granddaughter of Mary Louise Smith, who succeeded Bush as head of the Republican National Committee. Becky herself was just getting into politics as a volunteer in Bush's political action committee in Houston when Barbara approached her about the travel job in 1978.

"My grandmother is a friend of theirs but she did interview four people," Becky said. "We hit it off. One thing she said to me before she hired me was that she appreciated the fact that I had volunteered for her husband."

The two began traveling together in January 1979, four months before George Bush officially announced his candidacy for the GOP presidential nomination. Their first trip was to Birmingham, Alabama, where Barbara showed her China slides to a garden club.

"It was the first group of people and she was so nervous about doing it," Becky said. "She wasn't accustomed to speaking. But she was fabulous. She put the audience at ease."

Longtime friend Janet Steiger said Barbara's China slides were particularly popular because they showed American audiences what life was like in a country that had been closed to the West for decades. "After all, they [George and Barbara] were effectively the first American representatives back in China in the lifetime of most Americans. It was for most people the opening of a mystery."

Barbara soon got into a routine on the campaign trail. She and Becky would fly to a city and hook up with a local Republican who acted as a guide. They would do five or six events each day, each one lasting about an hour, then repeat the whole process the next day.

"It was every day," Becky said. "We would basically come home, maybe for a weekend, but it was never very long."

They each carried their own luggage, helping each other where they could. Barbara had a blue hanging bag that she called Big Blue and another case with multiple zippers. She tried to coordinate her clothes colors so she wouldn't have to carry so much. "She and I both tried to pick a color so we could mix and match everything," Becky said. "She had a steamer and she would steam her clothes in her hotel room."

Barbara always carried along panels of the family rug that she had started to needlepoint in China. She worked on it in any spare moments she had, traveling in a car or plane and in her hotel room. "That was one of my biggest responsibilities, not to leave or lose that rug," said Becky, who often wound up carrying the panels in a tote bag. "She worked very hard on it. She kept a very good log as to what animal or flower she had done on a certain day." Many of the designs were in celebration of family events—births, elections, graduations.

Becky did needlepoint as well. "I had done needlepoint when I was in school," she said. "In all our car trips, we'd always work on that. We got to be best friends, really traveling like that when it was just the two of us for so long."

They also collaborated on thank-you notes. Barbara sent thousands of them and Becky helped her get names and addresses and put them in a directory. "We'd try to get everybody's names and she would do thank-you notes practically before we were out of town," Becky said. "Each one was personal and she wrote them all herself. I didn't write them for her."

Barbara took along a supply of paperback books wherever she went. When she finished one, she would leave it on an airplane for someone else to read, which also meant she didn't have to carry it any longer.

Although the campaign days were long, Barbara always got up early enough to have some private time in her hotel room to read, work on needlepoint, and exercise. "She had a coil to make her own coffee in the morning," Becky said. "She'd get up about five-thirty. We'd frequently leave the hotels about seven-thirty."

Barbara did her own scheduling with help from state political parties and old friends. "They [the Bushes] have got friends all over the country and a lot of their friends would help us," Becky said. "They would pick us up and drive us across the state."

She recalled a typical week they spent in Michigan arranged by Patsy Caulkins, who had lived next door to the Bushes while George was a student at Yale. Mrs. Caulkins was not politically active, but still was able to put together a full schedule of events.

Becky and Barbara stayed overnight at her house in Grosse Point, then got up at six the next morning for a two-hour drive to Ann Arbor, where they had breakfast with a group of Republicans, not all of whom knew who George Bush was. "President of what?" one was overheard asking. After breakfast, Barbara had an interview with the local newspaper, where the reporter did not know who George was, and she met with the mayor and toured city hall. Lunch was in Lansing.

The next day she traveled to Grand Rapids, where Mrs. Caulkin's sister-in-law had arranged a fair-sized party. Barbara also had an interview at the local TV station. Later in the day, Mrs. Caulkins drove the party to Muskegon, where a friend of hers had agreed to throw a wine-and-cheese party for Barbara and also had invited all three women to stay overnight at her house.

Knowing what a busy day it would be, Mrs. Caulkins had packed a picnic lunch and en route to Muskegon she hunted for a roadside picnic table. Finding none, she simply pulled the car off the road and everyone ate. Before long, a policeman came by and asked if everything was all right. "I introduced Mrs. Bush and told him her husband was running for president," Mrs. Caulkins said. "He wasn't very impressed."

At the wine-and-cheese party, she noticed that both Barbara and Becky were writing down names. She was pleased to discover a few days later how many people had received a personal note from the candidate's wife— even the teen-age girls who served the hors d'oeuvres were remembered.

After Muskegon it was on to Midland, Michigan, where a woman the Bushes had known in Washington gave a reception for Barbara. That afternoon, Mrs. Caulkins drove Barbara and Becky to Bay City for a party and a TV interview and then on to Flint for another gathering, "all before supper."

On the final day of the Michigan visit, Barbara went to a shelter for abused women in Pontiac and attended two parties in nearby Birmingham.

It was a typical grueling campaign week, full to the brim. Both Becky and Mrs. Caulkins were hard put to keep up with the energetic Barbara. "It was exhausting," said Becky, who was in her twenties at the time. "She had a whole lot more energy than I did."

The events in Michigan were typical of the campaign, especially during the first year. "Early on, I'd say we met in people's houses mostly," Becky said, usually with no more than fifty people attending.

The two of them traveled to every state except Alaska but spent a disproportionate amount of their time in Iowa, which held the first-in-the-nation caucuses. A win in Iowa could catapult an obscure candidate like George Bush to the forefront. "I think she went to all ninety-nine of Iowa's counties," Becky said. "She spent a lot of time."

She recalled one harrowing day in Iowa where she and Barbara were riding in a single-engine private plane in terrible weather with a pilot who appeared to be in his eighties. The plane landed safely, but, said Becky, "I'm sure that was the last time we ever went on a single-engine plane."

Another time, in the dead of the frigid Iowa winter, "we were staying at a hotel in an itty, bitty tiny town and the locks to the car were frozen when we tried to leave the next morning. The girl who was driving us had to get a hair dryer and melt them."

Shortly before the Iowa caucus, when the entire family was campaigning full tilt, Barbara and George met by chance in Chicago. "Mrs. Bush and I were changing planes in Chicago," Becky said. "We didn't realize it but so were Mr. Bush and David Bates," his personal assistant. "We were literally carrying all our bags, a lot of them, and we look up and here come Mr. Bush and David. It was the first time they had seen each other in a week."

The Bushes kissed but it was a brief encounter. "We were off to catch another flight and so were they," Becky said.

Chance meetings and occasional weekends were the only times the Bushes were together for most of a year. The grueling schedule sometimes got Barbara down but she wanted to prove—to herself, her children, and her husband—that she could make a substantial contribution to the campaign.

"The majority of the time during the first presidential campaign, they were separate," Becky said. "Both of us would get a little frustrated being out on the road so long. She missed not only Mr. Bush but the kids. But she wanted to give it one hundred percent and she did."

The two women ate where they could—at receptions, luncheons, or even in the car, and Barbara was introduced to a new cultural experience along the way. "She had never been to a McDonald's until she met me," Becky said.

Becky found Barbara to have a sunny temperament. "I consider her to be one of the genuinely nicest people I've ever known," she said. "Any time she had a sharp tongue she was always right. . . . She never was upset about anything she didn't have a reason to be."

Occasionally thing would go awry. Becky recalled a fairly large event—a couple of hundred people—where Barbara was doing her slide show. She narrated and Becky flipped the slides—too fast, as it turned out. "She said later she could tell when I wasn't paying attention," Becky said. "I would hit the button faster to hurry her along. By that time, I knew every word she was going to say."

Shirley Pettis, who had just retired from Congress when George Bush began his presidential campaign, worked for him in California and invited Barbara to speak.

"She had by then found her own self, speaking-wise," Mrs. Pettis said. "I got an enthusiastic group of former constituents to join me for a brunch at the San Bernardino County museum, headlined Bar Bush with her pictures from China. She came out and stayed with me at Loma Linda. The event was very well attended."

When Barbara saw the large audience, her first thought was that the candidate himself should be on hand. "She said, 'Oh, my soul, George should be here,'" Mrs. Pettis recalled. As it turned out, the rally was a success with Barbara as the headliner, in part because she and Shirley Pettis shared with the audience the warm and teasing relationship they had developed as neighbors in Washington. "We had fun," Mrs. Pettis said.

Barbara stuck with her slide slow for about a year, then decided she could speak on her own without it. She worked out a basic speech with

George Bush as the focus, talking about their family life, his accomplishments and his goals.

Janet Steiger remembers Barbara giving that speech to a college audience in Beloit, Wisconsin, and was impressed that she could held the attention of college kids at a political rally. "She has the amazing ability to create rapport no matter what the generation," Mrs. Steiger said.

When Barbara looks back on the 1980 campaign, she remembers it fondly, not least because she and her children developed new relationships while working to elect George Bush president.

"I liked it for a lot of reasons, not the end result, but I liked the campaigning," she said. "I felt I was really helping George. I probably lost votes by the hundreds, but I thought I was helping. The children and I all got much closer to each other and to George. Every one of them did their part, and it's true that they now treat me as an adult for the first time."

The end result, she said, was that "I think they thought that I did a pretty good job campaigning and I know I thought they did."

When voting started in late 1979 and early 1980, it appeared that their efforts would pay off. George Bush won a straw poll—no actual delegates, but good publicity—in Maine in November, and the victory was seen as an upset because other candidates had spent more time in the state. Then, on January 21, 1980, Bush won the Iowa caucuses, coming in two percentage points ahead of Ronald Reagan. That victory pulled him out of the pack of candidates and marked him as the chief contender against Reagan, who had established his credentials as front-runner early on, based on his strong race against Gerald Ford four years earlier.

Suddenly, national reporters were paying close attention to the campaign, seeing a potentially successful challenge to Reagan. The Bush family was elated, and George Bush exulted that he had the "Big Mo," the early momentum.

Barbara, riding a plane out of Iowa after the caucus vote, was working on her needlepoint when *Detroit News* reporter Jerald terHorst asked what she was doing. "That's interesting," he said. "It looks like a seat cover."

Barbara replied, "It's for George and I'm leaving the needle in it. He's got to keep moving."[8]

The next major contest was the New Hampshire primary, which has knocked out many a political candidate over the years. What is best re-membered from that contest was a remark that Reagan, with his great sense of theater, made at Bush's expense before an important audience.

The incident occurred at a debate that had been arranged by the *Nashua Telegraph* between the two GOP front-runners, Reagan and Bush, three days before the February 26 vote. Reagan's campaign had agreed to finance the event. When other Republican candidates asked to take part, Reagan agreed. Bush did not.

When Reagan got onstage, it was clear the audience wanted all the candidates in the debate. Reagan took the microphone to say he agreed. John Breen, editor of the *Nashua Telegraph*, was angered at this change of plans and told a technician to turn off Reagan's microphone.

"I paid for this microphone, Mr. Green," Reagan said.

Although Reagan got Breen's name wrong, he won his point and the whole evening as well. The other candidates were kept out of the debate as Bush wanted, but what people remembered was how Reagan upstaged his opponent. Reagan won New Hampshire with an impressive 50 percent of the vote. Bush was second with 23 percent.

George Bush went on to win other primaries—in Puerto Rico, Massa-chusetts, his home state of Connecticut, Pennsylvania, and Washington, D.C. He also won the high-profile Michigan primary in May. But Reagan had won so many more states by that time that it was clear he would have enough delegates to claim the nomination at the party's presidential nom-inating convention in July.

Bush, finding he no longer could get substantial financial contributions in the face of the likely Reagan victory, dropped out of the race on May 26 and said he would support Reagan at the convention and in the general election.

He made the announcement at his home base in Houston. Barbara, standing at his side, held on to the shoulders of her four-year-old grand-son, George P., and blinked back tears. George was dry-eyed and, in typical fashion, had a party later in the day for members of the press who had been traveling with him.

Despite George's upbeat manner, the next two months were uncom-fortable for Barbara. She knew she had to go to the GOP convention in Detroit and put on a happy face. But her heart was not in it. Two years of campaigning had left her longing for the prize. "When we went to Detroit, my idea was to do the right thing and get it over with," she said years later.

With Reagan certain to get the presidential nomination, the only mystery at the convention was who he would choose as a running mate. George Bush knew he was a possibility, but any hope he might have had seemed to die when word spread among the delegates that Reagan was talking with former President Gerald Ford about the number-two spot. By Wednesday night of convention week, it appeared to be a done deal.

Bush was sitting with Barbara, son Marvin, and family friends in the Pontchartrain Hotel when the phone rang at 11:37 P.M. James Baker, who had managed the Bush campaign, picked up and heard Ronald Reagan's voice on the other end. Quickly Baker hustled everyone out of the room except for Barbara, Marvin, and convention aide Dean Burch. He handed the phone to George Bush.

Minutes later, Bush emerged from the hotel room to tell reporters that "out of the clear blue sky" Reagan had asked him to run as vice president on the Republican ticket. "I was surprised," he said. "I of course was very pleased. I told him I would work work work for his election."

Bush later told reporters he had been so sure Ford would get the nod that he had warned his sons he did not want to see "you guys grumping around here or down or something because something that nobody owed us didn't come to us." But he also tried to instill a little pride in them despite what he expected would be a hurtful loss. "Look, we've got twenty-four hours," he told them. "And by gosh, we're going to do this thing with a certain feeling and a certain style and then we'll figure out what to do."[9]

Barbara confessed that "a little competitive spirit" rose up in her during convention week and she was delighted when George won the contest for the number-two spot. "It's funny, everybody makes fun of the job, but everybody I knew there wanted it," she said.

George's new prominence elevated Barbara into the spotlight as well and she wasn't really prepared. At her first news conference at the convention, she was asked her position on the Equal Rights Amendment, which would have amended the U.S. Constitution to give women equal rights with men. Barbara had supported the measure in previous years but Reagan was opposed.

"I'm campaigning on the Republican platform," she said. Asked how that squared with her previous position, she simply turned away with a smile. She knew right away that her performance had been sub par and told a reporter later in the day, "I think I answered that question very badly. If I had another shot at answering the question, I would say, 'Do you have any idea, really, of how I feel about abortion and ERA? Because I'm not going to tell you. I'm not running for public office, George Bush is.' "[10]

She added, "I'm not a wave maker. I do not agree with my husband on everything and I'm not going to tell you if I don't agree. Because I am going to tell George Bush how I feel. Upstairs."

Her other answers had a similar defensive, snippy quality to them.

Did she regret dropping out of Smith College? If she had regretted it, she replied, she would have done something about it.

Did she miss having her own career? She had lectured on China, she answered, but found being a wife and mother more fulfilling. "I've always been a part of George Bush's life," she said. "He is a sharer. The role of a wife is to be supportive, and I've been very happy these thirty-five years. So don't rock my boat."

As she got into the fall campaign, traveling an average of six days a week, Barbara became more accustomed to the spotlight and showed she was a quick learner. By October, she had a better answer on where she stood on the Equal Rights Amendment, which was never passed but was a big issue at the time. While she supported it, she said, she had no problem with Reagan opposing it. "I feel my president should be solving problems—economy, foreign affairs, getting a strong inventive energy program, and strengthening our intelligence service and our defense," she said. "If you want to see ERA passed, you should elect congressmen who feel that way because the president should be giving leadership in these fields that are in crisis."

She took a complimentary, teasing attitude toward the Reagan campaign, saying she told his aides that if they had let people know earlier about Reagan's "decency, his sensitivity, his caring for people . . . we wouldn't have gotten so far in the primaries."

Barbara had nothing but praise for Nancy Reagan. She even managed to say something nice about Nancy's strained relationship with her children. "I think the way to judge a mother is by her children," Barbara said. "The thing I like about her children is their independence—which is the best thing you can give your children. They are the four most different children I have ever met but they have one thing in common. They say their father listens to them and they are very supportive of him."[11] This wasn't true, as it turned out, but by the time the nation learned details of the deeply dysfunctional relationships in the Reagan family, Barbara's comments were forgotten.

Barbara realized early on that she and Nancy Reagan were not going to be close. "We're not going to be able to have hobbies together," she said. "I jog and she rides; she probably would rather die than jog and I put riding up to the top of my rather-die list."

She also acknowledged that campaigning as the wife of the vice presidential candidate instead of going all out for her husband as a presidential contender took some adjusting. "You step back if you're the wife of the man running for vice president," she said. "You want to help as much as you can, but it's a whole different role."[12]

While she refrained from criticizing either Rosalynn Carter or Joan Mondale, wives of the Democratic opposition, Barbara did use Rosalynn to get in a dig at Jimmy Carter, saying Rosalynn must love her husband "a whole bunch because I would have been scared to death to go to a city where they had forty percent unemployment and have to tell them things are getting better."

The voters agreed with Barbara. In the fall election, the Reagan-Bush ticket won an overwhelming majority, receiving 489 electoral votes while Jimmy Carter and Walter Mondale got just 49. Barbara and George and their children watched the results in a Houston hotel. "We didn't imagine a sweep like this," George said.

The next day they flew to Los Angeles to join the Reagans in a victory celebration. They would spent the next eight years in the shadow of the presidential couple. But as it turned out, Barbara didn't mind at all.

7

SECOND LADY

On January 21, 1981, President Ronald Reagan and Vice President George Bush were sworn in to office on a bright day before one hundred thousand people by Chief Justice Warren Burger. The day was made all the more dramatic with the news that Americans who had long been held hostage in Iran had been released just as the new president took the oath of office.

Reagan wore a morning coat for the formal ceremony and Nancy Reagan sparkled in a scarlet coat and hat. Barbara, out of the spotlight, wore bright blue, the color that would become her signature.

In a sign of things to come for the extravagant eighties, four days of inaugural festivities cost $11 million, a record-breaking amount at the time.

The Bushes celebrated by bringing their entire huge family to Washington, an estimated one hundred thirty people, most of whom wore "Bush Family" tags so people would know who they were. Traveling in buses, they attended a reception given by the Republican National Committee, George's old workplace, went to a big party in Georgetown and to a reception at the vice presidential mansion.

At one of the inaugural balls, Barbara found the man who designed her blue satin gown. "Am I doing everything correctly?" she asked Bill Blass. "Glorious," he replied.[1]

When the parties ended, George and Barbara began exploring the thirty-three-room vice presidential residence on Massachusetts Avenue in northwest Washington, next door to the British embassy. It would be their home for eight years, the longest they had stayed in one place since they were married.

Barbara found the 1893 mansion in fairly good shape and she loved living in it. The house has big white pillars and is set among gently sloping lawns and wooded hills. With a porte-cochere entrance and broad veranda it offered plenty of space for Barbara's favored activities—gardening, jogging, tennis, and walking C. Fred, the family cocker spaniel.

Family friends and political allies raised $187,000 for the work the Bushes wanted done. Barbara replaced the abstract paintings that Joan Mondale had showcased with Oriental art and more traditional paintings. Over an elegant Chinese bureau, she displayed a painting by E. Martin Hennigs of two Indians on horseback, passing under a gold-leafed tree. She stretched, framed and hung two intricately embroidered gold-and-azure Mandarin Chinese jackets. She borrowed Impressionist art from the Corcoran Museum and the National Gallery in Washington and an Audubon print from the Houston Museum of Art. She put out myriad pictures of the Bush clan and filled the house with flowers. The living room wallpaper, a sunny yellow floral pattern, added to the bright, airy look.

As they always had, the Bushes began entertaining immediately, even before Barbara had all her decorating done. "George wants instant moving," she said. "When we moved to Houston, he had invited the King of Jordan for dinner before we even had a house."

In their first months in the vice presidential house, the Bushes gave a small party for President and Nancy Reagan, a dinner for six, a bash for old Washington friends who had helped house the Bush family members during the inauguration, a party for staff members, and more. A household staff of six helped with preparations, but Barbara had a dishwasher installed on the first floor of the house so she could entertain her friends without much help or interference from the chefs in the basement kitchen.

Barbara also had a busy schedule outside the house, full of minor but politically necessary public appearances. She visited charities, welcomed Texas students visiting the capital, met with Republican groups—mayors, governors, fund-raisers, and wives—and was regularly at George Bush's side for public dinners and speeches.

Her duties included several quaint activities, long established by Washington protocol—riding a crane to place a starburst ornament on top of the national Christmas tree, and leading a weekly craft session for Senate wives.

Although most of the nation's attention was focused on the new president, Barbara received a lot of letters, most of them supportive but many also wanting to know why she didn't dye her hair. "When we first got into office, someone wrote and said, 'Dear Mrs. Bush: This is a youthful administration. The vice president looks young, Mrs. Reagan looks young. Why don't you?'" Barbara said. "I wrote back, 'I'm doing the best I can. And besides, I'm the youngest of all those people.'"[2]

As the letters about her hair continued to pour in, she began sending back a standard, humorous answer: "I said, 'Please forget about my hair. Think about my wonderful mind.'"

She also found, much to her annoyance, that when she made public appearances, people were aware of her busy schedule and often asked if her feet hurt. "I want to put my mind and my soul into what I do and I'm bored with the hair," she said. "Feet and hair are boring. Who's interested in feet? When you go someplace, people ask if your feet hurt. If they did, I wouldn't tell them!"[3]

With her natural high energy level, Barbara had no problem meeting the demands of the vice president's office. Raising five children, moving dozens of time, and campaigning for almost two years had prepared her well. "I am now physically and mentally stronger than I was twenty years ago," she said.

Her day started at 6:00 or 6:30 A.M. with coffee and newspapers in bed. She and George took turns getting the coffee. By 7:00 A.M., she was exercising, sometimes using George's new treadmill while she watched the morning news shows on television.

Old friends found that she was still a friend.

"Whatever seems to happen to political wives didn't happen to her," said tennis partner Ellen Sulzberger Straus. "When you live in Washington, you notice that as these people get to the top they get stuffier and stuffier.

That just isn't the case with Barbara. She doesn't take herself too seriously. There is no phoniness about her."[4]

Longtime friend Andy Stewart was surprised to learn that Barbara had planned a large birthday party for her in cahoots with other members of the Stewart family. "I was completely surprised," Mrs. Stewart said. "My daughter and some relatives came from out of town. It was so thoughtful because my husband had died just a year before. It was a wonderful sit-down luncheon, maybe sixty people. I was so overwhelmed. I walked right in the door and didn't recognize my own daughter."

The thrifty habits Barbara had developed as a young wife at Yale and in West Texas stayed with her, even as her husband rose in prominence. While Bush was in Congress she had taken an automobile mechanics class and thereafter performed some of the repairs on the family cars herself. She also had picked up a little knowledge about electrical wiring, as a Washington contractor discovered when he got a call one day from the vice president's wife. She was at Marvin's house trying to rig the wiring when she ran into a problem. "Here was the wife of the vice president using her own tools stripping wires and fooling around with switches to save some money," said the contractor. "It was just like her, but I sent my electrician over."[5]

Barbara still made jokes and her repertoire had expanded to the rich and famous. After Prince Charles had dinner at the vice presidential mansion, she remarked that having him as her dinner companion was "like sitting next to one of my four sons only he's better dressed and more polite."

Noting that a highly visible job of vice presidents in recent years had been to attend funerals of foreign dignitaries, Barbara quoted family friend James Baker saying of George Bush, "You die, he'll fly."

She didn't always follow protocol. She noticed that the rigid dictates of seating in official Washington often left a visiting foreign official sitting next to the same person for three dinners in a row. When the party was at her house, though, she changed the seating so everyone would have someone new to talk with. And although an honored male guest at the vice president's house would normally sit at Barbara's table, that didn't always happen with Barbara in charge. "This poor man didn't come to the United States to sit next to me," she said. "So I'll try to put him at the table with George so they can talk. I always make it clear that this is not the vice president's idea and they're very nice about it."

She and George went to endless numbers of dinner parties themselves and found a way to amuse themselves even when the speeches were long and dull and the food close to inedible. "Sometimes, well, almost all the time, there'll be an after-dinner speaker who reminds us of something funny," she said. "I look across at George and get laughing, 'cause he knows what I'm thinking and I know exactly how it's going to grab him." She adds diplomatically, "Of course, I hope other people laugh at us, too."[6]

She laughed at her own mistakes. When the Archbishop of Canturbury visited Washington with his primates, they dressed in traditional red and purple. Barbara, forgetting the Church's colors, said, "I got up in the morning and thought, 'It's still cool enough to wear my purple dress and red coat'—so did they, all of them."

During a visit to Ghana, her duties included watching a man bite the head off a chicken. "I made up my mind that no matter what he did I wouldn't react," she said. "And I didn't react. But people around me were dropping like flies."

Barbara had always bought her own clothes right off the racks in retail stores as most people do, but she found as the vice president's wife she couldn't go shopping without causing a commotion. The secret service had to go along and other shoppers would come up and greet her. She began to have her clothes made but her taste was not extravagant and she never attracted the kind of attention Nancy Reagan did with her slim figure and costly designer dresses. "I spend time and effort but no one thinks of me as well-dressed," Barbara joked. "It takes a lot of strain off you."

For the same reasons she no longer shopped in public, Barbara couldn't spontaneously visit her children or old friends in other cities, a curb on her freedom that she learned to live with but sometimes regretted. "I can't just hop on a plane and fly to see my new grandson in Texas," she said. "The taxpayers would have to pay for the Secret Service agents who would have to go with me."[7]

Despite her busy schedule, she remained relatively low profile. She joked that a Swedish embassy reception in Washington, given in honor of her and George, was an exercise in humiliation.

"Usually you don't hear anything in a receiving line but this night I heard three things," she said. "One person gave me a quizzical look and said, 'Who are you?' Another person looked thrilled, recognition flooding her face and said, 'Well, hello Mrs. Schultz' [thinking Barbara was Helena Schultz, wife of Secretary of State George Schultz]. And the one I really loved was a darling man who got to me, warmly clasped my hand in both of his and said, 'Welcome to our country.' "[8]

Barbara loved the privacy that the wooded grounds of the vice presidential mansion provided and professed sympathy for Nancy Reagan living in the much more public White House. "I feel so lucky being here," she said. "I think how awful it must be for Nancy Reagan not being able to walk around the lawn, having strangers wandering through the downstairs rooms all morning."

There were times, however, when her own privacy was interrupted. Early one morning when Soviet foreign minister Eduard Shevardnadze was to have breakfast at the vice president's house, Barbara put on her bathrobe and started to take her dog for a brief walk outdoors. She was stopped short by a secret service agent, who warned her the grounds were full of photographers awaiting Shevardnadze's arrival. So she sneaked back into the house, went up to her dressing room—and found the photographers directly below the window. "I had to crawl to my closet to get my clothes," she said.

While Barbara was often humorous in public, she seldom spoke out on the major issues of the day, except in her chosen fields of literacy, home, and family. Even so, she learned that her husband's position put her much in demand. "I'm finding lots of groups that might not be too hot to hear you as just Barbara Bush, want you as a speaker because your husband is vice president," she said.

She had long been a supporter of a proposed constitutional amendment to guarantee equal rights to women but she also felt strongly that families, especially women, needed to pay closer attention to their children.

"I don't think men and women should have children and not take responsibility," she said in 1984. "Men are going to have to take a lot more responsibility. They will have to do more as their share. But women are also going to have to learn that they have to have priorities, that they have to make choices, and that they can't have everything. You can't, in my opinion, be a bank president and a full-time mother."

Realizing many women must work to help support a family—her own daughter would divorce and go to work a few years later—Barbara said she felt it was so important to have someone home with a child for the first four or five years that families should be willing to make sacrifices to ensure full-time parental care.

Later she would refine and change some of these views. Her support for the Equal Rights Amendment eventually faded when it became clear that the measure didn't have enough support in the states to win. But Barbara remained friendly to those who were working for the ERA.

During the inaugural parade in January 1985, Barbara and George were riding with the Reagans when they passed a group of women holding up signs in support of the amendment. Neither the Reagans nor George Bush acknowledged the group but Barbara turned, smiled and held up her fingers in a victory sign, according to Molly Yard, then president of the National Organization for Women, who was among the sign holders.

Throughout the 1985 reelection campaign, however, Barbara defended Ronald Reagan's record on women, noting that he had appointed Sandra Day O'Connor to the Supreme Court and had two women in his Cabinet. She argued that "women's issues" were the same ones that concerned men.

"I'm not as convinced anymore that the Equal Rights Amendment is half as important as seeing that women get equal pay for equal work, pension plans, deductions for child care, and seeing that husbands who are delinquent in child support are made to make payments," she said. "The main thing for women is that we have peace, that we have a strong economy, that we get inflation down, that people can buy a home and get jobs," she said. "Reagan has done a wonderful job on those things and that should count for women."

Because the Democratic candidate, Walter Mondale, had chosen Congresswoman Geraldine Ferraro as his running mate, Barbara was frequently asked what she thought about having a woman as vice president.

In a campaign speech in March 1984 to the National Federation of Republican Women, she said, "Just this morning two newscasters were saying that the only qualified women for vice president were Republicans. That's true. But we already have a vice president we like very much."

She was always ready to defend her husband and took any slight to him personally, a trait that Bush appreciated with a certain wariness.

"She'll go to bat for me, sometimes more than I'm inclined to myself," he said. "I'm glad to have her defend me. I'd rather have her on my side than not."

At the Republican convention that August in Dallas, Barbara was asked again if she thought a woman could be a good vice president. By that time, she had a different answer. "In my opinion, the vice president should be qualified to be president," she replied. "So the question should be, 'What do you think of a woman for president?' And I plan to vote for one surely before I die—and she will be a Republican."

Later in the campaign, Barbara got angry at Geraldine Ferraro and had an outburst that she came to regret. The incident occurred in early October as she was traveling on Air Force Two to a Columbus Day parade in New York. She walked back to talk with reporters and the discussion turned to accusations made by Mondale and Ferraro that rich people like the Bushes were out of touch with the needs of everyday Americans.

Barbara had gotten increasingly annoyed at the suggestion. Talking to the reporters, she blurted out that Mrs. Ferraro had more money than the Bushes and went on to describe her as a "four-million-dollar—I can't say it but it rhymes with rich."

Within hours, the story was being broadcast all over the country and Barbara realized she had made a mistake. She quickly called Geraldine Ferraro to apologize, and said publicly that she regretted the remark. Privately she cried and cried, knowing that such a remark could hurt the campaign. "It hurt me a whole bunch," she said later.

Geraldine Ferraro accepted the apology but her mother, Antonetta, was indignant at the insult. "I thought it was terrible," she told reporters. "I would not put myself in her category. So she apologized. Empty words."

As it turned out, her slip-up had little if any effect on voters. Reagan and Bush won in a landslide in the election a month later. They carried every state except Mondale's own, and the District of Columbia.

The inauguration in January 1985 was a flashy one, full of minks, limousines, big diamonds, showy shoes, and other signs of money. Having recovered from the deep recession of 1981–1982, the economy was hot, Wall Street was knee-deep in multibillion-dollar deals, and the mood of the country was one of celebration and extravagance.

Barbara took part in the festivities with pleasure but was careful as usual to leave the spotlight on Nancy Reagan and enjoy herself in the shadows. For the inauguration, she ordered a $6,000 white wool coat with jeweled buttons and a $10,000 white mink blouson jacket. Both were modest compared with the $100,000 furs wrapped around many inaugural guests.

Barbara and George had their own inaugural party one night before the more glitzy affair held for the Reagans. Frank Sinatra had been scheduled as emcee, but since he was to star at the Reagan gala, he turned his duties over to Merv Griffin, who joked to the Bushes, "Obviously, you couldn't get tickets to the Super Bowl either."

The Bushes didn't seem to mind. Although the six-thousand seat Washington Convention Center was not full for the vice presidential tribute, both Barbara and George looked to be enjoying themselves. It was typical of the political life the Bushes led as number two couple. They were seldom in the news or more than a sideline to major events of the day. Bush did not have the close relationship with Reagan that a later vice president, Al Gore, had with Bill Clinton.

Barbara would say later that she "got away with murder" during the vice presidential years. Since few people noticed what she did, she wasn't under the same kind of pressure that goes with being first lady.

Nancy Reagan wasn't above snubbing Barbara. The insult was especially apparent when Mikhail and Raisa Gorbachev visited Washington in 1987. Both Washington and Moscow realized from previous meetings that Nancy and Raisa didn't get along well and the Soviets indicated they would like Barbara Bush to accompany Raisa to the National Gallery of Art. Word came back quickly from the White House. "That was not to be encouraged," Bush aide Craig Fuller said. "It was made clear that this would not be looked upon favorably." Nancy made sure she would not be upstaged by Barbara.

Barbara has said repeatedly that she hated comparisons between herself and Nancy and she did what she could to blunt gossip. Nevertheless, except for official functions where they had to be together, the Reagans and the Bushes generally went their separate ways.

During her second four years in the vice presidential mansion, Barbara calculated how she allocated her days. "I spend fifty percent of my time doing charitable work and twenty-five percent on organizational things like running the house," she said. "Maybe fifteen percent on my husband and children and maybe ten percent on myself, exercising and playing tennis."

Her charitable work included a substantial amount of entertaining. Her style was much the same as it had always been. "It's not changed all that much," said longtime friend Jessica Catto. "They've always been gracious but informal and they had, as I remember, their friends and people in government."

The Cattos usually visited the vice president's house with a small group of old Bush friends, and it was inevitably an early evening. "We might go to a Chinese restaurant or something like that," she said. "They're pretty early retirers. The party would end by ten," at the latest.

For large groups, Barbara liked to do afternoon parties, especially teas. In the spring of 1986, *McCall's* magazine was on hand for a tea at the vice president's mansion in honor of a joint literacy campaign by ABC and the Public Broadcasting Corporation. While Barbara talked with a reporter, she drank a cup of tea with a lemon slice studded with cloves. She said she usually used Lenox china with the vice presidential seal for large parties, but for small, more personal gatherings, where breakage is less likely, she preferred her own Tiffany pattern.

The dining room table, a ten-foot-long mahogany, was bare to show off the polished wood. A floral arrangement in the center was surrounded by china and silver platters filled with tea sandwiches and cookies arranged in concentric circles over lace paper doilies. The sandwiches included watercress, smoked salmon, chicken and tuna eclairs, tomatoes stuffed with cream cheese and dill, and one hot hors d'oeuvre, cheese puffs. In addition, there were brownies, lace cookies, and pecan tartlets.

At both ends of the table were silver tea services and gold-rimmed cups and saucers marked with the vice presidential seal. Glasses of white wine sat on a tray on the sideboard.

Barbara said that while she consulted the chef and other staff members about decorations, she didn't worry if the final arrangements were not what she would have chosen. At the tea party, for example, the dining room had a number of vases filled with flowers in addition to the bouquet at center table. "Personally, I prefer one strong floral arrangement to a jungle like this," Barbara said. "But I'm not going to get disturbed about that. It's not essential to the success of the party."

She recalled that when Margaret Thatcher visited the vice president's house, the navy stewards for some reason changed the pastel icing on the petits fours to orange, purple, and red, much to Barbara's surprise.

"I just laughed," she said. 'It wasn't that important. If you have a good time, yourself, others will.'"[9]

During the eight years Bush was vice president, he and Barbara traveled extensively abroad on goodwill and diplomatic missions and to the many funerals vice presidents are required to attend. Barbara visited sixty-five countries while she was second lady.

One of her most emotional trips was to Africa in 1985 to call attention to areas struck by famine. During the weeklong visit the emaciated children Barbara saw brought tears to her eyes. "We're never going to be the same again," she said after walking through a refugee camp in the Sudan. Among the grisly sights were starving babies, their heads completely shaved except for one row of hair.

"They told us they had that so God can reach down and pull them up to heaven," she said.[10]

In the camp hospital, newborns had no incubators or sterile bottles. They were put on dirty cots among the sick. A nurse handed Barbara a four-pound premature infant—no rubber gloves, no surgical mask. "I couldn't help but compare, to think of our own premature grandchildren," she said. "We didn't touch them, you know. We put our hands in rubber gloves."

She also was struck by the size of the children. "When they told you the ages it made a tremendous difference in what you were seeing," she said. "What looked like a one-year-old was a four-year-old. If these kids lived, they are going to be the strongest, most immune kids you've ever known."

Throughout the African tour, the Bushes were welcomed by crowds wherever they went because the people felt that such a high-ranking American official would bring more attention and lead to increased relief efforts.

Barbara noted that she and the vice president were not always so welcome. During an earlier visit to Afghanistan refugees in Pakistan, she said, women were crying and yelling at her. Despite the obvious anger in their faces, the interpreter told Barbara the women were saying, "Thank you, Mrs. Bush, for the help you and your husband are bringing to us."

Annoyed at such a transparent lie, Barbara demanded to know what the women really were saying. The interpreter obliged. What the women wanted was guns, not sympathy. "Don't tell us you care," they said. "We don't give a darn about that. Tell us you'll give us guns and we can go back and fight for our homes."[11]

Such goodwill trips were eye-openers for Barbara and helped her develop an appreciation for the severe problems in the wider world. But she also spent a lot of time in elegant diplomatic halls abroad and met the leaders who will be part of history.

She tells a funny story about a dinner where she was seated next to Australian prime minister Malcolm Fraser.

"We were at a big formal dinner and I was too vain to wear my glasses," she said. "The first course was a big thing in the middle of the plate and I cracked right into it. The prime minister leaned over and whispered, 'Barbara, that's the adornment.' It was a lobster shell, which I naturally was trying to break and eat."[12]

That embarrassing gaffe sent Barbara to an eye doctor for contact lenses—with bifocals.

She had a better time when she first met Princess Diana. Before Diana came to the United States, Barbara said, "I didn't think I'd like the little princess from England. But Diana is the most outgoing lady. I took her to a hospice. She sat on the beds of people who were in the last two weeks of life, held their hands and asked how they felt. They glowed. She said, 'How are you being helped? Is the program working? Are you in any pain? Does your medication help?' And these people told her."

At a dinner party during the visit, Diana was seated next to George Bush. Barbara said to her afterward, "I hope my husband behaved." Diana replied, "He didn't."

Then, Barbara said, "She showed me that on his place card he had written. 'Stay awake. Only twenty-nine and a half minutes and I guarantee you'll be asleep. That is, if the speeches and the music don't go on too long.'"

While the Reagans were in the White House, Barbara attracted only minimal attention when she traveled. But the trips gave her a grounding in international protocol and diplomatic requirements that would prove invaluable in future years when she would be in the international spotlight much of the time.

8

THE BIG PRIZE

The rumors surfaced several months before George Bush announced that he would run for president in October 1987, and reverberated through Washington. Both *Newsweek* magazine and *U.S. News and World Report* reported that Bush had an affair with a female staff member.

He denied it. His oldest son, George W., furiously denied it. Barbara denied it. But she was hurt and angry. "How do you defend against something that didn't happen?" she said. "It was a large fat smear and I didn't like it one bit . . . I hate it for him. I hated it for us."

Her protective instincts toward George also were sparked by charges that George had played a bigger role than he admitted in a scandal involving Iran and arms for a group known as Contras in Nicaragua. It was, she said, "an example of the negative tone of the entire campaign. The ugliness of politics has been very bad this year, Democrats and Republicans . . . it's been very hurtful and I don't like that," she said."[1]

Then, in the Iowa caucuses in February 1988, George Bush had an unexpected and humiliating loss, coming in third after Bob Dole and televangelist Pat Robertson, which led to a lot of speculation about Bush's future. Barbara was so disgusted and disheartened about what she heard that she refused to watch television news or read newspapers for a while.

"George doesn't like me to say it because it makes you sound like a nincompoop when you say you don't follow the news," she said. "But . . . it's just hard to go out and campaign for twelve hours when you're hearing such depressing things."

As in previous campaigns, the question of her white hair and wrinkled face came up frequently, but this time in more brutal form. NBC's Jane Pauley told Barbara on camera that people were saying, "Your husband is a man of the eighties and you're a woman of the forties. What do you say to that?"

Barbara was stunned, but maintained her composure enough to cobble together an answer. Later, however, she admitted the question had hurt. "She's lucky I didn't burst into sobbing tears," Barbara said.

As questions about her looks continued, she responded in various ways, sometimes with anger, other times with a more temperate answer. "I'm not going to turn into a glamorous princess," she said shortly before the GOP convention in August 1988. "I'm not going to worry about it. I have plenty of self-confidence, not in how I look but in how I feel, and I feel good about my husband, my children, and my life."

At the same time, she told reporters she admired the looks of Kitty Dukakis, wife of Democratic presidential candidate Michael Dukakis. "I'd love to look like her if you want to know the truth," she said.

Barbara spent almost as much time on the road campaigning as George did. As in previous campaigns, she frequently used slides when she spoke before a group, most of them designed to show George Bush as a happy family man and a strong leader. A favorite of audiences was a snapshot of George and Barbara in bed early one morning at their summer house in Kennebunkport, Maine, with grandchildren bouncing around them and playing on the floor. There were also slides of George with world leaders, George at the Berlin Wall and George at the Wailing Wall. Sometimes there was a videotape of George describing Barbara's life, with an emphasis on humor.

One anecdote was set in a bookstore, where Barbara was signing copies of *C. Fred's Story*, the first book she wrote about the family cocker spaniel. A woman came into the bookstore looking for the dog. Told the dog was home in Washington, she was indignant. "You mean I came here for nothing," she said.

Barbara used this type of self-deprecating humor to great effect and soon became a favorite with campaign audiences. She also revealed little bits of family trivia that added to the enjoyment. "George Bush sleeps with two girls," she deadpanned, pausing for effect. "Millie and me."

Although she generally refused to discuss political issues of the day, Barbara occasionally aimed a stinger at her husband's opponents for the GOP presidential nomination. Campaigning in Texas, where Robertson had been showing strength, she was asked whether he was a threat. "We don't need anyone who sees missiles in Cuba when they're not there," she replied, referring to Robertson's unsubstantiated and sensationalist claim that the Soviets had nuclear weapons in Cuba.

But she had learned a lesson from her infamous 1984 statement about Geraldine Ferraro—rhymes with rich. During one campaign trip in 1988, she was steaming about remarks Senator Bob Dole had made questioning whether George would be tough enough as president. Talking with reporters on the campaign plane, Barbara was suddenly aware of George Bush coming up behind her. "I better get back to my seat," she said. "The poet laureate has retired."

Despite her anger at Bush's opponents, Barbara claimed it wouldn't be the end of the world for her if George lost. Having been through two losing Senate races and an unsuccessful presidential campaign with her husband, she knew life didn't end at the ballot box.

"No matter what happens, I'm going to have puppies next year by this time," she told the *Baltimore Sun*. "And I'm going to beg George to take me down the Inland Waterway by boat. I've always wanted to do that. And I wouldn't mind taking a barge trip through the French wine country. And I'd like to go to Baja fishing again. We did that once. And I'm going to dig in my garden, and I'm going to play with my ten grandchildren, and I'm going to read a lot more. I might even write some. I'm going to do a lot of needlepoint. I'm going to walk six miles every day. And I'll play with my friends, while they can still play."

She had to put off all those activities, however. After a shaky start, George Bush went on to easily overcome his political opponents in the GOP primaries.

Whatever her real feelings about the campaign, Barbara was able to put on the required happy face for the Republican convention, held in mid-August in New Orleans. She and George and several grandchildren had been in Kennebunkport in early August as usual, but if Barbara had regrets about leaving the cool oceanside estate in Maine for the steamy, crowded streets of New Orleans, she didn't let on.

Both she and Kitty Dukakis had agreed to write convention diaries for *USA Today.* Barbara used hers in large part to introduce the wider Bush family to the public. She started writing from Kennebunkport. By the Sunday of convention week all the family had departed from the summer house except for Barbara and Jeb's three children. "The four of us are sitting here right now thinking, 'Why aren't we there where all the fun is?' " she wrote. She and twelve-year-old George P. shared their jitters, since he was to give the Pledge of Allegiance the following Tuesday at the convention and Barbara had to give a speech.

"There are many pros and cons to being the grandchild of the vice president," Barbara wrote. "Tuesday night will be one of the pros. On the con side: He got into a knock-down, drag-out fight with another boy at camp a few weeks ago out of loyalty to his grandfather."[2]

George P. and his two siblings, the children of Jeb and Columba Bush, were the ones George Bush referred to affectionately during the campaign as "the little brown ones." The phrase offended many people but the initial buzz was quieted by the Bushes' outraged reaction that anyone would imply that George had demeaned his own grandchildren. Americans would learn later that he had an especially close relationship with George P., his first grandchild. And of course, George P. went on to become a star of his uncle's 2000 presidential campaign.

On Monday, the day before the Bushes arrived at the convention, Barbara closed up the Kennebunkport house, doing the kind of homey chores many women could identify with. She said she put fresh sheets on all the beds, emptied vases, bid farewell to her beloved garden, and gave the man who takes care of the grounds some final instructions. She didn't plan to iron her clothes until she got to New Orleans, but it was the first thing she did when she arrived.

The night before she left for New Orleans, Barbara had dinner with George's eighty-seven-year-old mother and his even older aunt, Margie Clement. "One of the great reasons Mrs. Bush has been a wonderful mother-in-law is that she always pretended her four daughters-in-law were the four most wonderful women she's known," Barbara said. "I've tried to do the same with my daughters-in-law but I know I'm Bossier."[3]

George and Barbara made a grand entrance into New Orleans, arriving in a riverboat filled with family and friends and the newly chosen vice presidential couple, Dan and Marilyn Quayle. "I was overcome with emotion," Barbara said. "It sort of hit me that this was really happening."

She said that while George had told her his choice for vice president during the plane trip to New Orleans, she had figured it out the night before by process of elimination. "I also think it's a sign of living together for forty-three years," she said. "You think alike."

Wednesday was the first full day of the convention for Barbara. She got up at four-thirty in the morning to prepare for a super-full day, including a round of breakfast meetings, each featuring a specific voter group—blacks, Latinos, Jews, and the elderly. At the breakfast with black Americans, she ran into an old friend from Houston, former American League football player Ernie Ladd. "I like to stand next to him," Barbara said. "He makes me feel tiny."

Later in the day she visited a day-care facility that doubled as a meeting place for senior citizens. "What an extraordinary place it is," she said. "The children had a little song for me and showed me their arts and crafts."

She practiced her speech and stood at the podium in the convention hall, both to get a feel for it and to combat the nervous sensation that hit her when she thought of addressing the thousands of delegates who would fill the empty seats and spill out into the aisles.

Wednesday night she had dinner with the extended Bush family—sixty-five people in all. "One of the brothers took a poll of all the family members to see who had the grayest hair, and he said I won," Barbara reported, adding a typical mother's lament of the era: "Unfortunately, Marvin was runner-up for the family member with the longest hair."

She noted that her Mexican-born daughter-in-law, Columba, had celebrated her thirty-fifth birthday that day and had also given a seconding speech for George Bush's nomination, first in Spanish, then in English. Columba had just become an American citizen that year, Barbara said, "and I'm bursting with pride."

Thursday, the final day of the convention, was also the most fun for Barbara. Not only did George give a widely admired speech that night but she was honored earlier in the day at a free-spirited luncheon filled with family and friends.

She awoke at 4:00 A.M. in nervous anticipation, checking her clock every ten minutes to see if it was time to get up. When she rose she washed her hair, ironed a dress, and was ready to appear on the morning news shows by 6:15. She joked that on the way to her interviews she saw a news reporter she knew sleeping soundly on the floor. "I stopped for a moment and wrote him a note that said, 'I came by to give you an interview. Sorry I missed you.' Then I signed my name and left it on his tummy."

At the luncheon in her honor, the highlight was a teasing display of affection between George and Barbara, a response to her earlier complaint that Kitty and Michael Dukakis were simply looking for votes with their lovey-dovey stance. "I don't like the faking. I don't like the holding hands and all those things," Barbara had said in a TV interview a week earlier.

When George introduced his wife at the lunch, he told the crowd that he had been instructed by his aides to loosen up and "be a little more demonstrative."

"So here we go," he said. "The introduction—with feeling. Come on up, sweetie pie."

Barbara Bush grinned as she moved toward the podium and gave her husband an exaggerated hug. "Thank you very, very, much, sweetie," she said. Then, turning to the audience, she added, "See if he looks at me as adoringly as I looked at him."

There were more tributes to come. Bush campaign manager Lee Atwater said that Barbara had "an uncommon degree of common sense" and was a buoyant presence on the campaign trail. "You can't imagine how tough it got out there for six or seven months, trudging around during this so-called Iranian mess," he said. Atwater recalled that when he was depressed and "sitting there looking a little sad, she'd always come up to me and say, 'Cheer up, jittery jattery.' "

Dorothy Bush choked up during a tribute to her mother, saying she was "someone who was always there," and a woman who had spent many years "on the front lines of domestic warfare ... putting up with my four brothers without hazardous-duty pay." At that point, she was interrupted with a loud boo from one of those brothers.

Barbara, clearly pleased, told the crowd she felt like the world's luckiest woman. "Nobody has ever had dearer friends, nobody ever had a greater, more precious family, nobody ever had a better husband," she said.

"You know, today, August eighteenth, is really a great day. Sixty-eight years ago today, August eighteenth, 1920, the Nineteenth Amendment was passed, giving us, the women of America, the right to vote."

Then, turning back to her family, she said, "Twenty-nine years ago today, one of the happiest days of our life, our precious girl was born. We named her Dorothy after Grandmother Bush, and Dorothy means gift from God and that she's certainly been. Now, this evening, my most beloved husband will accept the nomination for the presidency of the United States. What a day!"

Later in the day, George and Barbara joined the Quayles at a hokey fund-raiser where all four rode in an antique truck toward a facade of the White House. But nothing could diminish Barbara's spirit, not even, she said, her fleeting and somewhat catty thought that Nancy Reagan had worn the same dress to the convention that she had worn eight years earlier. "I groaned," Barbara said. "I could never fit into the same dress from eight years ago."

Her speech that night was short, humorous, and filled with homey portraits and praise for the candidate.

"You're looking at a woman who couldn't be happier with her life," she said. "That's a wonderful thing to be able to say. I have my causes, such as literacy. I have caring friends, such as yourselves. I have five wonderful children, each of whom has married an equally wonderful person, and in turn given me ten exquisite grandchildren.

"And I'm married to an absolutely marvelous man—and I want to take a few minutes to tell you why he should be president of the United States. I've loved George Bush since the day I laid eyes on him. Now, I realize that won't get him a lot of votes. So let me explain why I respect him.

"First of all, George was always there when the children needed him. You've probably heard to the point you're sick of hearing it of all the important, big-deal jobs George has held. And he has. All those jobs have demanded tremendous energy and commitment from him. But do you know what I respect about George? In spite of all those important, time-consuming jobs, our family has always felt an enormous part of his life. The children and I have always felt as important as the work he was doing.

This has given our children confidence.... A reporter once asked George what his proudest accomplishment was. He said that the kids still come home. He meant it.

"He's just always there when someone needs him. I'm not going to tell you when this happened or where this happened or the event leading up to it, but my husband once had to fire a man who was an alcoholic. He didn't pass this painful task off to someone else; he did it himself. But George didn't just fire the man. First, as support, he went with him to tell his wife. She said, 'Thank God. For ten years I've worried and wondered why no one knew.' It was as if a burden had been lifted from her. And then do you know what George did? He attended AA meetings with the man. And today that man is a friend and supporter of my husband's. He may be in the audience tonight."

Right after the convention the Bushes flew to Indiana to showcase the vice presidential choice, Dan Quayle, who had already gotten a lot of negative reaction. Barbara did what she could to create a warmer atmosphere for the Quayles, including the chilly Marilyn. At a barbecue she and George held for the Quayles in early September, Barbara noted that Marilyn was the only wife among the presidential and vice presidential couples who still was responsible for young children—ages fourteen, eleven, and nine. "She still has to worry about dentists and homework and piano lessons," Barbara said. "What a juggling act."

From Labor Day to the November 8 election, the candidates, their wives, and families were on the road campaigning almost nonstop, and all of them had some testy moments. One of Barbara's occurred in Roanoke, Virginia, where a TV reporter asked her how George Bush could enjoy his sleek speedboat *Fidelity* when people were going hungry in America. Barbara smiled icily, then replied, "The American people love boats. Everybody has to relax—and I've got sunblock on but that light of yours is much too close to my face and it's burning me."

There also were lighter moments. Barbara was campaigning with country music star Loretta Lynn and noticed that the singer was chewing gum. "Can you sing with chewing gum?" she asked. Loretta Lynn said that she could indeed, at least while she was in "Lake Tahoe or in a real dry climate." But elsewhere, she said, "I just put it on my back tooth and let it lay there."

Barbara spent more than half her time on the road with George. Both of them preferred it that way and figured it was a luxury they could afford in this campaign, so unlike the days when they faced the problem of "George Who?"

When Barbara traveled alone, many of her appearances were at women's clubs, hospitals, programs for the elderly, day-care centers, and elementary schools. She asked her schedulers not to send her to high schools and colleges, fearing a generation gap and also knowing that college campuses often produce a more critical audience.

"I'm not just one who can stand to jolly up the crowd, you know, sort of cheer along," she said. "I think they need younger people and we've got all these sons. I don't see myself as a great campaigner."

But, she added, "I love people so I'm very good, I think, at hospitals. I don't think I'm so bad at elementary schools. . . . I feel very strongly about my literacy program, programs for abused children."[4]

She had an easy time with young children, being one of the few people on the campaign trail who actually looked comfortable in a classroom. In Fayetteville, Arkansas, she visited four and five-year-olds at a Baptist day-care center. She walked in with a present for the children, a book titled *Blueberries for Sal.* Holding up the book, she said, "I pick blueberries in Maine. Maine is one of the four hometown states for my husband."

The children in turn had a gift for her, a homemade basket filled with apples straight from the tree. "Pretty nice," she said.

At a school for disturbed children in Tulsa, Oklahoma, she read a story to a group of ten-year-old boys. As she was leaving, one came up and asked for a hug. "As I leaned down, I heard someone else say don't forget me," Barbara reported. "The next thing I knew, I had an armload of all those precious children hugging and kissing. I could hardly keep from weeping, and I heard a emotion-filled voice behind me say, 'We wouldn't need all those expensive programs if these little ones were given love in the first place.' It was one of my Secret Service agents."[5]

Barbara's easy manner in small groups led not only children but also grown women to approach her in a familiar way.

"Barb, I love your hair," a fifty-seven-year-old salt-and-pepper-haired volunteer told her at a children's hospital in Tulsa. Barbara laughed. Then, looking at the woman's hair, she replied, "You're not there."

In Enid, Oklahoma, a woman said, "Those pearls must be awful special. I see you with them all the time." Barbara, who would later reveal that she wore the pearls to cover up her wrinkled neck, said with a smile, "They're all different and they're all fake."[6]

The big event in September was a televised debate between George Bush and Michael Dukakis. Afterward, according to campaign officials, Barbara gave her husband some advice, which he took. She thought his response to a question on the homeless had been inadequate and that his attacks on Dukakis were too strong.

By October, a month before the election, many Americans could identify Barbara by sight. Kitty Dukakis was not as well recognized, according to polls taken at the time. Ironically, Barbara's white hair was the key difference.

John Molloy, author of a book titled *Dress for Success*, told United Press International that neither Mrs. Bush nor Mrs. Dukakis had made an especially strong impression, but Barbara's hair had stuck in the memories of many people.

"The first thing they said about Bush's wife is she looks very old, probably the gray hair," Molloy said, citing a survey. "Most people, especially men, didn't know what Mrs. Dukakis looked like," he added. "She didn't make an impression, good or bad."

The survey found that most people did not want Barbara Bush to change her hair, and men felt most strongly on the point. "The men said, 'Oh, no, she's that way. It's sort of like going back on what you are.'"

Barbara managed to look neat and fresh on the campaign trail most of the time, despite days that might include ten different stops and a plane ride in between. She kept a bag of toiletries packed at all times and tried to coordinate the clothes she took on her trips—usually choosing skirts and dresses in blue, black, or brown—so she wouldn't have to take so many shoes.

One day a reporter complimented her suit, a brown skirt and light blue jacket. "It's Bill Blass," Barbara said. "Describe it as more practical than beautiful, but pretty stylish. The jacket can be worn separately. I think I've worn it every other day on the campaign."[7]

Barbara's style and common sense reminded some people of Eleanor Roosevelt, but she rejected the idea with some vehemence, saying there were other first ladies who would make better role models. "The ones I respected the most are the one who did their own thing," Barbara said. "I wish you wouldn't say Eleanor. I grew up in a household that really detested her. She just irritated my mother. I admire Pat Nixon for some reasons, Betty Ford for some reasons. Mrs. Nixon was one of the most courageous, loyal women I've ever known. She was the most down-to-earth. A lovely lady. And Betty Ford, she's almost now more than then. I admire her enormously. She's in great pain. She goes around the country working for arthritis, working for drug abuse programs."

By mid-October, Barbara confessed that she was "counting every single second" until Election Day. "I'm ready for it to end now," she said.

Much to her dismay, she had gained thirteen pounds during the campaign. She complained that she was "the only living human" who gained weight under such circumstances—her daughter, Doro, had actually lost fifteen pounds.

"I am the world's most disciplined soul except for one thing—food," she said. "I write all my letters. I keep my diary, pay my bills, fix the scrapbook, I'm just very disciplined. But I just fall apart when it comes to food."

She said there was no particular food that tempted her—it was simply the idea of eating. "Just anything," she said. "That's how I deal with tension. I just go eat something. It's like, 'That will show that person who said that ugly thing.'"

Barbara said that when she and George were alone, they ate simply, but "I think we're every doctor's horror. Last week we had an evening home alone and we had cheese omelets, bacon and toast. Just the wrong things, of course."[8]

True to her word, however, she was tightly disciplined about everything else. She carried needlepoint and books on the campaign trail so she would have something to do during lulls and waiting periods. One handy addition to her purse was a pocket computer diary that held her schedule, her credit card numbers, a list of the books she had read over the last eight months, the names and addresses of 154 friends, the sizes of her children's clothes, and a reminder of two baby presents that were overdue. She also carried a plastic-covered three-ring binder that she used to record names, addresses, and ideas she picked up along the way.

Barbara successfully avoided most of the controversies of the campaign and she was ultra-cautious about making a mistake. Campaigning in California, she confessed that she had rooted for the Los Angeles Dodgers against the New York Mets in the playoff game leading up to the World Series and also favored the Dodgers over the Oakland Athletics in the series itself. But she had second thoughts about taking a stand, even on a baseball game. "I'll get in trouble for my Dodger answer," she told an aide afterward.

She still refused to answer questions about major issues but she did discuss them on her own sometimes in a way that put her husband in a good light.

"There is no question that we are better off today than we were in 1980 [when Democrat Jimmy Carter was president]," she said. "The Chinese are turning westward. Russia is negotiating for the very first time in my lifetime. We are doing away with weapons. The Russians are going out of Afghanistan. There seems to be some sort of movement in the Middle East. Things look better—they're not great but they are considerably better. Inflation is going down, unemployment is down, interest rates are down. I think things are better today."

Then, she added with a smile, "Having said that, I am no politician."

Barbara always hated it when George was criticized but she found late in the campaign that she also disliked some of the tactics the GOP used against Dukakis. She objected strongly when the Illinois Republican State Central Committee charged that Dukakis was weak on crime, and put out a press release saying, "All the murderers and rapists and drug pushers and child molesters in Massachusetts vote for Michael Dukakis."

A day after Dukakis denounced the campaign literature as "garbage," Barbara appeared on a CBS news show and said she agreed with that assessment. She said she had asked campaign chairman James Baker about it, telling him, "Jim, I don't like that and I knew George wouldn't."

She also had sympathy for Dukakis when *The Washington Post* and ABC released a poll the day of the second presidential debate showing Dukakis running six points behind Bush. "I thought that put a lot of pressure on him," she said.

But when Barbara was in Los Angeles for the debate, she was angered to see signs featuring George Bush's face with the words, "It can't happen" and "here" written on his forehead. "My gut reaction was to stop and pull them all down," she said.

Then, on a personal note, she added, "The most beautiful creature in the world and they've got the ugliest picture up."

During the final week of the campaign, Barbara spent a day on a chartered bus for a trip across Illinois. She was joined by country singers Crystal Gayle, Peggy Sue, Moe Brandy, and Lee Greenwood. One of her stops was at a school for the deaf in Jacksonville, Illinois, where she put in a plug for sign language. "I've decided that I want to learn sign language," she said, "even though I seem to be all thumbs. It was an extraordinary visit, much like the one I had at the School for the Deaf in Fremont, California, except I was very impressed in Illinois with a class that taught siblings how to sign. In one particular class, there was a father, brothers, sisters, three cousins and even one little boy who wanted to learn how to sign so he could communicate with his friend. I remember I was surprised in Fremont to learn that some of the parents couldn't sign."[9]

With just days to go until the election, Barbara said both she and George were having trouble sleeping even though polls showed he was running well ahead of Michael Dukakis. Ever cautious, Barbara said she didn't "think the thing's in the bag," and she recalled her own first vote—it was for Thomas Dewey, the 1948 Republican presidential candidate who was thought to be a sure winner but lost in the end to Harry Truman.

Barbara said she and George had talked about the possibility of losing, and he favored getting in a car and driving right out of Washington after the inauguration if that happened. She joked that she objected, since as vice president he had always had the services of a chauffeur. "I said, 'You'll leave by yourself because I'm not leaving the White House in a car with a man who's never driven in eight years.'"

She told reporters that her worst experience in the campaign occurred at a fund-raiser where the guest speaker was a comedian who told tasteless jokes about childbirth. The audience wasn't laughing and as she considered the whole scene, she said, she "got the giggles. The thing I hate is that fifteen hundred people think I thought that man was funny."

Another embarrassing moment, she said, was when she turned around at one event to thank the person who had introduced her and realized she didn't know who he was.

Her strangest gift was a live baby pig—not easy to accommodate on the campaign plane.

On Election Day, November 8, the Bushes went home to Houston along with their children and older grandchildren. They voted early, 7:40 in the morning, by paper ballot at a Ramada Inn near the hotel where they were living at that point when they were in Texas. The sixty voters waiting in line let the candidate and his wife go first. Afterward they visited campaign headquarters, where banks of volunteers were calling supporters to urge them to vote. Bush called a few himself, noting that some of those manning the phones were the same people who had been there twenty-five years earlier when he first ran for office. "Very inspirational," he said. Then he went jogging and had lunch with an old friend.

That night supporters gathered at the Brown Convention Center to await the results. It wasn't long before the good news started to come in. Michael Dukakis telephoned Bush with congratulations after the California polls closed at eleven o'clock Eastern Time. Other calls soon followed—President Reagan, Democratic vice presidential candidate Lloyd Bentsen, Jesse Jackson, Dan Quayle, and Canadian prime minister Brian Mulroney. Nancy Reagan telephoned Barbara.

The two and a half months between the November election and the January 20 inauguration sped by, just as busy as the campaign had been but with far less travel. Barbara found herself deluged with requests for interviews and appearances. She said she sometimes felt she was "on the couch," being asked how she felt about everything.

Once she was home again, though, she was able to achieve one of her immediate goals—she sent Millie to Kentucky to be bred, so that there would be puppies in the White House.

She and George spent Thanksgiving at Kennebunkport alone. All their children, exhausted from the campaign, were at their own houses or with other relatives. Barbara and longtime housekeeper, Paola Rendon, cooked the turkey and George carved it. They had blueberry pie for dessert.

At Christmas, the Bushes sent out ninety thousand cards to friends and campaign supporters, though they didn't sign each one individually. Barbara, for the eighth year in a row, put the crowning ornament on the national Christmas tree and said she didn't want to relinquish the job to Marilyn Quayle even though the task has traditionally been performed by the vice president's wife. "I would only be offended if someone else did it," she said. "It's the only thing I've done more than anyone else."

In January, Barbara had lunch in New York with Nancy Reagan and Raisa Gorbachev. When photographers asked the women to smile, Mrs. Gorbachev said, "We can't see you. That's why we don't smile." Barbara interjected, "How do you say cheese in Russian?" As the translator interpreted for Mrs. Gorbachev, everyone broke into smiles and laughter. This time, Nancy Reagan could hardly object to Barbara sharing center stage.

During inauguration week, hundreds of Bush family members again crowded into the capital, twenty-eight of them staying at the White House, including the grandchildren. Barbara, accustomed to the hullaballoo, was delighted to have them. "We get enormous strength from our family," she said. "It's always been like that and more so now. Once you're in a position where you're really isolated from people, you count more heavily on your children and your closest friends."

She said she and George would continue to go to local restaurants and theaters and make other short trips that put them in touch with normal life because "It's very good for both of us to get out of the house, be among people who come up and talk to you."

On Inauguration Day, Barbara wore a turquoise wool coat for the official ceremony. She stood by George's side as he was sworn in, a slight smile in evidence as he took the oath of office. George said later that she had saved him from embarrassment. After he was sworn in, he and Ronald Reagan left the inaugural platform and walked to the front of the Capitol to say a formal farewell. As the Reagans' helicopter left, the House sergeant-of-arms came forward to direct Bush.

"Mr. President, he said.

Bush didn't respond.

"I'm standing there waiting for President Reagan," Bush told congressional leaders later that day, "and I feel something that was between an affectionate hug and kidney punch—the Silver Fox [Barbara] telling me to get going."

Bush was inaugurated on a bright, sunny day, and he and Barbara got out of their limousine during the parade to walk. They held hands along the way.

When they reached the reviewing stand, Bush found a blond grandchild

Barbara, age 5. She was the baby of the family until brother Scott was born that year. She doted on the baby but was jealous of the time her mother spent with him. *(Courtesy of the George Bush Presidential Library)*

Barbara, age 7. Her dad worked for *McCall's* and brought the pattern books home so Barbara and her friends could cut out the models and make them into paper dolls. *(Courtesy of the George Bush Presidential Library)*

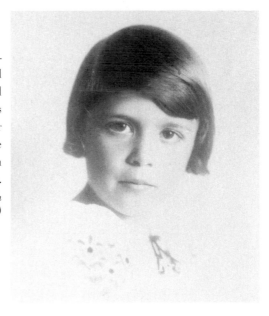

Barbara, age 18. She was a good student in high school, but at Smith she had lost interest in her studies. She was already planning to get married.

(Courtesy of the George Bush Presidential Library)

Barbara on Manursing Beach shortly before her marriage.

(Courtesy of the George Bush Presidential Library)

They're engaged. She said he was "the handsomest-looking man you ever laid your eyes on." *(Courtesy of the George Bush Presidential Library)*

The happy couple. The wedding was postponed once because George had been shot down while flying missions against Japan. Barbara was happy to reschedule. She and George were married January 6, 1945.

(Courtesy of the George Bush Presidential Library)

The Pierce family. *From right:* Jim, the older brother that Barbara often
fought with; Marvin, the family patriarch; Scott, the baby of the family;
Martha with her baby daughter, Sharon; and Barbara.
(Courtesy of the George Bush Presidential Library)

Barbara doting on her first-born son. He was the only one
of the Bush children born in the East, but he
grew up to be the most ardent Texan.
(Courtesy of the George Bush Presidential Library)

Barbara in 1953 with Robin, a curly-haired 3-year-old who developed leukemia that year and died seven months later on October 11. Barbara fell apart, but slowly recovered when she realized how much her two remaining children needed her.
(Courtesy of the George Bush Presidential Library)

In the summer of 1955 in Rye, New York, George and Barbara with their first-born son, 9-year-old George, looking much like dad. Barbara still had her dark, curly hair. *(Courtesy of the George Bush Presidential Library)*

The Bush family in Midland, Texas, in 1959, shortly before they moved to
Houston. Barbara is pregnant with Doro, the long-awaited girl.
(Courtesy of the George Bush Presidential Library)

A Bush family campaign photo taken in 1964 when George Bush was running for the Senate. He lost to the incumbent, Ralph Yarborough. George W. had just started school at Yale and introduced himself to the school chaplain, William Sloane Coffin. Coffin said, "Yeah, I know your father, and your father lost to a better man."

(Courtesy of the George Bush Presidential Library)

Another campaign photo of the Bush family in 1964.
(Courtesy of the George Bush Presidential Library)

The victorious candidate in 1966. George Bush won a seat in the House of Representatives that year, and the family moved to Washington for the first time. He was the first Republican from Harris County to win a House seat.
(Courtesy of the George Bush Presidential Library)

Barbara in the Waldorf Astoria apartment in New York City where she
lived in the early '70s when George was ambassador to the United
Nations. "I would pay to have this job," Barbara said.

(Courtesy of the George Bush Presidential Library)

Barbara at the Great Wall. *(Courtesy of the George Bush Presidential Library)*

George Bush was ambassador to China from October 1974 to December 1975. He and Barbara generally got around by bicycle. She loved the assignment because it gave her a lot of time with George.
(Courtesy of the George Bush Presidential Library)

The Bush family in 1978. *From left, top:* Doro, George, Barbara, Columba, Laura, and George W. *Bottom row:* Marvin and Jeb with Jeb's children, and Neil on the right. *(Courtesy of the George Bush Presidential Library)*

A Bush-Quayle campaign rally on October 30, 1988, shortly before their election victory. Finally, they were on their way to the White House. *(Courtesy of the George Bush Presidential Library)*

Barbara helps Millie learn a little history during the 1988 presidential campaign. *(Courtesy of the George Bush Presidential Library/David Valdez)*

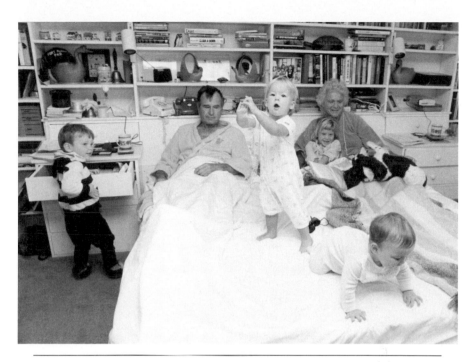

Morning at Kennebunkport with the grandchildren. Barbara said George Bush often read to the children while the family was in Maine, but maybe not at this early hour. *(Courtesy of the George Bush Presidential Library)*

Celebrating victory, 1988. *(Courtesy of the George Bush Presidential Library)*

Barbara, Millie, and the pups on the White House lawn. At one point, more than 100 photographers were on the grounds taking pictures of those puppies. *(Courtesy of the George Bush Presidential Library)*

George Bush at the Westin Galleria in Houston, November 3, 1992, conceding the 1992 election to Bill Clinton. Both Barbara and George took the defeat hard. *(Courtesy of the George Bush Presidential Library)*

George and Barbara celebrate their 50th anniversary in January 1995.
Back row, left to right: George W. Bush, Laura Bush, Jeb, Doro, Bobby Koch
(Doro's husband), and Neil. *Second row:* Barbara Bush (George W.'s daughter),
Marshall (Marvin's daughter), Columba (Jeb's wife), Lauren (Neil's daughter),
Sharon (Neil's wife), Ellie LeBlond (Doro's daughter), and Margaret Bush (Marvin's
wife). *Front row:* Jenna (George W.'s daughter), Ashley (Neil's daughter), Barbara,
George, Pierce (Neil's son), Walker (Marvin's son), and Marvin.

Barbara, celebrating her 75th birthday with three of her favorite
people. *(Courtesy of the George Bush Presidential Library)*

standing in his chair. He whisked her to the floor with a twirl, but his attention was soon diverted by a grandson showing him a Transformer. And so it went for the rest of the afternoon—wave to the crowd, talk to the children.

The evening, however was reserved for grown-ups. The Bushes had reserved inaugural balls at nine sites around the city to accommodate the thousands of people who wanted to attend and, as is traditional, they took a few dance steps at each one, beginning at Union Station.

"You can say you saw here first a lousy dancer trying to dance the first dance with the first lady of the United States," Bush said. Then, to the strains of "I Could Have Danced All Night," he took Barbara out on the floor. She wore a bright blue dress with a velvet top and satin skirt, designed by Arnold Scaasi. She said that blue was George's favorite color.

The dance at each subsequent stop was short. George had warned Barbara four decades earlier when she was wearing a green-and-red Christmas dress that he wasn't much of a dancer. And anyway, they needed to get home. They had a big day—four years' worth of big days—ahead.

9

MOVING IN

A couple of weeks before Barbara Bush moved into the White House, Nancy Reagan took her on a tour of the family quarters, including the second-floor kitchen and a third-floor laundry that she had not seen before. Afterward, Barbara was full of enthusiasm.

"It's the most beautiful house I've ever seen," she said. "I'm not going to change one thing."

As it turned out, she made quite a few changes, among them making room for First Dog Millie's new puppies where a bank of hair dryers once stood. But perhaps the biggest change was in the atmosphere at the White House. George and Barbara were both interested in the historic surroundings, and they invited scores of people in to share the fun of their discoveries. The quiet, formal world of the Reagans gave way to the more boisterous and open lifestyle of the Bushes.

Their first day in the White House was a Saturday and they celebrated with a personal welcome to four hundred tourists waiting outside the gates. George Bush randomly selected fifteen people from the group and took them through the rooms himself. "This is the people's house and it does seem appropriate on this first day that we welcome as many as we can," he said.

The Bushes brought to the White House their own bed and all their bedroom furniture as well as pieces from their sitting room and living room. Barbara packed a roomful of toys she had kept at the vice president's house for her grandchildren but other items were sent to the summer house at Kennebunkport or to Camp David, the presidential retreat in Maryland.

In the early weeks of the administration, both George and Barbara settled into a routine. Each tended to the business of the day—charity work, meetings, and interviews for Barbara, briefings, public appearances, and planning sessions for the president—and they returned to the family quarters about six o'clock. Evenings were devoted to more work but also entertainment—family, friends, and staff, lots of them. They were seldom alone.

"We just like to have people around," Barbara said. "That's neither bad nor good. That's us."

Most of those invited to the White House got a full tour from Barbara. "Everything glistens," she said, showing the house to reporters in early February. "It's so much more beautiful than I thought. Everything is beautiful in the White House. Honestly. The food is the most beautiful food you've ever laid your eyes on. Today I had lunch off of Wilson's plates, sometimes I have lunch off of Lincoln's plates, or Grover Cleveland's."

Moving to a window in the Yellow Room that showed of the South Lawn of the White House as well as the Washington Monument and Jefferson Memorial, she said, "This is the view right here. It's sensational." She remembered the room being yellow when Lyndon Johnson was president—he had invited the Bushes to the White House when George was elected to Congress from Texas.

The White House bedrooms also drew rave reviews. Barbara noted that England's Queen Mother had slept in the Queen's Bedroom, along with a number of other actual queens. She pointed out a secret stairway to the third floor, showed off the room where her grandchildren slept, and took a practical view of the historic Lincoln Bedroom. "It's not a thing of great beauty but pretty exciting," she said, with the only signed and dated copy of the Gettysburg Address displayed in one corner.

Barbara said she had quickly become comfortable in the White House and in the first weeks of the new administration was enjoying it much more than she had anticipated. "It's much more fun than I thought it would be," she said.

She worried, though, that she would become isolated. "I'm working on a theory," she said. "I'm going to go out so much that you're going to be saying, 'Ho-hum, there's Mrs. Bush out again.' I'm going to go to museums. I'm going to walk. I'm going to go out with friends. I'm just going to do things because I think there's a danger in.... I mean, look how pretty it is; who would ever want to leave it? But I think it's very important to get out."

And in fact she did get out and not only locally. Less than three weeks after she moved into the White House, Barbara accompanied George on a trip to Canada. While the two leaders discussed acid rain, Barbara went with Canadian first lady Mila Mulroney, a friend from the vice presidential days, to a preschool and read the children a story about owls and told them about her children and grandchildren, including one born that week.

The Canadians were interested in Barbara's style, especially in comparison with Nancy Reagan's. The contrast could not have been more clear. For that early 1989 visit Barbara wore a Bill Blass dress she had chosen for the presidential swearing-in ceremony weeks earlier and she paired it with an eight-year-old lavender coat. Marci McDonald, Washington bureau chief for a popular Canadian magazine, *Maclean's*, said that after she wrote about Barbara's relaxed style, "I got more requests for interviews about what this meant for Canadian women—could we stop holding our stomachs—and go a little easy on the wrinkle cream."[1]

Less than two weeks after the Canadian visit, the Bushes flew to Tokyo for the funeral of Emperor Hirohito. The emperor's death stirred anti-Japanese memories for some Americans since he had been a symbol of evil to the Allies during World War II. But Barbara urged the country to make an effort to look at modern-day Japan in a different light. "George was shot down by the Japanese and if he doesn't feel embittered, I can't imagine why anybody else would," she said on NBC's *Today* show shortly before she left for Japan. "These are allies of ours and business partners of ours, and this is the time when you put aside old grudges and you move on."

Because the occasion was a funeral, Barbara kept a low profile in Tokyo. She had tea with Naoko Takeshita, wife of the Japanese prime minister, a dinner with other prominent women in the country, and another tea with the wife of the Mexican president, but no public appearances.

Barbara's style of travel differed markedly from Nancy Reagan's, a distinction that was much noticed in Tokyo since it was a new administration. While Nancy's entourage included a chief of staff, personal secretary, hairdresser, and personal maid, Barbara took along one personal assistant, Casey Healey, and her press secretary, Anna Perez. She also had refused to allow the White House advance team to make arrangements ahead of time, a fact that caused considerable confusion and grumbling among the reporters traveling with her.

After the funeral, the Bushes made a brief stop in South Korea and then went to China, where Barbara relaxed and relived the days fourteen years earlier when she had been a resident of Beijing. Right off, she noticed that the city was undergoing a construction boom. "I mean, everyplace you look there's a crane," she said. "But the people are the same, the feeling is the same, the Forbidden City is the same."

She told reporters that her own experience in China "was about like now, except you weren't here. I used to ride my bike and give someone two cents to park it, and spend an afternoon with a house guest."

When she tried to convey the emotions she was feeling about being back, the words came out in an uncharacteristic jumble: "I feel good about China. I'm not good about telling my feelings. We went to church today. We saw the ministers we saw every Sunday when we lived here. This was a very happy time in our lives. I feel lucky to be able to be back here."

George Bush, speaking to the congregation of the church, also was feeling nostalgic. He said the church had been "our home away from home" when he and Barbara lived in China. "It's a little different though," he said. "Today we came up with twenty motorcars in a motorcade and I used to come to church on my bicycle—my Flying Pigeon."

One of the pleasures of the trip was seeing old friends, people they had known in the early 1970s. "We went to the International Club and saw our tennis-playing friends, the man who cut our hair," Barbara said. "We went to the U.S. embassy. They brought back some folks who had worked in the embassy. We saw the widow of our driver and lots of good friends."

Among the highlights of the trip was a luncheon given for Mrs. Bush by the U.S. embassy staff at an ancient ornate building. In addition to the head table, there were eleven tables of three women each. Barbara moved among them, talking to everyone. The women were all prominent Chinese—artists, teachers, authors, and doctors. She was accompanied on her rounds by a Chinese woman in a traditional long pink dress. When it was time to move to the next table—precisely four minutes was allotted to each one—the woman twirled and did a little dance.

Barbara's tour of the Forbidden City included a visit to the Hall of Supreme Harmony, a throne room that is off-limits to most tourists but was featured in the movie *The Last Emperor*. The occasion was marred by Chinese security guards who roughly shoved reporters and photographers and slammed Barbara's own White House photographer, Carol Powers, into a doorway, dislocating her jaw.

During the visit the Bushes gave a dinner for their Chinese hosts in the great Texas tradition—barbecue, baked beans, potato salad, and cold beer. It was a big dinner for five hundred people. Among the invited guests was China's leading dissident, physicist Fang Lizhi. Fang didn't make it to the dinner, however; he was stopped by security officials. The Bushes were unaware what was happening during the banquet but George Bush later told his hosts he regretted that Fang had not been allowed to attend. The Chinese replied that they didn't want any American interference in China's internal affairs, foreshadowing the stance they would take a few months later when the West protested the violent deaths of Chinese students who were demonstrating for democracy in Tiananmen Square. "We are heartbroken," Barbara said after watching the crackdown on TV.

Because she had become accustomed to constant attention during the presidential campaign, Barbara was prepared for the spotlight, both abroad and at home. But she still found it disconcerting at times. "We grew up in a world where you didn't talk about yourself all the time," she said.

She was delighted, however, to find that after years of being harangued about her white hair and full figure, she suddenly was getting widespread acceptance of her looks and appeared to be gaining in popularity. "I think people know I'm fair and I like children and I love my husband," she said. "I think people like that. People think it's nice to think you really love your husband and your children and your dog—I don't even mind cats."

Barbara said she had no plans to change her style—"I'm so old now that I don't have to pretend to be something I'm not"—and she had nothing but positive things to say about her much-criticized predecessor. "Of course I'm not going to be the same," she said. "She's a perfectionist and I'm not. Our lifestyles are very, very different. Would I like to be like her? You bet. But there's no chance of that . . . she has a flair that I'll never have."[2]

Although she still would not discuss most political issues, Barbara did speak out on subjects that interested her, usually involving women and work and literacy. She noted that an abortion had been performed on a woman who had fallen into a coma after a car accident in a case that drew national attention. While antiabortionists had protested the decision, Barbara said, "I agree with my husband on that. The life of the mother was at risk. I'm very grateful that it worked out as it did."

She still worried about mothers going to work when their children are young but said she realized it was an economic necessity for many. "There is a conflict there," she said. "But having said that, it's a fact of life."

While Barbara had been a full-time housewife for two decades, she understood the budget pressures families face, even if her own household had different problems from the average family. When the Bushes moved to Washington in the 1960s, they dipped into their oil earnings because they could not maintain a house in Washington and one in Houston and send their children to private schools on George's salary as a member of Congress. "Could we have lived on it? We probably could have," she said, but it would have meant a major change in lifestyle.

Early in the new administration Barbara ventured briefly into a hot and emotional topic—gun control—and came to regret her comments. Although George Bush was a member of the National Rifle Association, Barbara told reporters, "I myself do not own a gun. I'm afraid of them. I'm too afraid I'd shoot the wrong person." She described her first and only experience hunting with her husband.

"He told me to follow the bird and I followed the bird and his head came right through that little circle [the rifle scope]. I put down the gun, and said, 'That's it. I'm not going to do that again.' "

The discussion turned to a tragedy in California, where a gunman using a Chinese AK-47 assault rifle had killed five children in a schoolyard.

Barbara said she thought such weapons were illegal, and added, "They should be—absolutely."

While most Americans agree with that position, it turned out that assault weapons were not illegal at the time and George Bush did not favor a ban on them. A few weeks later, Mrs. Bush's press secretary, Anna Perez, announced that the first lady would not be talking about controversial subjects anymore. A short time later, though, President Bush moved to outlaw such guns.

Barbara found that almost everything she and her family did, no matter how insignificant, was of interest to the public, hungry for information about the new first family. "I guess I'm going to have to start thinking more," she said. But it wasn't really necessary with Millie around. During the early weeks of the administration, the cocker spaniel filled the anecdote quotient nicely. And her puppies got a stupendous amount of attention; at one point, more than one hundred photographers were on the White House grounds taking their pictures.

George Bush revealed that in the final days of Millie's pregnancy he had been banished to the Lincoln Room because Millie didn't like her own bed and wanted to be with Barbara. "The dog refuses to go to the doghouse," he said.

Both of the Bushes got teary-eyed watching Millie have her pups. "Really beautiful. It was unbelievable," George Bush said afterward. Asked if it was his first delivery, he said, "Yes, my first dog delivery." Barbara then put an arm around his waist and added that George had not seen any of his children born either.

She teased him about Millie, too. Visiting an adult learning center in Baltimore where questions about the dog came up, Barbara revealed that Millie liked to take showers. "Millie, of course, does not take them alone because she's too short to reach up," Barbara said. "But someone, a very high public official, elected to office, takes a shower with Millie every week or so." As she left the center she had second thoughts about her revelation. "I hope that same public official won't be sore at me," she said.

With the obvious affection she had for Millie, Barbara shocked some television viewers a few months later when she nudged Millie with her foot while the cameras were rolling. The incident occurred while ABC was filming a show featuring a tour through the White House with Barbara.

Millie tagged along and, having no sense of decorum, lay down in the Green Room during the taping and began to lick her private parts. Barbara nudged her and reporter Sam Donaldson chastised the dog, too, but did not touch her. Of course, he said, he got a lot of mail asking why he had kicked the dog.

One setback the Bushes suffered early on in the White House was illness—George and Barbara both had Graves' disease, a hyperthyroid condition that in Barbara caused an eighteen-pound weight loss in two weeks and vision problems that left her with puffy eyes. After she disclosed the illness, she was besieged with questions and concern for her welfare, all of which she found pretty irritating. In March, she told a group of volunteers that yes, she was feeling tired, but then went on to recite what kind of day she had put in: "I got up at eight and played tennis with three friends. I worked at my desk for two hours. I went to a lunch with George Bush. I just met with Martha Graham upstairs. I'm meeting with you now. And George and I are having a large reception this evening. Thank you for asking how I feel. I feel wonderfully well."

In April, she was treated with a radioactive iodine solution to shrink her thyroid gland, but she continued to have vision problems, including periods of double vision. In November she went to the famed Mayo Clinic—she would serve on its board of directors after her husband left office—to see if doctors there could eliminate the eye problems. They changed her medication and two months later she started radiation therapy at Walter Reed Army Medical Center in nearby Maryland.

The treatments, given over a ten-day period, helped somewhat but when they were completed, Barbara said she still had double vision at times even though she felt her eyes looked better. She said she and her husband had worried how the treatments would affect her personality, since there had been "an enormous change" in their daughter Robin during her radiation treatments for leukemia.

"So far everybody says I've been just angelic," Barbara joked. "I haven't changed a bit. I'm just as mean as ever."

Although the eye problem never did disappear entirely, it was not serious enough to slow Barbara down much. After her first one hundred days in the White House she found that she was not as isolated as she had feared. She went out frequently to charity events, museums, visits to friends, restaurants, just as she had said she would. She and the president read six newspapers each morning while watching the early television news shows on three channels. In the evening, they watched four news shows.

"The world comes to you," she said. "I mean, we're not as isolated as you might think. We've seen thousands of people." And those who couldn't manage to see her often wrote instead. In her first three months in the White House, she received 35,000 letters.

She often went to the "back fence" to talk with tourists and sometimes watched them from a White House window, noting with amusement that Americans who took a picture of the White House frequently started on the sidewalk, then backed into the street to get everything in, whereas Japanese simply crossed the street and took the picture from there.

She still managed to exercise, usually seventy-two laps daily in the pool on the White House grounds, under the watchful eye of a secret service agent. "Someone watches me swim a mile every day," she said. "Talk about watching the grass grow."

To relax, she said, she and George watched movies and some television shows, including *Murder, She Wrote* and *60 Minutes*, often with friends. She read short mysteries in the evenings, but with her full days and 6:00 A.M., rising time she had trouble staying awake. "By nine-thirty I am ready to go to bed," she said. "So I go to bed to read a book. I barely can keep my eyes open. He wanders in about ten."

She thought her fatigue might have been caused by her thyroid condition. "I'm lucky if I get through the days," she said. "I don't mean I'm overextended, but I am sixty-three years old and I need to be babied a bit."

Despite her age and her ailments, Barbara kept up the full social schedule that she and George had long maintained. It was not unusual for her to come home from a day of events to a house full of guests. While she now had plenty of help to take care of the cleaning, decorating, cooking, and cleanup, she still had to be on hand to entertain. Frequently guests were invited to a buffet with a movie afterward, usually the first runs of the day. Or everyone would pile into cars and go to the president's favorite Chinese restaurant in the nearby Virginia suburbs. By spring Bush had opened a horseshoe pit and he celebrated by holding a party around it— hamburgers, hot dogs, and a competitive game.

The guests included members of Congress, old friends, reporters, Cabinet members, governors, business leaders, sports stars and team owners, authors, members of the Supreme Court, and the White House staff. Unlike the Clintons who followed, the Bushes were not much into Hollywood.

Because the open-house style of the Bushes contrasted sharply with the closed society of the eight Reagan years, many people were surprised at the ongoing festivities at the White House. But people who had known the Bushes earlier recognized this party fever as just a continuation of their longtime penchant for entertaining. "So what's new?" Barbara said. "That's the way it's been for forty-four years."

She recalled that during their time in New York City, living at the Waldorf-Astoria while George was ambassador to the United Nation, he called home one night and said, " 'I've just been to a wonderful meeting and I asked all the newspaper publishers and their wives to come back for a drink.' I mean, we didn't have a kitchen there but we also had a hotel so we could cope," Barbara said. She added that she didn't mind such impromptu invitations. "With George, nothing's impossible. What's more, he's willing to help, not dump all of it off on me."[3]

For formal White House dinners, the Bushes worked on the seating plans themselves. When the social office drew up a plan and sent it to them, the arrangements often would go back with revisions. The same planning went into the entertainment at Camp David and Kennebunkport, but arrangements at both were much looser. Going into her first summer in the White House, Barbara explained to *House & Garden* magazine how the family lived at Kennebunkport in August.

"The difference between Washington and Maine is night and day," she said. "I play tennis, garden and plot and plan everyone's day. I try to see that one and all are included in some activity. I do have certain rules posted on the doors, which no one really keeps:

"Picnics should be planned early for the beach.

"Please pick up wet towels and use them twice.

"Please be down for breakfast between seven and nine or no breakfast.

"All rules are broken constantly," she said.

The entire family—all the children and grandchildren—tried to be together in Maine at least for a few days in August.

"The decor of the house is hodgepodge," she said, "three houses of furniture put in one, no antiques, fifteen-year-old slipcovers—a house where grandchildren are more than welcome. There are six bedrooms and six baths in the main house plus a girls' dormitory. My favorite room is the end room, painted aqua as it was in George's grandmother's time, with a large fireplace, latticework on the walls, and water on three sides."

Her garden was in the same spot the old garden had been, a mix of perennials and annuals. "There is a cutting garden so I can have flowers for the house," she said. "I mix my garden flowers with wonderful wildflowers and have big loose arrangements. My favorites are hard to say, but certainly lilies, gardenias, daisies of all varieties, phlox, and delphiniums."

Her early-morning routine at Kennebunkport was similar to the one at the White House, but without all the newspapers.

"The day starts with coffee in bed at six—children and grandchildren drift on down. They all have breakfast at the dining room table and there's a choice of pancakes or muffins, depending on the day. Many of us go our separate ways—boating, swimming, softball, tennis, horseshoes and golf. Many ages play together.

"Lunch, usually on the deck, is a big pot of soup—clam chowder, corn chowder, zucchini—with sandwiches or salad. The children eat dinner early but the two older grandchildren usually eat with us. I do not cook these days. Most of our meals are cooked on the grill, swordfish being my favorite and lobster a close second. We usually have a clear soup served in mugs in the living room. A favorite dessert is ice cream with Paola Rendon's butterscotch sauce—she's been with us for years. We entertain a lot on four round tables of ten—big family dinners and get-togethers mixing childhood friends with foreign friends or just out-of-town guests."[4]

Almost all guests at Kennebunkport spend the night, including a substantial number from overseas. Among foreign guests in the first year of the new administration were French president François Mitterrand and his wife, Danielle; Danish prime minister Poul Schluter and his wife, Anne Marie; and Canadian prime minister Brian Mulroney and his wife, Mila, and their four children. Good friends of the Bushes, the Mulroneys were invited back repeatedly.

Barbara also managed to keep the bedrooms at the White House pretty full, but not in the same sense the Clintons did, offering overnight stays to big financial backers.

Among those who slept at the White House during the first months of the Bush administration were Kentucky horse breeder Will Farrish, whose dog was the father of Millie's pups; childhood friend FitzGerald Bemiss, who was at the Bushes' wedding; Pennzoil chairman Baine Kerr, and former neighbor Shirley Pettis Roberson.

Although Mrs. Roberson was familiar with powerful Washington, having served two terms in Congress herself, she said staying overnight at the White House in a historic bedroom—she and her husband, Ben, were in the Queen's Bedroom—is "a storybook experience. . . . Everyplace you turn there is a sense of your forebears. Bar makes you feel you must know everything about this wonderful house, and because she knows every piece and tells its story, the whole floor comes alive."

Barbara had turned the Queen's Bedroom into a guestroom extraordinaire. A white princess telephone next to the four-poster bed came with instructions for dialing out and for obtaining White House services. A basket of fresh fruit was set nearby. In the adjoining bathroom she put a hair dryer and assorted toiletries and she could reel off the names of the famous people who had been guests in the room—Prime Minister Winston Churchill, the English Queen Mother, Queen Elizabeth II, Queen Fred ericka of Greece, and Queen Juliana of the Netherlands. During the inaugural ceremonies, George Bush's mother, Dorothy, had the honor.

When Barbara took guests on tours of the house, she also pointed out the Lincoln Sitting Room where Richard Nixon prayed with Henry Kissinger during the dark days of Watergate two nights before Nixon resigned as president. "This is the little sitting room that's only notable because supposedly, remember, when President Nixon and Kissinger went in—it had a fire in the fireplace and air-conditioning on in July."

She also showed off the Bushes' private sitting area, a small room in the back of the White House that had been used by Ronald Reagan as a study. Barbara put her big needlepoint rug on the floor and hung the mounted kimonos that she had displayed on the walls of the vice presidential mansion. Bush family photographs were on display around the room, which included a television with a remote control bearing the presidential seal.

She and George usually ate dinner in the President's Dining Room, whose walls are covered with revolutionary war scenes. The room was turned into a dining room by the Kennedys; earlier presidential families had to go to the first floor to eat. "This used to be Tad Lincoln's and much later, Alice Roosevelt's bedroom," Barbara said. "Jackie Kennedy made this an upstairs dining room."

She said that when Alice Roosevelt had the room around 1901, "there were no West Wing offices and in the other end of the hall from this room, all the affairs of state were conducted. Six children running up and down the hall . . . and the business being carried on in the other end."[5]

The Bushes completely redecorated the president's office. "This room was the Treaty Room and it was very dark," Barbara said. "Jackie Kennedy changed it from the Monroe Room to the Treaty Room and before the Monroe Room, it was the president's office."

On the wall, George Bush had hung a picture of President Lincoln talking with generals aboard a riverboat on the Mississippi. He said he drew inspiration from it, seeing the president and his men as peacekeepers. Among the framed and autographed pictures on the president's desk was one of Mulroney, who had written, "George, believe me it only gets better."

Behind the desk was the president's electric typewriter—he used it himself—and a word processor that he would later take lessons on. "George loves this room," Barbara said. "These were Nixon's old curtains. We found them in storage."

During the spring, Barbara accompanied George on a weeklong trip to Europe for a meeting of NATO. While the European journey didn't have the same sentimental value as China, it was full of fun for Barbara and without any underlying political tension. On the plane to Europe, Barbara showed off a $7,000 gold watch from Tiffany that she had received from the Ladies of the Senate, a club she had presided over for years. She said she was feeling good, except for her eyes, which were still red from her thyroid condition.

The first stop was Rome. Barbara, showing her practical side, wore a red suit with matching pumps for her initial event, but an hour later, when she was to tour the ruins of the Arch of Constantine, she switched from pumps to red loafers. Asked if she had changed into her walking shoes, she said, "You bet I did." Seeing the photographers' interest, she warned, "Now, don't focus on my feet."

She visited a center for homeless women, bringing along a gift of six dozen sheets and towels. She helped serve food for almost half an hour and said afterward she was impressed by the facility. That afternoon she went for a swim at the U.S. embassy, had her hair done by an Italian stylist at four o'clock, and was ready at five o'clock for a tour of the Vatican and a meeting with the pope, a quick-change schedule that amused and amazed the Italians. For the Vatican meeting, Barbara wore a black suit by Arnold Scaasi. She had to go to a dressy dinner immediately afterward, but that was no problem clothes-wise—she simply took off the suit jacket to reveal a lacy white top.

She told her staff she wanted to stop at Ferragamo, a top Italian shoe-maker, but she didn't have time and in fact didn't do any shopping on the trip. "I'm not a good shopper," she said. "I'm a good sight-seer."

Sight-seeing yielded one surprise in Italy. George Bush made a spot decision to visit the USS *Guadalcanal* off Anzio Beach, and during the tour Barbara ran into a startled seaman who was just getting out of the shower, wrapped only in a towel.[6]

In Belgium, Barbara went to gala luncheons, concerts, and dinners but also visited a village outside Brussels that was built especially for the mentally handicapped, one of five such government-subsidized towns in the country for adults capable of living semi-independently under supervision. "It's an absolutely wonderful project," Barbara said. When she arrived, two residents presented her with flowers. Then she was taken on a tour to see the many workshops in the village—candles, baked goods, and fabrics all produced and sold to the public in a competitive market.

As Barbara was getting ready to leave the village, she was given a gift by one of the residents, a twenty-year-old woman named Beatrice, who had made a puppetlike witch on a broomstick for the first lady. Having presented the gift, Beatrice began to cry from the emotion of it all. When Barbara realized what was happening, she went over and patted the young woman on the shoulder. "I wish I could say what I really feel in French," she said. "But all I can say is *merci beaucoup*."

The highlight of the European tour was London, where Barbara stole the spotlight by spontaneously reaching for the hand of Denis Thatcher—husband of Prime Minister Margaret Thatcher—and planting a big kiss on it. The incident occurred as Barbara arrived at 10 Downing Street to join her husband, who had been meeting with Mrs. Thatcher. Denis Thatcher greeted Barbara with a kiss on the hand but some photographers missed the shot and asked for a repeat. At that point, Barbara quickly reached for Denis Thatcher's hand instead. This time all the photographers got the picture and it ran in newspapers all over the world.

Earlier in the day, Barbara had toured Brixton, a poor immigrant neighborhood in London. She stopped in at an adult education center to see how the English cope with illiteracy and talked with students from Angola, Ghana, Ethiopia, and Zaire as well as with school officials. She told them that in some places in the United States, "there are enormous waiting lists for literacy. It's heartbreaking."

In a lighter moment, she joined in a cooking class that was making strudel, which she said she had not made before, adding "My pie crust is nothing to write home about." At the school's day-care center, the children presented Barbara with a brightly colored paper teapot, which inspired her to recite an English nursery rhyme. "I'm a little teapot short and stout. Here is my handle, here is my spout," she sang, extending her left arm as a spout. "Do you know it?" she asked the three-year-olds. They looked bewildered.

Lunch that day was at Buckingham Palace. George took Barbara's hand as the photographers snapped their pictures. Queen Elizabeth's staff served salmon mousse, duck, asparagus, and for dessert, mango ice cream.

That night, the Bushes wound up their weeklong, nine thousand-mile journey at a dinner given by the Thatchers. When they got home they went straight to Kennebunkport for a rest.

Just five weeks later another European trip was scheduled with stops in Poland, Hungary, Paris, and the Netherlands. Barbara, having learned from the rigors of the last trip, decided to pack more clothes this time—"just everything in my closet"—and to have a fresh outfit for every appearance. On the previous trip, she said, she had forgotten that the president's wife is widely photographed each time she gets on a plane and gets off. "I forgot that of course you can't just throw on something and get on an airplane and then change your clothes on the plane," she said. "You've got to be seen getting on and off."

With careful planning that took several days, she filled a hanging bag with clothes for each of the four countries she would be visiting. Having gone to so much trouble, she joked with reporters about her efforts. "I hope you have noticed," she said. "I've killed myself."

Her husband, she said, did his own packing as usual and got through the job in about twenty minutes. He even packed two tuxedos on the advice of an aide, in case he spilled something on one of them.

The first stop was Poland, a country full of excitement at the time over the retreat of communism and the growth of the democratic Solidarity movement. In Warsaw, the Bushes gave a luncheon at the U.S. ambassador's residence, mixing longtime Communist leaders with major figures from Solidarity. Barbara's table included both Communist party leader Wojciech Jaruzelski and Solidarity's chief spokesman, Janusz Onyszkiewicz, who emphasized how much Poland had changed. "If you take into account that a year ago I was in prison it was rather strange," he said.

Barbara later said she found Jaruzelski nothing like the stone-faced Communist he often seemed in public appearances. When George Bush invited the men at the luncheon to take off their coats, she said, Jaruzelski told her he would have to sneak out and take off his suspenders as well. Later, when he stood up to give a toast, he joked, "Well, I better be careful. I've gotta remember I don't have my suspenders on."

That night Jaruzelski held a dinner for the Bushes and also invited many Solidarity and Catholic Church leaders. Barbara, making good on her clothes promise, changed from the navy-and-white cotton she had worn during the day to a spectacular red-flowered dress for the evening. Outside the dinner, held in a seventeenth-century palace, demonstrators shouted, "May Bush live one hundred years." And "Down with communism." Bush, in his toast, said, "Poland is entering a new era. It is beginning once again to command its own destiny."

Before leaving Warsaw, George Bush presented a gift to the Polish people—Little League charters and enough uniforms and baseball equipment for ten teams. "Perhaps nothing is more American than Little League baseball," he said. "Well, few things show America's love for Poland like bringing our national pastime to you."

The next day the Bushes flew to Gdansk to have lunch with Solidarity leader Lech Walesa, who in later years would replace Jaruzelski as head of Poland's government. Walesa and his wife, Danuta, lived in a two-story stucco house. Even though it was a modest dwelling, Walesa said he was able to buy it only because of payments he got from Solidarity. "If I were an ordinary Pole, I would not be able to afford, it," he said.

Lunch was substantial and rich—salmon, eel, a cold vegetable soup, turkey, roast beef, schnitzel and pork loin with Jell-O for dessert. Bush, who drank a small glass of vodka with the lunch, ate heartily. "My mother taught me to eat what's before you," he said. "In this house, I would weigh three hundred pounds."

After lunch, the Walesas took their guests to the Solidarity Workers Monument. Huge crowds lined the roads along the way, singing a traditional Polish song, "One Hundred Years." George, Barbara, and Lech Walesa all got out of the limousine to shake hands. It was a moving, emotional experience for everyone involved. Americans and Poles, sharing a realization that democracy was taking hold in a country that had long been ruled by Communists.

Barbara said later that Walesa kept saying, "Oh my gosh, oh my gosh, oh fantastic, fantastic." She added, "I'm sort of cleaning up the 'oh my goshes,' but it really was exciting." Recalling her last visit to Poland in 1987, she said, "I think there was an awful lot of hope that we did not see the last time, an enormous amount of hope tempered with a little bit of caution."

During the stop in Gdansk, Barbara went out on her own only once, with Jaruzelski's wife, Barbara, to the town hall. Her schedule called for a stroll around the building to look at its medieval architecture but crowds near the structure were so enthusiastic that security guards got nervous and sent her straight inside instead. Barbara said later she had noticed major changes in the Polish leader's wife—she had lost considerable weight and learned English since the Bushes' last visit to Poland. "She was always lovely, but I said, 'I just can't get over how thin you are,' she told us that she wanted her husband to get out of politics. I don't know if that's true or not, but they were just more open, much more open."

In Hungary, the next stop on the tour, Barbara played a more substantial role, visiting a camp the Hungarians had set up to help Romanians fleeing from the despised government of Nicolae Ceausescu, who later would be vengefully executed by his own people. The refugee settlement, located on an island outside Budapest, was set up by Hungarian lawyer Ferenc Jana to protect ethnic Hungarians from the Transylvania area controlled by Romania. The five hundred refugees described a society intent on eradicating their culture—one young woman said authorities had tried to force her to change her baby's name.

Barbara met the families and had her hand kissed many times in traditional European fashion. "I have often thought the worst thing that could happen to you would be to have your country taken away from you," she said. "And the second worst thing would be to have no one accept you to their country with loving arms."

Barbara also visited a center for handicapped children run by the Catholic Church in Budapest. Eleven of the children sang and recited a biblical skit for her and her companion, the wife of Hungarian prime minister Miles Németh. Mrs. Németh broke into tears during the performance. Barbara wrote in the guest book, "I feel God's love in this wonderful house. God bless you all. Thank you for letting me share in this great moment. I will care more, thanks to you."

That night the Bushes hosted a party for the Hungarians. As in Poland, it was a mix of Communists and leaders from the opposition parties. A Hungarian band played country and western music and the ambassador flew in American shrimp for the occasion.

Afterward, on the flight to Paris, Barbara said she had been especially impressed by the changes in Hungary since her last visit in 1983. Poland, she said, always had "enormous pride and spirit, more than any other Eastern European country I'd ever been in, so I wasn't surprised to see it again. Just more so. But Hungary, I think, has changed enormously since we were there."

When the Bushes arrived in Paris, they found it in a festive mood, celebrating the two hundredth anniversary of the French Revolution and also hosting an economic summit for the seven major industrial nations. The first day, Barbara attended a luncheon given by Danielle Mitterrand, wife of the French leader. Afterward she went to the Louvre and then to the American Hospital in Paris to unveil a plaque dedicating a new wing. Engraved on the plaque was a notation that Barbara Bush had dedicated the hospital wing "on the occasion of the visit to Paris of George Bush."

Barbara, recalling that George had torn up his speech in Budapest and given a short talk instead to a rain-soaked crowd, decided to do the same thing at the hospital dedication. "I'm going to show you that I learned something from my husband in Hungary," she said. "I'm going to give up my speech and just tell you that speaking from the heart, as he did, this is one of the nicest things that ever could happen to me, and selfishly, I feel like you've stretched my life a little bit because now I'm on a plaque."

She also stopped in the hospital for a visit, talking with a man who had developed acute appendicitis while visiting Paris and telling a surgeon from New York City, "so am I but don't tell anybody. Don't tell them down in Texas."

Besides the plaque bearing her name, Barbara received another surprise from the Parisians—a rose that will always have her name. Cross-bred to get a red-and-white color, it was planted in the Bagatelle Rose Garden in the Bois de Boulogne in Paris, which includes strains of roses named after many famous people, including John Kennedy and Princess Grace of Monaco. But the Barbara Bush rose was the first named after an American first lady. Barbara was presented with a large bouquet. "It's almost like having a baby," she said, sniffing the roses. "I feel like a grandmother with a new child. They'll still be here when I'm gone. I adore them. I love the color combination."

Horticulturist Henri Delbard, who developed the rose, promised Barbara a bush of the flowers for the White House Rose Garden. "We'll have to plant it," Barbara said.

The Paris trip included numerous luncheons and dinners. Barbara found that her hosts didn't follow her own practice of breaking protocol occasionally to make sure that foreign guests weren't seated next to the same person meal after meal. "I have now become glued to Mr. Mobutu," she said, referring to the president of Zaire, who was her dinner companion a number of times. "I teased him because he doesn't eat vegetables and I told him when he comes [to the United States] I'm going to only give him regular water and artichokes because he certainly doesn't drink regular water and he certainly does not touch artichokes."[7]

The last stop on the European tour was the Netherlands, where Barbara unveiled another permanent structure bearing her name. This one was the cornerstone of the American School of the Hague, which had just begun construction. The stone read: "This cornerstone unveiled by Mrs. Barbara Bush, first lady, July 17, 1989, on the occasion of the first visit by a president of the United States of America."

Perhaps the most interesting stop during the short visit to the Netherlands was at a church in Leiden, where President Bush gave a speech and learned from the mayor that two of the Bush family ancestors had lived in the city and sailed on the Mayflower to America in 1620. Mayor

Cornelis Goekoop told Bush that Francis Cooke, a signer of the Mayflower Compact, and Hester De La Noye, had a daughter named Jane, who was Bush's "grandmother" eleven generations back. The mayor said that Hester's sister Marie had a child named Philippe whose grandchild—seven times removed—was Franklin Delano Roosevelt. "Two sisters, two presidents," Mayor Goekoop said.

The trip was a success from Barbara's point of view, exhilarating but also tiring. While George had jogged every day, and had gained no weight despite the rich meals, she hadn't done any exercise. "I've been trying to keep my diary up and my thank-you letters in the spare time and so I've sort of been a slug," she said. "But I'm up to date, so that's not bad."

Back home, her popularity was soaring. An NBC-*Wall Street Journal* poll found that Americans preferred Barbara to Nancy Reagan by a 3–1 margin; at the same time, George Bush topped Ronald Reagan 2–1.

American women began to emulate Barbara. The three-strand fake pearls she always wore became a big seller. The National Needlework Association said her interest in sewing had brought new adherents to the craft. And designer Arnold Scaasi said, "Having Barbara as first lady means that women who weren't buying a new dress because they were a little overweight are buying new dresses now. It means you don't have to try to look like your daughter anymore."

"Not since the 1950s has there been a first lady who so perfectly fitted our traditional ideas of how a first lady should be," said Barbara Kellerman, a professor who studied presidential families for a 1981 book, *All the President's Kin.*

"Mrs. Bush is really a throwback—in the good, not the pejorative, sense of the word—to a time when what a first lady did, how she looked and the activities in which she was engaged seemed very clear to all of us, when there was some consensus of what was appropriate."[8]

Even lobbying groups that were vehemently opposed to the president's position on social issues often had a kind word for Barbara. Kate Michelman, executive director of the National Abortion Rights Action League, said that although Barbara publicly supported her husband's opposition to abortion and refused to say what her own view was, she set a good example for politicians pondering the issue.

"She's why politicians should trust women to make decisions for themselves," Michelman said. "She's thoughtful, caring, concerned and compassionate, not only about children's lives and the quality of family but about the role of women in the society and the world at large."

Barbara herself said she was a liberal on social issues but added that she considered the Republican party to be liberal on social issues as well. "Now, you may not look at it that way or you may not look at me that way, but I think of us both as caring enormously about people and looking—it's very hard, you know, easy when you're one civilian, but when you're the president of the United States, you have to look at all the people."

Newsweek magazine reported that the Bush family had a discussion about abortion around the dinner table in January 1990, after Bush had been in office one year. The magazine said all the men at the table had been against abortion and the women for it. But George W. told reporters the report was "totally inaccurate." He said he didn't know what meeting the article referred to "nor do all the males come down on the same side." George W. said that he and his father were opposed to abortion but not all of his brothers were. Barbara, of course, revealed after her husband left office that she favored abortion rights.

At the end of Bush's first year in the White House, the United States invaded Panama and ousted strongman Manuel Noriega. Women were prominent in several of the skirmishes that occurred. Barbara was asked, in an interview with reporters at the White House, what she thought about women in combat. She replied that while she thought women would have no problem handling the job mentally or emotionally, she had reservations about the physical side. "The average man is better at throwing a hand grenade," she said. "I myself am very athletic but I have never been able to throw a ball as far as a man." She said she also worried that most women would not be strong enough "to carry a buddy to safety" if his life were endangered.

But she had a clear opinion on a noncontroversial aspect of the war: the capture of Noriega. "He cost thousands of lives," she said. "He's a bad man. Also, I'm glad he is here and will stand trial."

Turning to a scandal of the day, she said she was as shocked as the rest of the nation to find out that a white man in Boston had killed his pregnant wife and then convinced police that the couple had been attacked by a black man, a story that later unraveled. "First of all, it made me sick,"

Barbara said. "All of it, the whole thing. I have to say I can understand what turned out to be an overreaction to this crazy man's story because it's inconceivable that a man would kill his own wife and shoot himself so he would be incapacitated."

Such grim subjects aside, Barbara said that after a year in the White House, she was still surprised at how much she liked it. Completely gone was the pity she had expressed years earlier for Nancy Reagan having to live in a fish bowl. "The wife of the president of the United States is probably the most spoiled woman in the world," she said. "You'd have to be awfully spoiled if you lived the life we live and wished for something else."

Early in her second year as first lady, she donated her inaugural ball gown to the Smithsonian Institution, a long-standing White House tradition. She invited both her hairdresser, Yves Graux, and her favorite designer, Arnold Scaasi, to the museum for the occasion. "I vividly remember visiting here as a child," she said. "I remember the awe and the excitement I felt in our very own history. Who would have ever guessed that fate and an extraordinary husband would actually make me part of that history. I am grateful beyond words."

Her dress, blue satin and velvet, went onto a mannequin in the first lady collection, along with the pearls she had worn to the inaugural ball, a cape, and an evening bag.

Barbara continued to get thousands of letters from admirers and she let it be known that some of them got on her nerves, however well intentioned the sender. As Mother's Day neared, she asked people not to send her cards, letters, or other endearments and expressed some irritation that people treated her as though she were part of their family when she didn't even know them. "Please don't write me," she said. "I have children of my own. I'm not your mother."

She made the same request in anticipation of her sixty-fifth birthday, coming up just a month after Mother's Day. "People who don't love you—I mean they like you but they don't love you—send you flowers and things," she said. "And it's so sweet. But it should be a very private, personal thing. So I walk around like Scrooge in this house saying, 'Anyone who mentions it, I'll cut off your head.' "

Barbara explained that she received hundreds of cards on her birthday from complete strangers and felt obligated to answer each one. "I just want to celebrate it with my husband and children and maybe one friend," she said, "and I can't think of that one."

Ironically enough, George Bush was not home on Barbara's sixty-fifth birthday. He was in Chicago on a fund-raising trip for Republican congressional candidates. The president told the audience he had telephoned his "birthday girl" and found that "she seems unexcited about her sixty-fifth birthday."

And although she said she wanted a private celebration, Barbara spent part of her birthday in a very public forum, reading a story to a dozen children on ABC's *Good Morning America*. The children listened quietly but later blurted out, "Happy Birthday, Mrs. Bush." She seemed genuinely pleased. "Oh, how'd you know?" she said. "Who told you that secret? Thank you very, very much."

Besides the unwanted birthday cards, Barbara had discovered another unpleasant aspect of White House life—the public interest in and media scrutiny of the first family had been hard on her children, especially Doro, who had recently separated from her husband.

On the positive side, Barbara said she loved to be part of such happy occasions as the release of a hostage in Beirut. She recounted how thrilled she had been to be with the president when he greeted former hostage Robert Polhill, and said she was moved to tears when Polhill telephoned Frank Reed, another hostage who had been released just hours earlier.

In the spring and summer of 1990, Barbara had several major foreign affairs duties. The first was a May trip to Costa Rica where she represented the United States at the inauguration of president Rafael Calderón. It was her first trip to Costa Rica and her first time heading a diplomatic mission. Her support crew included Spanish-speaking son Jeb, a friend of the Calderóns, and White House chief of staff John Sununu.

The trip got off to a late start because Barbara uncharacteristically left the White House without one of her suitcases and had to return to get it. She also noted ruefully that almost everyone in the delegation spoke Spanish except her.

Barbara carried a letter from President Bush to Calderón that wished him well. At the bottom he wrote by hand, "Barbara, Jeb, and Columba are thrilled to be with you on this great day." But Columba, Jeb's Mexican-born wife, had to cancel at the last minute because their son was sick.

When she arrived at the airport Barbara was met by outgoing president Oscar Arias Sanchez. "Our main purpose for being in San Jose is to join all Costa Ricans in celebrating those most precious democratic activities—the recognition of the will of the people, the rule of law, and the peaceful participation of all citizens in the selection of their leaders," she said. At the inaugural ceremonies, she got more applause than any other delegation leader except Violeta Chamorro, who had recently been elected president of Nicaragua, knocking the leftist Sandinistas from power.

Before the ceremony, Barbara had breakfast with Calderón, his mother, his wife, Gloria, and their four children at the family's house. Calderón predicted that Barbara would be warmly welcomed. "Our wives are more popular than we are," he said. "Barbara, picking up on the line and perhaps recognizing a hint of condescension, looked with amusement at Gloria Calderón. "How come we're not presidents?" she said.

While she appeared to enjoy her diplomatic mission, Barbara emphasized that she would not make a habit of it, and she stuck to her policy of avoiding major political questions. "Nobody said, 'Don't speak about politics, Bar,'" she said, then paused. "And nobody was right."

That same month, the Bushes played host to Soviet leader Mikhail Gorbachev and his wife, Raisa. The Bushes first met the Gorbachevs in 1985 when the vice president was sent to represent the United States at the funeral of Konstantin Chernenko, Gorbachev's predecessor. Barbara and Raisa talked during that visit at a tea following the funeral and they hit it off immediately after discovering they had a common interest in education. The two women found on subsequent meetings that they could get along well and the goodwill held through the 1990 summit. Barbara took Raisa with her to the commencement at Wellesley College and invited her to historic Williamsburg, Virginia, Mrs. Gorbachev declined the Williamsburg visit, however, saying she preferred the alternative that was offered—a relaxing day at Camp David.

Two months later leaders of the seven big industrial powers had a meeting in Houston and Barbara took four of the wives to San Antonio to see the Alamo, the symbol of Texas independence. They also visited the Mission San Jose, established in 1720. It was the kind of outing many foreigners had not been on before, as Barbara acknowledged. "I wanted to show off a different part of Texas," she said.

Animals continued to play a part in Barbara's life. She had two early summer encounters with them, one a lot of fun and the other pretty alarming.

The fun occurred on a fishing trip she took with her husband to Alabama. They fished on a fifty-five-acre private lake owned by Ray Scott, founder of the Bass Anglers Sportsman Society of America, who quoted longtime fishing buddy George Bush saying that "Barbara is the only person I know of who can fish and read a book at the same time."

Scott reported that on this outing, Barbara had not been reading but she did carry on a lively conversation with him, and "Who do you think caught the biggest bass? Barbara. It weighed six pounds and twelve ounces."

He laughed. "Then she had the nerve to turn to George, who was hunched over his rod in his boat about forty feet away. She said sweetly, 'George, darling, would you like to have your photograph taken with my fish?' "

But Barbara portrayed George as the hero of a misadventure she had at the White House swimming pool. She was moving along in the water for her mile-a-day swim when she encountered a large rat. "I swim with a mask so as it went by right in front of me—I mean, it was enormous," she said. "Fortunately, George Bush was there and drowned the beast. It was horrible." The White House, surrounded by parks and munching tourists, has long had a problem with rats and mice. Barbara said that after her encounter she asked the guards to check the pool every day before she got in to make sure nothing else had gone in ahead of her.

By the end of 1990, Barbara was back where she had been ten years earlier—up on a lift, putting an ornament atop the national Christmas tree. She invited Doro's two children, six-year-old Sam and four-year-old Ellie, who wore a new red coat her grandmother had given her as a birthday present. The classmates of Sam and Ellie were on hand as well, urging Sam to jump as he rose in the lift.

All in all, it was a jolly occasion but it ended on a somber note. Asked what she wanted for Christmas, Barbara, mindful of Iraq's invasion of Kuwait, said, "We're all wishing for peace. We want our people home."

10

A DEFINING SPEECH

Barbara Bush dropped out of Smith College in her sophomore year to marry the first man she loved. Now, forty-six years later, she was sitting in a white tent at the graduation ceremonies of Wellesley College, ready to give a commencement address to a new generation of women who questioned her credentials.

She didn't apologize for her lack of formal education or express regret that she had no career. Instead, she stood up for the values that have shaped her life—loyal wife, loving mother, cheerful homemaker, and volunteer worker.

"For several years, you've had impressed upon you the importance to your career of dedication and hard work, and of course that's true," Barbara told the 1990 graduating class. "But as important as your obligations as a doctor, a lawyer, a business leader will be, you are a human being first, and those human connections with spouses, with children, with friends, are the most important investment you will ever make.

"At the end of your life, you will never regret not having passed one more test, winning one more verdict, or not closing one more deal. You will regret time not spent with a husband, a child, a friend, or a parent."

Those sentiments were not predominant at Wellesley in 1990, as Barbara was well aware. She noted that for more than fifty years it had been said the winner of the school's annual hoop race would be the first to marry; now it was said the winner would be the first CEO.

"Both of those stereotypes show too little tolerance," Barbara said. "So I want to offer a new legend. The winner of the hoop race will be the first to realize her dream—not society's dreams—her own personal dream. Who knows? Somewhere out in this audience may even be someone who will one day follow in my footsteps and preside over the White House as the president's spouse."

She paused.

"And I wish *him* well."

The six hundred Wellesley graduates and five thousand friends and relatives loved it, giving Barbara a hearty ovation.

She won them over with humor and honesty, a refusal to pretend to be something she wasn't, but also an acknowledgment that members of the Class of 1990 at Wellesley might make different choices from those of the class of '47 at Smith College, which Barbara would have been part of if she hadn't quit school to marry George Bush.

Two years later, Wellesley students chose Hillary Clinton as their commencement speaker during the campaign between Bill Clinton and George Bush. Hillary, a graduate of Wellesley, a powerful lawyer and an architect of the Clinton campaign, had much stronger professional credentials than Barbara, but interestingly chose to speak on the same themes as her rival—children and family values and women's choices.

At Wellesley, the commencement speaker is chosen by popular vote. Hillary was the first choice the year she spoke; Barbara was not, having lost out to novelist Alice Walker, who declined the invitation. A year later, when Barbara was commencement speaker at Northeastern University in Boston and received an honorary degree for her campaign against illiteracy, she got a laugh by recalling the situation at Wellesley. "I want to thank you for making me your first choice," she said. "I needed that."

Her humorous tone was not shared by the Wellesley students who protested her appearance. The backlash was led by seniors Susana Cardenas and Peggy Reid, who asked Wellesley administrators to reconsider the invitation.

"Wellesley teaches that we will be rewarded on the basis of our own merit, not that of a spouse," the petition said. "To honor Barbara Bush as a commencement speaker is to honor a woman who has gained recognition through the achievements of her husband, which contradicts what we have been taught over the last four years at Wellesley."

About one hundred and fifty women—25 percent of the senior class—signed the petition. When reporters arrived on campus to ask questions, Susana Cardenas told them that Barbara Bush was "the furthest she can be from the ideals of a progressive, feminist institution where you're taught to work hard to be recognized for your own contributions. If she hadn't been married to this guy who happens to be president, we never would have heard of her."

When word of the protest got around it caused a national debate, with almost everyone lining up on Barbara's side, including the president. "I think that these young women have a lot to learn from Barbara Bush and from her unselfishness and from her advocacy of literacy and of being a good mother and a lot of other things," he said.

Barbara said: "I think George cared much more than I did." But she added, "I don't think they understand where I'm coming from and that's all right. I chose to live the life I've lived and I think it's been a fabulously exciting, interesting, involved life. I hope some of them will choose the same exciting, interesting, fulfilling, involved life. In my day, they probably would have been considered different. In their day, I'm considered different. *Vive la différence.*"

During her fifteen months as first lady Barbara had become increasingly popular, and her defenders were outspoken and highly critical of the Wellesley students.

"I'd like to spank some of those young women," said Carol Johnson Johns, a medical professor and onetime acting president of Wellesley. "I think they're missing the boat if they don't appreciate the satisfaction and fulfillment of a significant relationship with someone important to you and with your family, as well as the things you can contribute as a volunteer. . . . I think to put her down because she doesn't have a professional degree or a professional career is a miscarriage of value systems."[1]

Martha Hood, a Wellesley alumna and president of Hood College, said the seniors appeared to be "seeing Barbara Bush in terms of the one issue that's most prominent on their minds—getting that first job that they've prepared for. I hear them, but I think they're ignoring another important side of themselves—their role as a volunteer and her role as a volunteer. She's exemplary, in my view, of the qualities I hope will be instilled in our undergraduates—generousness of spirit."[2]

Some alumnae pointed out archly that the young protesters seemed to have forgotten Wellesley's motto: *Non Ministrari, Sed Ministrare*—"Not to Be Served but to Serve."

Barbara also drew a strong defense from editorial writers and newspaper columnists, even those who were frequently critical of George Bush.

"These young women are probably right when they say that except for her marriage, the country would never have heard of Barbara Bush," *The New York Times* said in an editorial. "She'd be just one more of those millions of unsung Americans, female and male, who believe that raising decent children is the most important job. But these young women are wrong when they question Mrs. Bush's self-affirming qualities. She has said she's never regretted the choice she made at nineteen, and to contemplate the life she's made for herself and her family is to know she's telling the truth. By most people's lights, Barbara Bush has been self-affirming all along."[3]

Syndicated columnist Ellen Goodman of the *Boston Globe* thought the young graduates were expressing anxiety about their own lives by objecting to Barbara Bush and what she stood for. "So, in many ways, this may be a proper match for a commencement day," Goodman said. "In the audience, a class of women with diplomas as fresh as a new deck of cards. Each holding fifty-two options, wondering which one to play, how many at once and whether it's easiest at solitaire. On the podium, a woman who took some of the cards that were dealt her and rearranged them into the best order. A woman who has played her hand with grace and character."[4]

Back at Wellesley there were attempts to defuse the controversy. Nan Keohane, the school president, said the protest had been blown out of proportion. "Every year we have students who don't like the choice of speaker and every year somebody signs a petition," she said, adding that the protest against Barbara Bush was "largely a generational thing."

Wellesley class president Julie Porter came to the first lady's defense, sort of. "I support Mrs. Bush coming here," she said. "She's a very interesting and successful lady who lived in a different time."

The two students who initiated the petition were overwhelmed by the response. Susana Cardenas, who at first was the most outspoken against the Bush choice, received threatening phone calls and letters telling her to go back to her native Peru. Peggy Reid, the other main backer of the petition, expressed her outrage over the reaction in an article in *The New York Times*. She did what people under siege often do—blamed the media.

> All right, I've had enough. As a Wellesley college student and coauthor of the petition that started this whole Barbara Bush mess, I'd like to set the record straight. Over the past month and a half, I've witnessed an outrageous perversion of what in reality is a very simple issue of discontent over Barbara Bush's speaking at this year's commencement address. The media have succeeded in creating a sensation by misrepresenting and misconstruing our original position. They have vastly misled the general public. Not once have we condemned the first lady for her role as a mother and a volunteer. We are not, as some would have you believe, "careerists" who look down their noses at any woman who does not hold a paying job....
>
> We do not advocate, as a commentator in the *Boston Globe* put it, "a vision of feminism defined exclusively as success in the world of traditional masculine work." Please do not be misled: Wellesley students did not miss the point in Feminism 101!
>
> So what was it we were protesting when we wrote a petition that called Barbara Bush an inappropriate commencement speaker? If we support motherhood and volunteer work, what is it that we have against Barbara Bush as a commencement speaker?
>
> The plain simple fact is that Barbara Bush was not chosen as a speaker because of her commendable role as a mother; nor was she chosen for her admirable volunteer work. If such were the case, why were other equally dedicated mothers and community volunteers not chosen? The bottom line is that these women are not married to George Bush. Barbara Bush was selected because of her husband's accomplishments and notoriety, not those of her own. So it is not the validity of her choices in life that we are calling into question, but rather that fact that we are honoring not Barbara Bush but Mrs. George Bush.

Ms. Reid's argument did nothing to satisfy her critics. "Of those highbrow Wellesley seniors who object to Barbara Bush's forthcoming commencement appearance on the grounds she was invited because she is 'George's wife,' I wonder how many were able to afford four years of tuition, room and board at this costly, exclusive New England college only because they are 'daddy's daughter,'" a reader wrote to the *Los Angeles Times*.[6]

Barbara defended Wellesley against the critics. "The poor girls, they're so bored with it now they could throw up," she said. "I've gotten so many letters about Wellesley from people saying, 'I'm never going to give to Wellesley again.' I'd like to write a letter saying, 'Please give to Wellesley.' This is very normal. I understand it. It's no big deal. I mean, I'm very sorry that it all happened. Well, there are them who don't approve of me and them that do. But I'm just sorry for Wellesley."[7]

Two weeks before the commencement, the White House announced that Barbara would be accompanied to Wellesley by Raisa Gorbachev, wife of the Soviet president, since the Gorbachevs would be in Washington that week for a summit meeting.

The news guaranteed that Wellesley's commencement would be in the national spotlight and it put more pressure on Barbara. Raisa Gorbachev had an advanced degree and had taught at the college level, a fact noted in a rather graceless way by one Wellesley student.

"I'm really excited," said senior Angie Hickman of Mrs. Gorbachev's appearance. "She might have something more interesting to say."[8]

The day of the speech, June 1, was hot and sunny. On campus, the illwill that had preceded the event was muted but it had not disappeared. A third of the seniors wore purple arm bands, which they explained, in letters left on all the folding chairs, were to "celebrate all the unknown women who have dedicated their lives to the service of others."

The fuzzy symbolism of the armbands didn't detract from the festive atmosphere, though; it was the first time the wives of the presidents of the United States and the Soviet Union had shared a public podium and the day had the exultant feel of history in the making. When Mrs. Bush and Mrs. Gorbachev arrived, accompanied by both secret service and KGB agents, the applause was thunderous.

Barbara spoke first. She started with acknowledgments and praise for Wellesley. Then she told a story about the importance of tolerance, quoting from a speech given a year earlier at Smith College by the student body president. The young woman had related a tale told by writer Robert Fulghum about a pastor who thought up a game called Giants, Wizards, and Dwarfs for a group of children in his care.

"You have to decide now," the pastor told the children, "which you are—a giant, a wizard, or a dwarf."

At that, a small girl asked, "But where do the mermaids stand?" and the pastor told her there are no mermaids. And she said, "Oh, yes there are. I am a mermaid."

"Now, this little girl knew what she was, and she was not about to give up on either identity or the game," Barbara said. "She intended to take her place wherever mermaids fit into the scheme of things. Where do the mermaids stand—all of those who are different, those who do not fit the boxes and the pigeonholes? Answer that question," wrote Fulghum, "and you can build a school, a nation or a whole world."

Barbara continued: "As that very wise young woman said, 'Diversity, like anything worth having, requires effort.' Effort to learn about and respect difference, to be compassionate with one another, to cherish our own identity, and to accept unconditionally the same in others. You should all be very proud that this is the Wellesley spirit."

It was the most gracious of rebukes, an acknowledgment of the months of controversy and a clear statement of how Barbara Bush felt about it. She followed up immediately with a lighthearted remark that left everyone laughing.

"Now, I know your first choice today was Alice Walker—guess how I know—known for *The Color Purple*. Instead you got me, known for the color of my hair."

That brought applause and Barbara turned to the heart of her message.

"As you set off from Wellesley, I hope many of you will consider making three very special choices. The first is to believe in something larger than yourself, to get involved in some of the big ideas of our time. I chose literacy because I honestly believed that if more people could read, write, and comprehend, we would be that much closer to solving so many of the problems that plague our nation and our society.

"And early on I made another choice, which I hope you will make as well. Whether you are talking about education, career, or service, you are talking about life, and life really must have joy. It's supposed to be fun.

One of the reasons I made the most important decision of my life, to marry George Bush, is because he made me laugh. It's true, sometimes we laugh through our tears, but that shared laughter has been one of our strongest bonds.

"Find the joy in life," she said, "because as Ferris Bueller said on his day off, 'Life moves pretty fast and if you don't stop and look around once in a while, you are going to miss it.'"

This reference to one of the day's popular movies got a lot of applause. Barbara deadpanned, "I am not going to tell George that you clapped more for Ferris than you clapped for George."

Turning serious again she told the seniors that her third choice in life had been to make her family and friends paramount.

"Whatever the era, whatever the times, one thing will never change," she said. "Fathers and mothers, if you have children, they must come first. You must read to your children and you must hug your children and you must love your children. Your success as a family, our success as a society, depends not on what happens in the White House but on what happens inside your house."

Wellesley gave Barbara an enthusiastic standing ovation, then settled down to hear the first lady of the Soviet Union speak. Mrs. Gorbachev, who has a doctorate from Moscow State University, spoke through a translator. Her speech was much more political than Barbara's, focusing on the upheavals in her country at the time and her hopes for world peace. "In renewing our country, we want to make it open to the world," she said.

"The Soviet people know the value of peaceful life. We wish to have good relations with Americans and other people."

The audience also gave Mrs. Gorbachev a standing ovation and Mrs. Bush embraced her. The two women were mobbed by well-wishers as they made their way out of the tent. But afterward, many people commented on the fact that Barbara Bush, emphasizing family values and her personal beliefs, had given a more interesting speech than Mrs. Gorbachev. TV network commentators and the major newspapers called the day a triumph for Barbara Bush.

"Our first lady sure beats their first lady," wrote *Washington Post* TV critic Tom Shales. "Not that it was a contest, of course, but Barbara Bush's speech to graduating seniors at Wellesley College in Massachusetts yesterday, aired on all the networks, was a rock-'em-sock-'em smash hit, while Raisa Gorbachev's was just your standard graduation address."[9]

The New York Times said the speech was "a triumph for Mrs. Bush, who not only won over most of her audience but to many listeners delivered a more interesting talk than Mrs. Gorbachev, who holds the Soviet equivalent of a Ph.D. and was a university professor before her husband became head of the Soviet Communist party."[10]

NBC's Tom Brokaw said on the air that Barbara's talk was "one of the best commencement speeches I've ever heard."

The Wellesley speech seemed to solidify Barbara's popularity. Americans had liked her since her earliest days in the White House. Now she had new admirers and respect, demonstrating skills and know-how that many Americans had not realized she possessed.

"I have never actually had much interest in Barbara Bush, but her refreshing speech at Wellesley College's commencement really impressed me," wrote Rania Nagulb, a student at California State University, in a letter to the *Los Angeles Times*. "I would be quite fortunate to follow in her footsteps."[11]

Others felt the same way. By the thousands, they wrote to the White House to express their admiration. By now Barbara had become accustomed to such accolades and she had an explanation: "I know they find me no threat and they know I care about them—I hope."

If she was sometimes more popular than her husband, something she didn't like to talk about, she had an explanation for that, too. "I don't have to make any major decisions. I don't have to take stands on issues. I don't want to take them on. I have chosen the cowardly route, which is to pick issues I'm very interested in and work for them."

Barbara went on to speak at a number of commencements, but none of those speeches were as controversial or drew as big an audience. In 2001, a decade after she left the White House, she gave an address at Kent State University in Ohio and once again drew protesters. This time they were protesting her $45,000 speaking fee.

"It's sort of flattering to be yelled at again," she told the audience. "When I was just Mrs. now-out-of office George Bush, no one even showed up to yell at me."

11

SETTING A GOOD EXAMPLE

Barbara Bush was watching a rock star on a TV talk show. He was telling the host that he had made millions of dollars in Britain. "What did you do with all that money?" the interviewer asked. "Well, I think I sniffed it up my nose, ha-ha-ha," the rock star replied. The reporter joined in the laughter.

Barbara failed to see the humor. As the rock star and the well-paid reporter sat there laughing, all she could think about were the damaged babies she had seen in hospitals around the country. Their parents also had sniffed drugs up their noses, she thought angrily. And no one who had seen those children would be laughing.

"We've got to stop having someone on television say, 'I sniffed it all up, ha ha ha,' and having the reporter laugh," she said.... "We cannot have television showing role models of people doing things which are wrong. I just was shocked ... I just couldn't believe that was on. They were laughing away at it.

"We've got to stand up and say, 'Enough.' "[1]

Coming from some public figures, such a statement might seem hypocritical. They visit hospitals in election years, make a show of cuddling a sick baby or holding the hand of an elderly patient, but have little interest in such problems once they get in to office.

Barbara had earned the right to speak out. She started volunteering in hospitals long before she became famous. She did the kind of work—even emptying bedpans—that gave her close-up experience with many patients.

With five children, she had been busy at home, but as George Bush's oil business prospered she was able to hire household help. While she didn't have a paying job, she put her energy into charity work. Her friends are unanimous in saying that when she decided to join a cause, she became an active participant. She was never just a name on the masthead.

By the time George Bush became vice president, Barbara estimated that she was spending 50 percent of her time on volunteer work. With her higher profile, much of the work shifted from hands-on help to showcasing good causes, especially reading. She joined the national board of Reading Is Fundamental and became a sponsor of another literacy group, Laubach Literacy International, and she traveled all over the country to get people to focus on the issue.

Sometimes she had a wide audience. In 1987, for example, she appeared on an ABC-TV Fourth of July special celebrating the bicentennial of the U.S. Constitution. Her part in the show was to introduce sixty-three-year-old former sharecropper J. T. Pace, a South Carolina man who had learned to read just a year earlier. His job was to read the preamble to the Constitution during the dramatic finale.

The program was to be broadcast live from St. Louis, and Pace was to meet the vice president's wife there for the first time. As show time approached, however, he got nervous, telling producer Vince Maynard that he didn't understand all the words in the preamble and that he couldn't go on with the show. The producer tried to change his mind but without success. Finally, Maynard suggested that Pace talk with Barbara Bush. Pace agreed. Barbara, using what her brother Scott called her "spectacular people skills," was able to empathize with the former sharecropper. She told him she sometimes had difficulty with big words herself, in fact, all readers did. She kept on talking for a while and then took the man's hands.

"What if you and I read the preamble together? she asked.

Pace smiled. "I'd like that," he said.[2]

When the time came, the two of them stood at the podium side by side and began reading. Pace stumbled on some of the more difficult words at first, but his confidence grew as he talked and Barbara Bush's voice faded into the background.

" 'We the people of the United States, in order to form a more perfect union, establish justice, insure domestic tranquillity, provide for the common defense, promote the general welfare and secure the blessings of liberty to ourselves and our posterity, do ordain and establish this Constitution for the United States of America.' "

When Pace finished, he and Barbara embraced and the audience gave them a standing ovation.

The ABC show had an emotional impact on millions of TV viewers, but more often Barbara's literacy work was on a smaller, less showy scale. Typically, during the vice presidential years, she would appear at a local school where children were being honored for reading a certain number of books, or to present a check to officials for programs designed to improve readings skills or to get parents more involved in the education of their children. She also cited her own childhood experiences to interest children in reading. "We all read aloud as youngsters," she told grade schoolers in Alexandria, Virginia, in 1981. "Our favorites were the Oz books. My brother got the whole set, lucky duck."

By 1983, *The Washington Post* had run more than one editorial praising Barbara for the work she was doing in reading and the attention she had brought to the cause of literacy.

"She is much more than a fancy name on a charity letterhead," the *Post* said, referring to her success in raising money that provided more than 200,000 books to Washington schools. "The beauty of this program as well as the contribution of Mrs. Bush is in its directness—no endless series of planning meetings or busy work, no splashy annual appearance at a fancy 'do,' but face-to-face, on the scene help that delivers immediate, visible results."[3]

Besides appearing at numerous schools and literacy events, Barbara talked up the issue with other people who could do something about it. Harold McGraw, retired from the publishing firm McGraw-Hill, credited a dinner party conversation he had with Barbara as his inspiration for starting a business council on literacy. She agreed to be on the board of directors after he got it going. "I believe if we can lick the problem of people being functionally illiterate—unable to read or write at the fifth-grade level—we will then go on to solve most of the other major problems besetting this country," she said.

By 1985, she told an audience in Los Angeles, she had given more than three hundred speeches on adult literacy alone, and the issue was seeping into the consciousness of more and more Americans.

"I do it every day . . . and the media is wonderful about reporting it," she said. "You probably don't hear about it here, but in Topeka, Kansas, I was very big. It gets out."

While schools and civic groups were her main audiences, she also spoke at prisons, sometimes with amusing results. "She once told me that she met a guy who had been in prison for stealing," nephew Jamie Bush reported. "She went to a literacy program for prisoners and the man told her his story. He got caught because he couldn't read the exit sign on the door of the supermarket he was robbing. She urged him to develop his reading skills—and then put them to good use!"[4]

During the 1988 presidential campaign, Barbara continued to talk about literacy, but she also put more emphasis on programs designed to help the disabled, the poor, and the homeless. In Enid, Oklahoma, she sat in on a workshop for the retarded, listening to a young woman describe her efforts to find a job. With crowds of onlookers and cameras around her, the woman began to stammer. Barbara immediately leaned over and put a hand on the woman's arm. "Are you nervous with all the cameras," she asked. The woman nodded, relieved to get the problem into the open, and she was able to continue with her story.

Staying in hotels all over the country, Barbara realized that the management put more soap in each room than any visitor was likely to use and she began to take the extra bars with her. When she got enough, she gave them to a homeless shelter.

"I share with George the information I gather about the homeless," she said. "In fact, he teases me when I take soap and shampoo from the hotels to send to women's shelters. For instance, when we stay in a hotel, we are given five bars of soap. George and I share one and I send the other four to the shelters so each woman can have her own soap."[5]

Barbara's charity work generally was praised by Democrats and Republicans as nonpartisan, but during the heat of the 1988 campaign, politics loomed over the good works. In New Orleans, Barbara visited a day-care center for both adults and children funded with federal, state, and private funds, the kind of mix favored by George Bush. Before she got inside, though, she had to walk past angry, sign-carrying women and youths complaining that the Republican administration had not done enough for the poor. "For the past eight years, where was George when the poor people needed him?" one sign said, picking up a theme from the Democratic political convention. Barbara ignored the protesters and went inside to talk as planned.

In the daily column she wrote for *USA Today* during the campaign, Barbara often wrote of the good works she had seen and sometimes her remarks had a distinctly partisan overtone. "What I really want to write about this week are the thousand points of light George talked about at the convention," she said in an October 3 column. "I saw them everywhere I went and through the people I met."[6]

She described two day-care centers, one run with private money and the other federally funded. "Both centers have professional and volunteer staff," she said. "Both are different programs and, under George's child-care plan, the parents would get to choose which one their child attends."

Barbara also lauded two programs run almost entirely by volunteers and praised a city—Hot Springs, Arkansas—that was being renovated with a mix of government and private funds. The "point of light" theme caught on and in 1990, a Points of Light Foundation was established in Washington, D.C., to highlight volunteer efforts.

The same theme ran through Barbara's initial efforts once she got to the White House. Her first trip, two weeks after she became first lady, was to Martha's Table, a few blocks from the White House. The nonprofit group used volunteers to distribute donated food to the homeless and also provided meals at an after-school center for children. Barbara's half-hour visit to the center drew fifty reporters and numerous camera crews. She took along a box of cookies made at the White House and a book to read to the children, *How Fletcher Was Hatched*. But she stopped first to talk with volunteers who made seventeen hundred sandwiches each day for delivery to homeless men and women. While she talked, Barbara put on a red apron, washed her hands, and made eight sandwiches.

She said she chose Martha's Table for her first outing "because I'm hoping Americans will look at this range of volunteers and realize how important it is, what a job they do and how really important it is to help people who need some help."

When she got to the children's room, she quickly commanded attention, telling the thirty-five children, "Everybody quiet. Everybody sit down, please." In a lively manner she read the story about a dog hatched from an egg, frequently turning the book toward the children so they could see the pictures. Afterward, she asked the children questions about the story and got them to howl like dogs.

A few days later, Barbara visited a thrift shop in suburban Virginia, another privately run organization that helps poor families. She brought along seven plastic bags of clothes and toys as a donation and talked with the people who ran the program. Later she told reporters, "You know, I don't think anybody realizes—or I didn't realize—that seventy percent of the people who are helping are working poor."

Philadelphia was chosen as the site of Barbara's first out-of-town appearances as first lady, thanks to persistent invitations from Sheila Whitelaw, executive director of the city's Friends of the Free Library. "The next thing I knew, they called me," she said with delight.

Barbara's book of the day was *Alexander and the Terrible, Horrible, No Good, Very Bad Day*, by Judith Viorst. The grade school children who heard the story joined in the refrain with the first lady: "I could tell it was going to be a terrible, horrible, no good, very bad day."

On Valentine's Day, Barbara visited a place that had long ago won her heart—the Washington Home and Hospice, a long-term-care facility. Accustomed to her visits, which started shortly after George Bush was elected to Congress in 1966, the residents wanted to know what life was like in the White House.

Barbara told them about the inauguration and how her own grown children had celebrated. "Some of those children of ours had danced till three or four in the morning so they were not a lot of fun at breakfast," she said. "But the grandchildren—we had ten in the house—they came in and climbed on the bed and played. And we did have a wonderful time."

The residents gave her a giant Valentine inscribed "Always the First

Lady in Our Hearts," and she had cards for each of them as well. "I really mean, I love you all," she told a group of elderly men and women who surrounded her with their wheelchairs."[7]

A few weeks before Valentine's Day, Barbara had recorded an appeal to Washington residents for donations and valentines for the city's abused children. Local radio stations picked up the tape and ran it during prime commuting hours. The result was more than ten thousand valentines delivered to Children's Hospital in the city and donations totaling more than $140,000. The money was split between the hospital and the local chapter of Childhelp USA, which named Barbara as national honorary chairman for the year.

"The impact on the morale of campaign workers was just tremendous," said Richard Tubbs, director of the Have a Heart campaign. "It's the best you can find in America when she took the time to reach out."

A couple of days later, Barbara flew to Denver to see her newest grandchild, ten-day-old Ashley Walker Bush, daughter of Neil and Sharon Bush. After she landed at the airport, her first stop was at the Food Bank of the Rockies, an organization that distributes supplies to groups that help find the needy. Neil joined his mother at the Food Bank, then took her home to meet the baby.

The next day, back in Washington, Barbara spotlighted an elementary school in a depressed area of the city as part of a celebration of Black History Month. Student Milton Law, who gave a dramatic recitation of Martin Luther King's "I Have a Dream" speech, said later he was impressed to see Barbara Bush swaying with the glee club and singing "We Shall Overcome." She knew all six verses.

In early March 1989, educators, publishers, and community leaders were invited to a White House luncheon for the formation of the Barbara Bush Foundation for Family Literacy. She told the audience she had already received commitments of $1 million for the foundation, which would be privately run, and she would serve as honorary chairman. The idea was to develop programs that helped entire families with reading problems.

"In ten years of traveling around the United States of America visiting literary programs, libraries, kindergarten groups, day-care centers, single-parent classes for high school dropouts, public housing projects, food banks—you name it, I've visited it—it has become very apparent to me that we must attack the problem of a more literate America through the family," Barbara said. "We all know of adults with reading problems tending to raise children with reading problems."

President Bush dropped in on the gathering to support his wife's efforts. "I'm the observer, I'm the fly on the wall in this project, and as interested as anybody in this room," he said. "I've studied with Barbara Bush on the importance of all of this and I've learned a lot."

Later Barbara was asked why she was putting so much emphasis on family literacy instead of concentrating on individuals. "I've visited a lot of Project Head Starts and they're wonderful," she said. "But they really aren't as wonderful as they could be because, in many cases, they're not working with the mothers and fathers. That's one thing that sort of got me. I mean, I could have had just a Barbara Bush Foundation for Literacy but in the last three or four years it has come to me that the family is what makes the difference.

"The home is the child's first school. The parent is the child's first teacher. Reading is the child's first subject."[8]

Barbara's emphasis on family learning led her to seek out examples of programs that cater to the idea. One of them was All Children's House in New York City, where preschool children of the affluent mingle with those from poor and homeless families. One of the mothers on hand for Barbara's visit was a school dropout working to get a high school equivalency degree from a program at her son's elementary school. "The people here encourage us all to go to school," she said.

Staff director Gretchen Buchenholz said, "Children of all backgrounds benefit by just being kids here together. But for children who come from unstable families, you have to reach out to their parents. Our program can be replicated and collateral services can be extended into school grades. That what I hope Barbara Bush sees."

A few months after Barbara started her literacy foundation she got a big boost—King Fahd of Saudi Arabia contributed $1 million. Barbara herself eventually exceeded that amount with her earnings from *Millie's Book*, all donated to the foundation. More information on the program is available on-line at www.barbarabushfoundation.com.

Barbara also stayed active in the foundation after she left the White House. In September 2001, she wrote in the group's newsletter:

Dear Friends,

   *Since the launch of the foundation more than twelve years ago, I've
had many opportunities to hear truly inspiring stories from adults who
have improved their lives and helped their children as a result of hard
work done in one of the more than three hundred family literacy programs that we've funded. The reports we receive from our program administrators back up these heartwarming testimonials with facts and
figures that document: significant gains in reading levels; high school diplomas earned; more and better jobs; and increased time that parents and
children spend reading and learning together during those critical early
years. Although there is so much more work to be done, I'm happy to say
that the news we get is very heartening! Of course, none of this would be
possible without your help, for which we are sincerely grateful! Thank
you for all you do.*

Aside from her emphasis on literacy, Barbara highlighted other issues of
the day. In her early months in the White House she visited Grandma's
House, a Washington home for four abandoned babies infected with the
AIDS virus. At the time, many Americans believed that the virus could be
spread just by touching an infected person. Barbara's mission was to dem-
onstrate that such fears were unfounded. She cradled an infected infant,
kissed a lively twenty-month-old toddler, and hugged an adult AIDS vic-
tim. Volunteers who work with AIDS patients were overjoyed at the image,
played in newspapers across the country, of the first lady hugging a baby
with AIDS.

   "You can't imagine what one hug from the first lady is worth," said
Jim Graham, administrator of a clinic that treats AIDS patients. "We've
had so much trouble with all the talk about the dangers of personal contact. Here the first lady isn't afraid and that's worth more than a thousand
public service announcements."[9]

   Indeed. Barbara's visit to Grandma's House resulted in a huge number
of calls from people volunteering both time and money to help AIDS
victims. Unfortunately, the support she drew from the AIDS community
later faded because AIDS activists felt that the Bush administration had
not done enough to help victims of the disease. Feelings against George
Bush ran so high that there were demonstrations at Kennebunkport and

even after the Bushes left the White House, they dropped out as sponsors of an AIDS event because of protests against their presence.

There were no such sour feelings about Barbara's support for the Ronald McDonald House in Washington, part of a privately funded national network that provides housing for families who must travel out of town to treat a sick child. "It makes an enormous difference to have a beautiful house where other people know what's happening to you," Barbara said on Mother's Day 1989. "This particular house has sixty volunteers without whom it couldn't run at all. They need more volunteers. They need money—and it just gives something to people who have a tragedy."

Then, noting that the house had a plaque describing the Bushes' loss of three-year-old daughter Robin, Barbara, on the verge of tears, said, "I'm going to try and tell you that Robin's name is in this house and I like that very much."

She might have said more. But as often happens when she talks about the daughter who died of leukemia, Barbara got teary-eyed and had to turn away from the TV cameras. In 2002, she is still active in the Leukemia Society of America.

Despite her emphasis on volunteers, Barbara has made clear she is aware that the best social programs also have strong paid staffs. "The meat of the program really is the professional," she said. "And you need money for that. You have to have the professionals who put everything in place and keep the program going and keep the volunteers coming in."

In the spring of 1989, Barbara was invited to dozens of colleges as commencement speaker. She chose a small school for black women in North Carolina for her first outing and agreed to speak at the college she had attended for one year—Smith—where she was to get an honorary degree.

The choice of Bennett College in Greensboro, North Carolina, site of a famous sit-in during the civil rights movement of the 1960s, was designed to highlight Barbara's commitment to equal rights for black Americans. But most of those at the ceremony didn't seem much concerned about symbolism. Parents and students alike were just glad that graduation day had at last arrived and they considered the first lady's visit as icing on the cake. "God, how I've waited for this day. It's been a long, hard time. I couldn't be happier," said Yvonne Roberson, whose daughter, Michelle, was getting a degree in health sciences—the first member of the family to receive a college degree. Having Barbara Bush as speaker is "giving me another chill," Roberson said. "It's about the best honor we could have."

Some of the graduating seniors also saw a practical benefit of the visit. "She's putting Bennett on the map," said twenty-three-year-old Regina Hucks. "They're going to know all about us when we go for job interviews."[10]

In her speech, Barbara talked about people, including Frederick Douglass, who had learned to read against all odds and who had gone on to greatness. "I can't tell you all the people I've known who have escaped the bondage of ignorance," she said. "You graduates have recognized this. And I urge you to help the young out there today . . . enslaved by ignorance."

The visit to Smith was also an emotional day for Barbara. She told the graduates she had no regrets about leaving college after one year to get married at age nineteen and have a baby, but lamented that her father was not still alive to see her finally get a degree, even an honorary one. Later, she told reporters she thinks it is important for young women to have a college diploma—"very important. I think most women would not have been as lucky as I was, but remember, we're talking about forty-five years ago."

She also urged students to put off childbearing until they complete their education. "I'm saying to young women, 'Wait, you've got years to have a family.'" Then, realizing how all this advice conflicted with her own example, Barbara grinned. "It sounds like 'Do as I don't,'" she said.

For every visit Barbara made, she turned down many others. She visited a center for runaways in New York City, listening to the sad tales of young survivors of the streets. She decided not to appear on an episode of TV's *Golden Girls* to promote the Special Olympics, feeling it was inappropriate for her to be seen in a comedy. But she read a story to Big Bird, Count von Count, and five preschoolers on *Sesame Street*.

Barbara's heavily publicized good works inspired many Americans to write and ask how they could get involved in her projects. She replied that a much better alternative was to find someone who needed help in their own communities. "Walk out your door and help someone," she said. "Whether you help them in the library or whether you adopt a school and are a volunteer in the public school, whether you go to a shelter and help somebody, whether you go volunteer in a hospital—whatever you do, you're helping me."

She said she realized that many people had busy lives but "Everybody has something, whether you have time or money or know-how or space. Today you can no longer say, 'The drug problem worries me' or 'Crime worries me' or 'Illiteracy worries me.' If it worries you, then you've got to do something about it."[11]

Traveling around the country seeing so many people involved in helping others inspired her. She said she senses that more people are feeling a sense of social responsibility and that many Americans are able to use their neighborhoods as extended families, much as she and George Bush did when they were a young couple without any nearby family in Texas. "I sense that young people are beginning to think in terms of extended family again," she said. "The extended families may not even be related. They may be neighbors, friends. People are saying 'What affects me affects my neighbors.' When problems arise—crime, drugs, bad schools—each person says, 'This isn't good. I have to do something about it.' "[12]

Barbara also used her high profile and popularity to urge women to take care of themselves. She was the guest speaker when the National Cancer Institute launched a campaign to make women more aware of the dangers of breast cancer and how mammograms can lead to early detection and live-saving intervention. "As you know, three of my predecessors— Happy Rockefeller, Betty Ford, and Nancy Reagan—faced the challenge of breast cancer," she said. "At a time when their lives were so public, these three shared with us all their private battles." (Less than a year later, Barbara had surgery to remove a small cancer from her lip.)

Because breast cancer strikes one of ten American women, she said, all women over age forty should have regular mammograms. "Pick up the phone and make a life-saving appointment."

She urged women who work to give their children priority, and asked that employers be accommodating as well. "It's hard on you but you have to put your children first," she said. "And I think your boss has to accommodate a little bit. I mean, if you need to go to school to see your child in a school situation, they should make accommodations for it. You'll have to make it up, but that's just a fact of life."

During her first Christmas at the White House, Barbara dropped in at the Central Union Mission, a charity that had been around for more than one hundred years and was helping needy mothers, serving meals to the homeless, distributing clothes, and providing shelter. Mothers with young children crowded into the center for the visit and Barbara read the Christmas story from the Bible. "This is a good story," she told the children, "so good it lasted almost two thousand years." Afterward, she and the mothers and a few of the children sang "Away in a Manger."

During the rest of her time in the White House, Barbara followed a similar schedule, always keeping her primary emphasis on literacy. In the fall of 1990, her family literacy group gave out awards totaling $500,000 to public and private groups that targeted what Barbara called an "intergenerational cycle of illiteracy."

In October that year, she wrote an article for *Reader's Digest* offering advice to parents and others who read aloud to children, based on her own experience with five children, twelve grandchildren, and numerous sessions in schools and libraries around the country. Here are excerpts:

1. Get started now. You can't begin too soon.
2. Make reading aloud a habit. Years ago, I usually read to my children at bedtime. Most evenings we'd snuggle together with a few favorite books. The kids came to love this special time. They learned passages from their favorite books by heart, which we'd recite together. It doesn't matter when you read but it is helpful to do it at the same time each day, for at least fifteen minutes. Over twenty years ago, University of Illinois researcher Dolores Durking studied 205 children who learned to read before starting school. They had one thing in common: Their parents made reading to them a habit.
3. Involve the whole family. Children enjoy being read to by people besides their mothers. Many people read to me when I was little: my father, a brother, a grandmother, even friends barely older than I. Today, both parents often work and may not be able to read as frequently as they would like. Baby-sitters, child-care providers, and older siblings can sometimes help by reading to their charges. George doesn't get much chance to read to our grandchildren in Washington but he does better when we're in Kennebunkport. Each morning at six

o'clock, the grandchildren race into our room, bounce into bed with us and wave their favorite books. Often it's George who begins our morning reading time. Children like it when the men in their family read to them. Educators hear this over and over around the country. When a girl in elementary school chose a book on football, her teacher asked why. "My dad likes football," the student replied.

4.   Keep books handy. Research shows that growing up in a house filled with books often helps children become an early reader. For my grandchildren, I keep stacks of books at Camp David, at Kennebunkport, and at the White House. There are Bible stories, Barbara Cooney's *Miss Rumphius*, Martin Handford's picture books, *Where's Waldo?* and several nearly worn-out copies of *Old Mother West Wind* stories by Thornton W. Burgess, which I treasured as a child. A home library need not be expensive. Low-priced children's books are available, even in supermarkets. You can watch for garage sales, trade books with other families, and ask relatives to give books as gifts. The best bargain, of course, is at the country's fifteen thousand public libraries.

5.   Choosing good books. Children need books appropriate for their interests, their ages and their ability, educators say. They also need variety, so experts suggest we read different things to our children—newspapers, magazines, street signs, even the backs of cereal boxes. That way we show the importance of words in every aspect of life. Youngsters love to hear the same stories over and over. I read Robert McCloskey's *Make Way for Ducklings* so many times to my children and grandchildren that the book fell apart. Repetition improves vocabulary and memory and helps children understand how stories work.

6.   Make the written word come alive. In reading to my children and grandchildren, I always try to involve them. In the middle of a sentence, I'll leave out a word and wait for a child to supply it. I also ask questions: "Now what do you think will happen?" And I read all the words, explaining any that might be unfamiliar. To make your reading lively, first spark your children's interest. Before you read a new book, let the youngsters study the cover. Ask what they see and what they think the book is about. Next point out the pictures in the book. Ask "What do you think is happening here?"

7.   Finally, keep reading to them after they can read for themselves. Most

children's listening comprehension is much higher than their reading comprehension, so they get more out of hearing a book. Reading to older children also enables you to introduce books they might not explore on their own.[13]

About the same time she wrote the essay, Barbara began a ten-week series on the ABC radio network titled *Mrs. Bush's Story Time*. She read from favorite books, offered reading tips, and interviewed celebrities.

Barbara says the best time to start reading to children is "as soon as they will sit still, even for a minute." She fondly tells of the time that granddaughter Noelle, daughter of Jeb and Columba, informed her grandmother that "I love Moses."

"I was so surprised, and said, 'Oh, really. Who was Moses?' " Barbara recalled, "She didn't have the slightest idea and couldn't say why she loved him. So I got some books on Moses and then she really did love him."[14]

In June of 1991, Barbara delivered the commencement address at a vocational high school in the Bronx. She told graduates of Grace H. Dodge that they were fine examples of what could be accomplished at a vocational school. And she urged them to go back to their rough neighborhood and help those who had been left behind.

"Counsel teenagers on the edge, comfort parents who have lost their own children to violence, drugs, or despair," she said. "And if and when you have your own children, love them, listen to them, read to them, be gentle with them, put them first . . . show them how to care for others—that's the greatest gift you can give."

The advice she gave them was similar to what she tells audiences wherever she goes—get involved, help someone in greater need than yourself. A decade after she left the White House, Barbara Bush was still doing work for the Leukemia Society of America, the Ronald McDonald House, the Mayo Clinic Foundation, and for Americare.

12

THE GULF WAR

When the White House announced that America was going to war against Iraq, Barbara, sitting with her daughter Doro and evangelist Billy Graham, watched the events on television along with the rest of the nation.

The three were in a room in the private quarters of the White House, a place made cozier by Barbara's needlepoint rug, which had much of the family's history woven right into the fabric.

Months later, Graham told a news conference that he had been invited to the White House the day before the announcement. Graham said he asked her, "Is this it?" She smiled and nodded.

He said the president came in thirty minutes later and told Graham, "I know I have done the right thing."

Barbara herself said very little, according to a source who was with the family at the time. "There was an intensity of focus that seemed singular to me at the time," the source said. "There is usually a lot more joking around her, a lot more teasing. There was none of that. There was just none of the usual razzing."

Like most Americans, Barbara was disappointed that Iraqi strongman Saddam Hussein had failed to back down under an ultimatum the United Nations had issued—withdraw Iraqi troops from Kuwait or face a multinational attack. For months after Saddam's Aug. 2, 1990, invasion of neighboring Kuwait, Barbara had remained optimistic that war could be avoided.

A month after the initial attack, Barbara told reporters that the invasion was the worst crisis President Bush had faced while in office. "I don't think it's ever off his mind, but does he dwell on it?" she said. "No. He does what he can."

She responded with scorn to Saddam's charge that a U.N. embargo was hurting the children of his country. "That's not what's killing the children of Kuwait or Iraq or Egypt or anyplace else," she said. "He went into a country and attacked it. We can't forget that."

Despite the crisis atmosphere that settled over Washington after the invasion, the Bushes decided to take their usual three-week vacation in Kennebunkport. It was a calculated decision. Bush remembered how Iran had succeeded in making Jimmy Carter a virtual prisoner in the White House a decade earlier while Americans were held hostage in Tehran. Bush was determined that Saddam would not gain that same kind of power over him.

A few weeks after the vacation, the Bushes were in Finland when a reporter asked Barbara whether it was right for her husband to be relaxing at the ocean while American troops were in danger in the Persian Gulf. She bristled.

"My husband spent most of the time on the telephone," she said. "He was not going to become a hostage in the White House to that dreadful man."

In another interview, she sought to put the vacation in perspective. "There is a certain stability about Maine and that was a reason George was there," she said. "You know this is not the United States against Saddam Hussein. I think occasionally we forget that. George stayed in Maine because it sent the right message."

Bush actually spent a lot of time in meetings with top aides who looked out of place at the shore in their white dress shirts and stiff black shoes. The telephone calls from Washington, some jangling in the middle of the night to inform the president of the latest developments, were out of public view. And, according to Barbara, the president made more than one hundred calls to foreign leaders during his stay at the shore.

"You know you're not away in this job no matter where you are," she said. "George even talked to one head of state from aboard the boat."

The president had one notable accident during the vacation. On a fishing trip that included Canadian prime minister Brian Mulroney and Jeb Bush, a fishhook caught Bush's ear. Reporters, following in another boat, thought that Mulroney was the culprit and he didn't deny it. "It was not a hostile act," Mulroney said. Barbara, however, didn't want to leave the wrong impression. She summoned Jeb, who grinned, and when asked if Mulroney had hooked the president, replied, "That is not really true." Then he walked away. The White House later confirmed that Jeb was to blame. Bush got a tetanus shot but was otherwise unfazed.

Barbara herself spent the vacation as she usually does, focusing on the grandchildren—twelve of them at that time—all of whom visited at some time during the twenty-five-day hiatus.

She got up at five-thirty each morning and was greeted by Millie and Millie's pup, Ranger. "My eyes would open and I'd go out and push the automatic coffeepot down, feed the dogs, walk them," Barbara said. "Then we'd climb back in bed and read the papers and the grandchildren all came down. We have that hour where we're watching the news and the kids are listening to their grandfather."[1]

When the children asked about the Gulf crisis, Barbara said, "I reminded them that a perfectly peaceful country was sitting there and another country invaded it and we cannot have that."

In the waning days of summer, Barbara handed out Popsicles and supervised at the beach for long periods so the children would not interfere with the visiting heads of state. When Prince Saud of Saudi Arabia came for a visit, though, the children were flush with excitement, their imaginations fired by tales of the Arabian Nights.

"Who could imagine what a full-fledged Arab prince looked like," Barbara said. "But I kept the children at the beach all day long. I thought it was a genius job on my part keeping them entertained."

She took some of the older children shopping for back-to-school clothes and made sure they did their summer reading—*Tom Sawyer* for thirteen-year-old Noelle, daughter of Jeb and Columba. When she wasn't with the children, Barbara went antiquing with Betsy Heminway and did some reading of her own—*The Burden of Proof*, a thriller by Scott Turow;

Slim, an autobiography by Slim Keith; and *Memories of Midnight* by Sidney Sheldon.

She exercised like crazy, swimming a mile each morning in a heated pool, then an hour on a stationary bike, and in the afternoon a toning session with a tape on the VCR. "I really built myself up, darn it, to be very strong," she said.

Still, it was not a typical summer. Both Bushes had daily reminders that hundreds of thousands of young Americans were stuck uncomfortably in the hot sands of Saudi Arabia, their futures uncertain. Barbara looked at their plight from a mother's point of view.

"I hate it because families are being broken up," she said. "I feel just like any other mother would. How do you think George feels—that's what kills me—because he really feels each one of those [young soldiers] are his."

Her worry extended to the hundreds of foreigners, including Americans, who had been trapped in Iraq after Saddam's troops invaded Kuwait. Now they were being held hostage in Baghdad and some were taken by force to chemical and nuclear facilities that Saddam figured were most likely to be bombed if the West decided to challenge his invasion. Saddam denied that the foreigners were hostages. He said they were simply guests of his regime for the time being.

In early September 1990, Barbara made a personal appeal to the Iraqi strongman to free the hostages. In an interview with Knight-Ridder newspaper, she said, "Let your guests go and then let's talk about this."

Asked how she would feel if she had a child serving in the Gulf, Barbara replied with two voices, one as a mother, the other as a patriot. "I'd be sick with worry . . . but I would also feel very proud. They are the only thing that's keeping any kind of peace in the Middle East."

During November, the Bushes traveled to Europe for an economic summit and stopped first in Czechoslovakia for a day. Even there, though, the Gulf crisis was much on their minds. Barbara, visiting with a group of eleven-year-olds, read excerpts from her book about Millie and told the children that the dog had the run of the White House, regularly attending meetings of the National Security Council. "So Millie knows more about the Persian Gulf and Czechoslovakia than I do," she said.

As Thanksgiving approached, the White House announced that President and Mrs. Bush would spend Thanksgiving with the troops in Saudi Arabia. When reporters noted Barbara would be going to three Thanksgiving dinners, she replied, "You know, I was built for the job."

She also showed off a bracelet she had been wearing for a couple of weeks, given to her by daughter Doro. It read: "Operation Desert Shield—A Call to Freedom." Barbara in turn ordered the bracelets for son Marvin and his wife, Margaret. "I think it's a nice reminder," she said. "It snags on everything I wear. It cuts into me at night. It reminds me. I think it's important."

Barbara said money from sales of the rough bracelet would provide "those wonderful voice messages that families can leave for their sons or daughters in Saudi Arabia. And it also facilitates telephone calls back home."

On Thanksgiving Day, George and Barbara were in Saudi Arabia, including Dhahran, just eighty miles from the Iraqi-guarded border with Kuwait. Barbara wore a camouflage jacket, khaki pants, white jogging shoes, and pearl earrings. She posed for numerous pictures with individual soldiers, signed autographs and answered questions about Millie. "It is clear to me that Millie is the most popular member of this family," she said.

With the troops, she joked and teased.

"I feel like I'm signing checkbooks," she told a marine.

"I don't know whose camera I'm looking at," she said to another.

"You look familiar to me," she teased, as she put her arm around his waist for a picture. "Didn't we just do this a minute ago?"

She had one dinner with an army tactical unit, another with marines and British Desert Rats. She took names and promised to call families when she got home.

Before the visit, Barbara had been shown how to put on a gas mask in case of an Iraqi chemical attack, but neither she nor the president carried their masks around. There was no escaping the guns and tanks, however. They were everywhere. "I rarely hug guns," Barbara said, pulling back when she came up against one on the arm of a marine.

General Norman Schwarzkopf, commander of the Gulf troops, watched her move easily among the soldiers and pronounced the Bush visit "wonderful for the troops."

"These kids here are so proud to be here. Doesn't it make you want to cry? It makes me want to cry," he said.

E-4 Kelly Fischer of El Paso, Texas, was among the soldiers who saw the first lady up close. "I admire her very much," he said. "In fact I wanted to see her more than I wanted to see the president. That's terrible to say."[2]

Afterward, Barbara said the visit had been "pretty exciting . . . and pretty moving."

"I was amazed by how many cameras the troops had," she said. "They asked us to autograph everything—pictures of their babies, pictures of their dogs, their springer spaniels. They asked me to sign pictures of their wives, their hats, their coats, their Bibles."

Like the soldiers, the Bushes brought home souvenirs. The president revealed that he got "a little patch" from the famed British Desert Rats.

"We were sort of tucking things in pockets," Barbara said. "It was very moving. I have to confess every time a helicopter took off, I felt like crying. It just—seemed so final."[3]

She said she had been touched by her visit to the *Nassau*, an amphibious assault ship stationed in Saudi Arabia, where one sailor who had a wife and four children at home passed her a note that said; "Don't forget our wives, who are so courageous at home. They're really the brave ones. You and the president keep them in your prayers."

Said Barbara, "I thought that was so sweet. We do pray, every night."

A few days later on December 1, when the White House Christmas tree was delivered, Barbara was asked about her Christmas wish.

"We wish for peace," she said. "We want our people home."

Did she think there would be war?

"No," she said. "I have great faith."

A week into the New Year, she visited elementary schoolchildren at the Church of the Immaculate Conception in Washington, and told them that "like everybody else in America," she and the president were praying for peace. "You may think the president is all-powerful but he is not," she said. "He needs a lot of guidance from the Lord."

She wore a paper necklace made by kindergartners. It was filled with doves.

A week later, however, she was watching with the rest of the nation as

American bombers, along with Allied forces, began a steady, pounding attack on Saddam's forces.

Once the war began, the president was busy all the time and Barbara did what she could to make life easier for him. "I think she worked very hard to clear the decks for him, to provide a haven, a calm," a White House source said. In normal times, many people ask Barbara to pass along messages or information to the president. Although she prefers that anyone with something to say to George Bush talk to him directly, she usually complies with the requests.

"People would think of her as a back channel to the president, and on most occasions she would pass it on to the president," the White House source said. But during the war, "she started winnowing it. If she thought it wasn't something he needed to hear at that particular moment, she wouldn't pass it on. As this point during the war, she was selective in what she passed on."

Barbara also became more careful in drawing up the White House guest lists. The Bushes continued to entertain, but she made sure the guests were people that the president could have fun with, people who would not "hammer him about his conduct of the war, people he could relax with."

She was happy and amazed to find that George Bush remembered little things about what was going on with the children and grandchildren and asked about such events regularly despite his preoccupation with the war. "If the children were having problems in their own lives, they would not talk to their father about it," the White House source said. "When they called, it was very upbeat, stuff about the grandchildren."

Two days before the war started, Barbara fractured a bone in her left leg. It happened at Camp David while she was sledding with her grandchildren and actor Arnold Schwarzenegger. Although the president was standing atop the hill, yelling, "Bail out, bail out," Barbara lost control of the saucer and held on tight as she crashed into a tree.

"She doesn't know why she didn't bail out," her press secretary Anna Perez said. "She just held on and the next thing she knew, there was the tree."

The White House doctor looked at her injury and sent her by ambulance to a hospital in nearby Hagerstown, Maryland. She returned to Washington later the same day, using a wheelchair from the helicopter on the South Lawn to the White House door.

The president, walking beside her, said, "It smarts a little."

Barbara smiled. "Easy for him to say."

Although she didn't need a cast, Barbara was told to stay off her feet for a while, so during the first week of the war she was mostly confined to family quarters in the White House, using a wheelchair instead of crutches to get around.

Ten days after the accident she made her first public appearance, hosting a reception for women taking part in a conference on breast cancer. Barbara told reporters that talks with her grandchildren had made her realize how scared children are of war and what parents can do to calm their fears.

She said a weekend at Camp David with Doro's children, Sam and Ellie, and Marvin's daughter, Marshall, illustrated for her that the youngsters were alarmed by the war footage on television. So she sat down with them to discuss what was happening."

"We just talked about it, the things we were looking at," she said. "I answered their questions. They were little kids so they didn't ask too many."

The children were especially alarmed when they saw Scud missiles hit Tel Aviv. "They were saying, 'Daddy, Daddy,' " Barbara said. She explained that the missile attacks were far away but that Americans were involved in the war so it was still important to them.

"My kids aren't different than anyone else's," she said. "I just think parents should monitor their children and just be sure they they're understanding what they're seeing so they're not getting terrible nightmares. I just think you ought to be careful of your children."

She described her husband during this period as "steady and stable and calm. He's on the phone a lot of the time. He's like anybody else. Every single one of those soldiers are his."

At the end of January 1991, Barbara made her first out-of-town trips since the start of the war, flying to Boston for an event sponsored by the president's nephew, Jamie Bush. Fear of terrorist attacks was strong in Washington, so security for Barbara's visit was extraordinary. The event was a benefit dinner at the Boston Park Plaza Hotel to honor students at the Mather School who had been assured by a foundation of a fully paid college education if they graduated from high school. In the hotel, security men were stationed every twenty feet.

Barbara seemed absolutely at ease even though she had to use a cane—a black wooden souvenir from Africa with her name on it—to get around. "Don't kick me in the leg," she joked.

A student asked what she thought of the war.

"I don't like war but I am also thinking that one fellow can't be allowed to brutalize a country," she said. "Sometimes it's easier to stay home and not do anything. This wasn't one of those times."

There were not many large protests against the war but there was some opposition. In mid-February while the Bushes were attending a church service in Kennebunkport a man sitting a few feet away in the front pew stood and demanded that the United States stop bombing Iraq. The minister thanked the man for his comments and then urged him to sit down, but he replied that "the spirit of the Lord is upon me" and continued to talk. He was led away by police. The Bushes sat quietly throughout the outburst.

Patriotism was high in most parts of the nation and especially on Capitol Hill. When President Bush gave his State of the Union address at the end of January, he got enthusiastic responses from both Democrats and Republicans on the war issues. Barbara came into the chambers unannounced before the speech began but was spotted immediately and got a standing ovation.

Six weeks into the war, air traffic had fallen dramatically because of fear of terrorist attacks on airplanes, just as it would a decade later after terrorists crashed planes into the World Trade Center and the Pentagon. Barbara, heeding the president's call to keep life as normal as possible, decided to do her part. She took a commercial jet from Washington to Indianapolis, flying coach.

"I want people to know the airports are secure," she said. "I'm trying to say to the public that our airlines and our airports have a lot of security and we're safe."

After a one-day visit to a VA hospital and Grissom Air Force Base, she took a military jet home.

Barbara was upset to find that a few small-minded Americans were taking out their anger at Iraq on people in the United States who looked as if they might be of Arab ancestry, just as some did after the World Trade Center attacks. Telling reporters that tolerance would be her theme at commencement addresses in the spring, she described a sad letter she had received from a young girl in the Washington suburbs whose father, originally from Afghanistan, was a taxi driver.

"It was a wonderful letter saying she just didn't understand why—because people thought she was Arab that they came by and trashed her father's cab and hurt their house and scared them all to death. And she said, 'We're not Arabs. We're from Afghanistan.'

"Well, it didn't matter to me whether she—the story is a horrible story—it doesn't matter if she's Arab or not. What matters is, we don't turn on our fellow neighbors and citizens like that."

The letter led Barbara into thoughts about all kinds of tolerance and how parents are the ones who instill such values in their children. "I'm concerned about parenting correctly and tolerance," she said. "I'm concerned about sort of the sloppiness in not being tolerant of people who are different. Whether it's handicapped or racially different or religious differences or whatever, that concerns me a lot. And you know, I think that Desert Storm sort of made that all come into light because people worked side by side—I mean, Arabs and Jews and blacks and whites and Muslims and Christians and Catholics—their lives depended upon each other.

"When those soldiers return home and find intolerance in their neighborhoods and on campus, it seems to me very sad," she said.

Barbara followed the war day by day on television, along with everyone else, and she had her favorites among the Desert Storm military "briefers" who gave updates on the status of the war each day from both the Pentagon and war headquarters in Riyadh, Saudi Arabia.

A reporter told Barbara that the president had mentioned her being in love with a different briefer every day. "That's about true, too," Barbara replied. "I did write Niall Irving [a British officer who briefed in Riyadh] a little note and got an adorable little note back from him."

Barbara's trip to Fort Grissom was one of several she took during the war. At Fort Campbell, Kentucky, she was met with uproarious chants of "U.S.A., U.S.A." She met privately with family members of units stationed in the Gulf, sang "God Bless America" with country singer Lee Greenwood, told the crowd, "You are serving your country extraordinarily well," and made a joke about her sledding accident, saying she taught her grandchildren to sing, "Over the river and into the tree, to grandmother's house we go."

Toward the end of February, it was clear that the ground war, added to the six weeks of bombing that Iraq had endured, was having the desired effect on Baghdad. On February 27, Barbara visited marines and their families at a base in Quantico, Virginia, and told them the war was "very close to over."

"This country is really, truly wrapped in yellow ribbons," she said.

The next day, President Bush announced the end of the war. "Kuwait is liberated," he said. "The Iraqi army is defeated."

Like most Americans, Barbara was elated that the fighting was over, but her job wasn't done yet. She continued to visit military bases for several months. In early March she made a solo trip to the Mayport Naval Air Station in Jacksonville, Florida, and told the families they had been an important part of the war effort, simply by going about their daily lives while their spouses were at the front.

"Keep life at home on an even keel," she said. "This relieves their worries about you and it helps ensure a wonderful homecoming for them. By tending to daily life, by making sure that the dentist appointments are kept and the mortgage payments get made, the homework gets done, Little League games get watched, you are doing the most essential service of all."

Then she paused and told the military families that she could empathize with what they had been through.

"You know, many years ago, when our country was fighting another just war, I was a college girl in Massachusetts. But my heart was not in the classroom. At least, that's how I explained my grades to my parents then. My heart and thoughts were somewhere in the Pacific on the USS *Jacinto*, a converted light cruiser, with a wonderful young naval pilot to whom I happened to be engaged. So we do understand a little bit of what you've been through."

In mid-April, Barbara was at Fort Gordon, Georgia, meeting privately with wounded veterans in an army hospital and chatting with some of them before the cameras, joking and signing autographs. For one man who had won the Purple Heart after stepping on a land mine, she wrote to his children, "You must be proud of your dad. Best Wishes. Mrs. Bush."

Life in the White House returned to normal, bit by bit. It had been closed to tourists during the war and for a month afterward and Barbara said she was happy to have people back when it reopened. "I missed the tourists," she said. "I missed having them come through the house. And I felt . . . I think the house missed them, too."

She said she was still getting letters related to the war, including an apology from a woman who had written a testy letter earlier.

"She wrote and said, 'Please send my husband back—I don't think anything is worth his life and please tell your husband' . . . and I wrote her back, and said, 'I can certainly understand how you feel and sometimes there are bigger things than we are and I'll pray for your husband.'

"So she evidently showed her husband her letter and my letter and he said to her, 'That's a very rude letter.' "

But Barbara said she had not considered the letter rude at all because she understood just how the woman felt. "I thought it was just exactly what a normal wife might write when she was desperate."

Like many Americans, Barbara was moved by the sight of an American soldier telling surrendering Iraqis who fell down and bowed at his feet, "Get up, get up, you're safe now." And she was amused to learn that many grateful Kuwaitis were naming their babies "Bush." One Kuwaiti woman, awaiting the return of her son who had been held captive in Iraq, told *USA Today*, "Thank you, Barbara Bush. You know what it is like to be a mother." The woman said she would welcome her son home in the old Bedouin way: "I will kill a camel and share it with everyone."

Barbara had nothing but loathing for Saddam Hussein, who was still in power when her son became president and prepared for a different kind of war.

"I'd like to see him hung . . . if he were found guilty," she told reporters at a White House lunch. "I mean, we're talking about thousands and thousands of lives that have been tortured and . . . I'm sure you have all talked to people who came back from Kuwait. But it's just horrible, the stories they tell."

She said she also would not be opposed to putting Saddam on trial for war crimes. "I guess he broke many, many international laws and I guess that would be only fair," she said. "He certainly is right up there with the people they tried after World War II."

Barbara's desire to see Saddam hanged was shared by so many Americans that her venture into policy issues caused the White House no political problems but it did provide the president with some good opening lines in his speeches for several weeks. "I seldom differ with my wife," he said. "I doubt if I'll differ with her here."

A few months later when Barbara once again ventured into a controversial area, someone reminded her that her marriage had survived the Saddam remark. She rolled her eyes. "Barely," she said.

The Gulf War saw, for the first time in America's experience, many young mothers going off to Saudi Arabia and leaving very young children behind with husbands or other relatives. The situation brought into conflict two of Barbara's strongly held beliefs—one, that women should be home with their infant children, and two, that when you make a choice in life, you should strive to be content with it instead of complaining. She resolved the conflict in this instance in favor of military mothers doing their duty to country, saying she would not favor an exemption for women with infants or young children going off to war.

"It's hard but you have to make choices in life. It's your choice," she said. "Nobody's making you do that. Now women who are in the service, particularly the reservists, will know what they've gotten into."

The war had also reinforced one of Barbara's most cherished beliefs— that she had married a wonderful man.

"You know, I would have told you that after forty-six years, you know your husband pretty well. But the truth is, I really was in awe of him. And I don't mean that I was going to fall down and kneel in front of him but I just have enormous respect for his stability and his ability. I knew he had it, but these were very difficult times. And yet, he managed to stay on a very even keel with absolutely no blips. I think that's amazing."

Most of the nation seemed to share Barbara's opinion. The president's popularity soared in the weeks after the war ended. And Bush seemed to revel in the patriotic spirit that swept over the country.

It was a satisfying end to a dark ordeal.

13

AFTER THE WAR

In the political afterglow of the Gulf War, all expectations were that President Bush would run for a second term and be reelected. The White House did nothing to discourage this speculation, although Barbara occasionally talked about her desire to get back to private life.

"It has to do with, will I still be able to bend over and work in my garden when he gets out of office, or will we be able to travel with our grandchildren or will George be able to take me down the Inland Waterway in a boat, that kind of thing, selfish things," she told CBS in August of 1991.

Throughout the year she expressed similar feelings but always came to the same conclusion: "I don't think I can be that selfish." She said repeatedly that she thought her husband would seek a second term and that she would be happy with whatever decision he made.

"The truth is, I think he has to run," she said.

The months following the Gulf War had been busy ones. President Bush suffered a personal setback in early May. While jogging, he experienced heart fibrillations, which doctors said were not serious. But the president was hospitalized and it turned out he had a variation of Graves' disease, the thyroid problem that struck Barbara two years earlier and affected her eyes. The family dog Millie also had an autoimmune disease, lupus.

Barbara told reporters that she was swimming at Camp David when a secret service agent informed her that the president had been taken to a hospital. She wrapped herself in a robe and rushed off to see him. He was on an examining table hooked up to a heart monitor.

"I wish I hadn't mentioned (the heart flutter)," he told her.

"George, come on, don't be dumb," she replied.

Doctors soon had the president's thyroid stable but he suffered from fatigue for a couple of weeks and like Barbara had to take pills to control the illness.

Because it is unusual for two humans and a dog to suffer from variations of the same illness, experts examined the water at the White House, Camp David, and the summer retreat at Kennebunkport, but nothing came of the search. Barbara said she thought that the stress of the Gulf War had triggered Bush's illness. "The fact that you send other people's children to war—don't let anyone ever underestimate that," she said. Her own illness, she added, might have been sparked by the stresses of the 1988 campaign and inauguration.

Barbara also told reporters that the president, who liked an occasional vodka martini, had given up alcohol entirely because of the medicine he was taking for the disease.

While the president was still "dead tired" from the illness and the effects of treatment, Britain's Queen Elizabeth arrived for her first official visit to the United States since 1976. The Queen presented him with a set of silver-plated horseshoes and a copy of *America Is Lost*, written in 1782 by King George III. The Bushes gave the queen a Steuben crystal flower bowl engraved with quotations from Shakespeare.[1]

In a colorful thirty-minute ceremony replete with military pomp and eighteenth-century music, Bush and the queen both referred to the successful war collaboration of the United States and Britain. "Years from now, men will speak of American and British heroism in the Gulf, as they do today of our cooperation in two world wars and forty years of peacetime alliance," Bush said.

The queen said she was especially pleased that the visit "comes so soon

after a vivid and effective demonstration of the long-standing alliance between our two countries."

What was remembered most about the queen's speech, however, was
the fact that no one in the audience could see her face as she spoke, only
the brim of her purple-and-white hat. Due to a White House gaffe, no one
had thought to provide her a riser after the six-foot-two Bush spoke. Not
too long after this incident, the White House chief of protocol, Joseph
Reed, left his post.

After the ceremony, the Bushes took the queen and her husband,
Prince Philip, into the White House for a luncheon that featured red snap-
per and a saffron rice timbale. Barbara told reporters later that she and
the president showed Queen Elizabeth burn marks on the Truman Balcony
overlooking the South Lawn. "This is where the British tried to burn down
the White House," she said. "We showed it to the queen when she was
here." Barbara added that she had to mumble when describing for the
queen wallpaper in the family dining room that showed scenes of the
revolutionary war and the American triumph over England.

The next day, Barbara accompanied the queen to a house built for low-
income residents in southeast Washington. They were greeted by the
owner, sixty-seven-year-old Alice Frazier, who upon seeing the queen im-
pulsively gave her a hug. It was a breach of protocol—no one hugs or even
touches the queen in public—but Barbara saved the moment by stepping
forward to hug Mrs. Frazier herself.

Although Mrs. Frazier had prepared fried chicken and potato salad for
the occasion, the queen declined to partake since she doesn't eat in public.
The food didn't go to waste, however. Housing Secretary Jack Kemp, on
hand to tout the building program, had some potato salad along with Mrs.
Frazier's extended family.

"I told her this was my palace," Mrs. Frazier said.

Later in the day, after a private luncheon at the Library of Congress, a
crowded garden party for eighteen hundred at the British embassy, and a
reception, the queen went—at her own suggestion—to a baseball game in
Baltimore. The Bushes accompanied her to the game, between the Orioles
and the Oakland Athletics, and they sat in the box of Orioles owner, Eli
Jacobs. The Athletics won, 6–3.

During the queen's visit, she had a brief exchange with George W. Bush, who at the time was not yet a governor, much less a president. *The Washington Post* said that George W. was under orders from his parent to maintain decorum with the queen, but he slipped.

The queen asked young Bush, who was part owner of the Texas Rangers, if he were the black sheep of the family. "I guess so," he replied.

"All families have them," the queen said.

"Who's yours?" Bush asked.

Barbara Bush stepped in at that point. "Don't answer that," she said. The queen didn't.

Two months later, the Bushes were in London for three days for an economic summit. While the president met with other leaders of industrial democracies Barbara joined the wives on a boat tour down the Thames, accompanied by a steel band. That evening, they saw a performance at the Old Vic Theater. Barbara appeared to be enjoying herself. She reported that Soviet leader Mikhail Gorbachev approached "and whispered, 'Barbara, I want to take you to all the nightclubs, the next time you're in Russia.' "

"I have been to Moscow before," Barbara said, "but I have only been to funerals, so anything is up."

Another day, accompanied by Princess Diana, Barbara visited AIDS patients at a London hospital. One of them told her he had studied at Indiana University in Bloomington and would like to return to the United States but was barred by U.S. rules because he had AIDS. He asked the first lady to see what she could do about getting the policy changed. Barbara replied that she had recently lunched with the president and several health officials who favored a change in the regulations. And in fact, the rule was changed a few months later.

Barbara described the "big treat" of her London trip as meeting Diana's sons, William, nine, and Harry, six, at the U.S. ambassador's residence and offering them an opportunity to see the president's helicopter. The boys responded eagerly and were taken by limousine for a private tour while their mother and Mrs. Bush did hospital duty.

At the end of the three-day meeting, Bush and Gorbachev announced an agreement on a new arms control treaty, clearing the way for a summit

in Moscow a few weeks hence. But first, the Bushes had the rest of their
tour to finish—stops in France, Greece and Turkey. Among the sights in
Istanbul was a performance by a whirling dervish—a Muslim mystical sect
of devotees who whirl as a spiritual act.

Barbara made news briefly during a cruise on the Bosporus Strait where
she wore one red sneaker and one blue. Asked about her shoes, she replied
that the president "gave me twenty pairs for my birthday. How else will I
ever wear them all? Now I'm the Imelda Marcos of Kennebunkport." But
she later changed to plain pumps.

The trip was wearing on both of the Bushes. Longtime White House
reporter Ann McFeatters of Scripps Howard News Service captured some
of the small details that made the first lady's life a little more difficult:

> As Bush made a lengthy speech in 99-degree weather in Athens, Bar-
> bara sat in a folding chair in the hot sun. As he finished, she stood
> up gratefully, eager to get to the air conditioning of their black lim-
> ousine. Oblivious of her, Bush strode past and went ahead without
> her.
>
> In Paris, he once left her standing at the bottom of the steps as
> he ran up them to a formal reception. He's left her standing in the
> rain in front of dozens of TV cameras as he's gone off with their
> umbrella to greet someone.
>
> At the London economic summit, Mrs. Bush found herself unable
> to communicate with many of the people who rushed to speak to her
> because, unlike Bush, she usually does not have interpreters.[2]

Shortly after that trip ended the Bushes were in Moscow for the summit
that had been arranged in London. Barbara spent much of her time with
Raisa Gorbachev, whom she had befriended during the Wellesley speech
a year earlier. "Mrs. Gorbachev, who often wears a somewhat pinched,
prissy look, broke into a broad unmistakably sincere grin as she welcomed
Mrs. Bush in the Kremlin . . . with a bouquet of roses," the *Los Angeles
Times* reported.[3]

The two women held hands as they strolled around the Kremlin and
they cut a ribbon at a local park to dedicate a bronze sculpture of a mother
duck leading eight little ducklings, a gift from the United States to the
children of the Soviet Union. Mrs. Gorbachev had admired a similar statue
when she was in Boston. Robert McCloskey, whose popular 1941 book

Make Way for Ducklings inspired the statues, was on hand for the ceremony. "I couldn't imagine this ever happening," he said.

Not long after the Moscow summit there was an unsuccessful coup attempt against Gorbachev and he and Raisa were held captive by armed men for three days. When he was freed, Gorbachev quickly telephoned Bush, who had been trying unsuccessfully to reach him during the upheaval. Barbara listened in on the call, which was taken at Kennebunkport during the Bushes' usual August vacation.

Raisa Gorbachev, who had seen the crisis coming and confided some of her fears to Barbara during the summit, became distraught during the ordeal and suffered a nervous breakdown. Once the crisis had settled down, Barbara sent her a personal note.

The Bush vacation was interrupted not only by the attempted coup but also a hurricane. The president had already returned to Washington to deal with the Russian crisis when the storm hit but Barbara and the rest of the family, who had stayed on in Maine, were evacuated. She went to stay with a friend. An even worse storm would do a heartbreaking amount of damage to the house just a few months later, the same frightening one that destroyed a fishing boat later featured in the book and film *The Perfect Storm*.

In late October, a northeaster destroyed the entire first floor of the Bushes' oceanfront house, perched on a rocky promontory in Kennebunkport. It obliterated the living room, the master bedroom, and several others, along with many mementos, and caused hundreds of thousands of dollars' worth of damage.

Luckily, Barbara had removed some family albums from the house during the summer hurricane. She inspected the house in early November after the northeaster and however she felt privately, kept a stoic face in public. "It's really pretty bad, but worse things happen in life—a lot worse," she said. "It teaches you a lesson. We're very lucky."

She did, however, allow herself a quick expression of pain: "All that nice living room went out to sea," she said.

One reason both George and Barbara talked circumspectly about their heavy losses at the beach house was that the economy was rapidly deteriorating and the unemployment rate rising. President Bush's high numbers in the polls were beginning to fall as well.

Stung by charges that he was neglecting domestic policy with all his foreign trips and interests, Bush launched an education initiative in the fall of 1991 and sent members of the Cabinet out into the cities to promote it. Barbara was part of the team as well, assigned to a school in Maryland, where she was mobbed with well-wishers more interested in seeing her than in hearing details of the president's plan.

But the main domestic issue during the summer and fall that year was the nomination of Clarence Thomas to the U.S. Supreme Court. Bush nominated the black conservative judge on July 1. Thomas was confirmed by the Senate on October 15 after graphic sexual testimony that riveted the nation and made college professor Anita Hill famous. Hill, working with liberals trying to defeat the Thomas nomination, said that Thomas had harassed her when she worked for him earlier. Thomas denied the charges.

While the outcome of the Senate vote was still in doubt, Barbara told reporters in New York that she didn't believe Hill's testimony. "I don't believe the allegations against him," she said. "I know him to be a superb, superior individual." She and the president watched the vote together on TV, then telephoned congratulations to Thomas.

"It's one more bit of evidence of how strong George Bush is and the degree to which he controls the political process and the agenda," said Steven Hess, a political analyst at the Brookings Institution in Washington.[4]

It wasn't all heavy politics for Barbara during this period.

In September, at a White House state dinner for King Hassan II of Morocco, the president said in his dinner toast, "Barbara and I felt like movie stars as we came down the stairs tonight. To steal a line from Humphrey Bogart, I call this place Casa Blanca. [White House]."

Later, the president asked, "Did you get it? You know, Casablanca. White House?"

Barbara replied, "Terrific. Did you hear everybody laugh?" She said he had rehearsed the line before dinner and "He read it about eight times and I'm the only one upstairs who got it."

And in the movie *Naked Gun 2½*, actor Leslie Nielsen, playing a bumbling detective, knocked over a Barbara Bush look-alike as he crept through the White House, and later accidentally hit her with a lobster. In the end, he knocked her off a balcony. After the movie came out, Nielsen was invited to a state dinner. How would he be received?

"The darn trouble is, she looks exactly like me," Barbara said. "She has the pearls. She has the mannerisms. I recognized myself. My children, those dirty dogs, called and said, 'Mom, don't go see *Naked Gun 2 ½*, and I said, 'We saw it and I loved it and Dad loved it.' And Doro said, 'Oh, good, because we died laughing.' "[5]

Neilsen said when he got the invitation to the White House, he asked if the president and Mrs. Bush had seen the movie, "just in case they would rather meet me in Siberia. The man got back to me the next day, and said, 'Don't worry. The president and his wife loved the picture. They thought it was very funny."

At the dinner, which honored Czechoslovakian President Vaclav Havel, the Bushes posed for a picture with Nielsen. In the photo, Bush is scowling and Barbara is holding two fingers up behind Nielsen's head.

Barbara also revealed that year just how fond her husband had become of another girl. She said the president "came in the other day with some stranger and he said, 'Come on in, I want you to meet the love of my life—here, Ranger.' "[6]

In the final months of the year, Barbara had a rose named after her, as well as the Mrs. Barbara Bush tulip during an economic summit in the Netherlands, and she topped the Gallup poll's list of the ten most admired women. She and George also made *People* magazine's list of the twenty-five most intriguing people of the year.

The Bushes were already preparing for the coming campaign year. In early December, abrasive White House chief of staff John Sununu resigned, under pressure from Barbara and George W. it was widely believed. His departure had been rumored for months and denied by both Barbara and the president. But there was a palpable sense of relief in the White House when the decision to oust Sununu finally was made. He was replaced by the much more affable Sam Skinner, a former federal prosecutor from Chicago.

Embarrassment over the Sununu dismissal was not the only problem the president faced. By the end of 1991, the economy was falling into a frightening recession, affecting tens of thousands of blue-collar workers and leading to widespread job losses among middle managers. When the unemployment rate reached 7 percent in October that year, Bush expressed sympathy for those suffering losses but remained focused on the area where he had achieved the most success—foreign policy.

At the same time, Bill Clinton was on the campaign trail exhibiting his superior people skills along with a populist-leaning message that was well-received by many, including the conservative Democrats who had defected to Reagan at the beginning of the eighties.

To top it all off, Republicans had been in power for twelve long years. In the view of many Americans, it was time for a change.

If George and Barbara were aware of these ominous portents, they didn't let on. They both seemed to think that, in the end, he would pull through.

In mid-December, Barbara went to New Hampshire to file the president's candidacy for the first political primary, kicking off his reelection campaign and paying little heed to polls that showed Bush below 50 percent in favorability ratings for the first time in his presidency. "He's not going to have any trouble," she predicted of the president's campaign chances. But, she added, "He's got a lot of work to do and he knows it."

Her own popularity remained high. She often gave tours of the White House, made interesting remarks in interviews, and commented on the events of the day. And she never forgot how interested people are in the minutiae of the White House and its occupants. Barbara was featured on the cover of the *Ladies Home Journal* in December that year after telling reporter Myrna Blyth all about her holiday plans.

"This year, we'll probably spend the holiday as we spent the last two," she said. "We've gone to Camp David with the children. I went up earlier in the week last year and stuffed all the stockings and hid them, so it made life considerably easier. I make a rule now—the children can only bring one present for each child, and then they exchange among themselves. The first year it was a disaster. I mean, one child brought enough for the whole of America. One brought one tiny something..."

Barbara told the *Journal* that the presents she gives her children and grandchildren are fairly traditional. At age eight or nine, each granddaughter gets a gold cross and chain. And one year, she bought each of her grown children an electric train set for their entire families. "I thought I was brilliant," she said. "Even though some of them have only girls, I think every home needs an electric train."

Barbara also revealed that she recycled Christmas presents, a practice that had caused Nancy Reagan some embarrassment. "What am I going to do with 400 scarves?" Barbara said. "So I just rewrap them." But she said she passed along these presents only to friends who had admired them.

As for her own presents, there are none, at least from the president. "George and I do not do presents," she said. "We have everything we want in life. If we don't have something and one feels they need it, one gets it. I need a lot of clothes so I go buy them. Maybe I could say George gave me this or that. He gave me every darn thing I have. But I don't have to ask for it. Don't feel sorry that we don't exchange presents."

The White House was decorated lavishly for the holidays as usual. That year there were 1,370 handmade needlepoint ornaments, many of them looking much like Barbara Bush.

"There are a lot of white-haired, fat, pearled ones," Barbara told reporters while showing off the decorations. And under the tree was a toy train—much like the ones Barbara gave her children—whose cars were filled with yarn and trees. The little train moved between villages marked Houston and Washington, D.C.

The next year would tell where the final junction would be.

14

THE '92 CAMPAIGN

For George Bush, 1992 started off on a really sour note and got worse. He became embarrassingly ill in Japan, there were devastating riots in Los Angeles, the economy was in deep recession, and his popularity reached new lows.

In contrast, Barbara had a number of shining moments and got glowing reviews wherever she went. But she took little pleasure in her own triumphs. Out of long habit, she put her husband and his fortunes first. She took his defeats personally.

In early January, the Bushes went on a goodwill tour of Asia, stopping first in Korea, where President Tae-Woo gave Barbara forty-seven red roses for her wedding anniversary. As usual, she and George didn't exchange presents.

Then it was on to Japan, where George had a very embarrassing public incident and Barbara got a chance to show her stuff.

The problem occurred at a state dinner. George was sitting between Barbara and Japanese prime minister Kiichi Miyazawa. Suddenly, the president slumped toward Miyazawa and vomited into his lap. Barbara was horrified and reached out to support her husband, clearing the vomit from his mouth. Secret service officials got the president onto the floor and he recovered enough to be taken out of the room.

Barbara made clear she had learned a lot during her long years in diplomatic service. Seeing that her husband wasn't in any real danger, she stayed at the banquet and spoke in his place. She was at her best, immediately putting the somber crowd at ease again.

"You know, I can't explain what happened to George because it's never happened before," she said. "But I'm beginning to think it's the ambassador's fault."

Michael Armacost, the U.S. ambassador to Japan, smiled uneasily.

"He and George played the emperor and the crown prince in tennis today and they were badly beaten," she said. "And we Bushes aren't used to that. So he felt much worse than I thought."

By the time she finished speaking, having made clear that George Bush had only a minor illness, she had the crowd laughing with relief. She got compliments galore in both the Japanese and the American press.

Barbara's spokeswoman, Anna Perez, said the first lady knew her husband was okay when he said to Miyazawa, "Why don't you just roll me under the table and let me sleep it off."

"She immediately made the decision not to leave the dinner," Perez said. "She was really frightened for a moment, seeing the president go down, but doctors were there immediately and his color came back immediately. She called it a combination of a rigorous schedule, playing tennis and this bug going around the White House staff."[1]

Although Barbara had no prepared remarks, she had become by this time pretty expert at pinch-hitting. "The woman was born prepared," Perez said.

The same political savvy was on display at domestic campaign events. Barbara was a regular visitor to New Hampshire, the state with the strategically important first primary election. While Bush had no real competition from regulars within the Republican party, he was being attacked from the right by broadcaster Pat Buchanan and from the populist point of view by billionaire Ross Perot.

Barbara refused to mention either Buchanan or Perot by name and she kept a rigorous schedule—seven or more events on a typical busy campaign day, trying to reach as many people as possible.

Perez claimed that Barbara enjoyed the campaign trail, noting that she made forty-two appearances for thirty-nine candidates in the off-year elections in 1990 ("And she wasn't married to any of them. This time it's even more fun.").

Maybe so, but Barbara, in a candid moment while campaigning in California a month later, admitted that the best part of the 1992 effort was "knowing that this is my last campaign." That, of course, didn't turn out to be quite true.

Barbara drew favorable crowds wherever she went, even among those who didn't like the president. "We like you, Barbara, but you're sleeping with the enemy," said a sign held by an unemployed schoolteacher in New Hampshire.

Democratic pollster Celinda Lake concluded that Barbara was more important to the campaign in 1992 than she had been four years earlier. "The strongest part of Bush's domestic issues is being supportive of family values," Lake said. "She is key to that. He has very little credibility now, so he says, 'Barbara and I care.'"

Sheila Tate, who had been press secretary to Bush in his 1988 campaign, put a more positive twist on Barbara's popularity, saying she had "the likability factor. Nobody is better credentialed to talk about the human being that George Bush is than Barbara Bush. She reminds people how much they like the Bushes. And that is an important ingredient in reminding them how to vote."[2]

Barbara had also learned to control her temper on the trail, though she still could get snappish when asked a question she didn't like. But, perhaps recalling the negative scene she created by calling Democratic vice presidential candidate Geraldine Ferraro "... rhymes with rich" in 1988, she had nothing but kind words for Hillary Clinton in 1992.

At a time when women who stayed home to raise children had been put on the defensive by the choice of so many others to have careers, Mrs. Clinton had stumbled into a cultural crossfire when she said dismissively that she had chosen a career instead of staying home to "bake cookies."

Barbara, representing a generation that had mostly stayed at home and had baked cookies galore, declined to criticize her rival. "Everybody's different and that's a great thing," she said, but added, "We're talking about two men, and I've got the better candidate."

Part of Barbara's ability to inspire positive press stories was that she almost always managed to connect with regular people on the campaign

trail. At a child-care center in Seattle, she barely missed a careening toddler as she entered a playroom. "Uh, uh-oh, who do we have here?" she
asked. Then seeing a shaggy black dog in the middle of the floor she said,
"And my, what a nice big dog. Does this dog have a name?"

As it turned out, the dog had just been given a new name in honor
of the first lady's visit—Eleanor Roosevelt Kennedy Bush. "Are her politics
changing?" Barbara said. "Not that it matters, of course. Does it,
Ellie?"³

At tax time, Barbara scored another coup. The Bushes, like all presidential couples, release their tax returns publicly, and it turned out that
in 1992, the first lady had earned scads more than the president. *Millie's
Book*, about the "first spaniel," had earned a whopping $889,176 in roy-
alties. In contrast, George Bush's own book, a 1987 biography titled *Looking Forward*, brought in a paltry $2,718 in royalties.

White House spokesman Marlin Fitzwater said that the difference in
earnings on the books "is somewhat embarrassing but the president is
taking it very well."

Almost all the money from *Millie's Book* went to charity. After deduct-
ing money to pay taxes on the income, Barbara gave $789,176 to the
Barbara Bush Literacy Foundation.

The tax returns also showed that while damage to the Bushes' summer
home at Kennebunkport from the northeaster was estimated between
$300,000 and $400,000, insurance had covered only $185,000. The pres-
ident decided not to take advantage of federal benefits that were available
to him because he had declared the area a federal disaster area, thereby
making the assistance available but creating a conflict of interest for himself.

The White House, realizing that Barbara was a campaign asset, made
the most of her talents. A few days before the big California primary, she
sat down for an hour-long interview with the *Los Angeles Times*, which
ran much of the interview in question-and-answer format and started out
with a bittersweet question:

Q: You've heard, no doubt, that you are the better half of the presidency, you're more popular?

A: Then they're crazy. They ought to love George Bush. He's the most wonderful man. . . . We're talking about apples and oranges and that's what really counts. The orange is what counts. I'm the apple."

Q: Are you comfortable with the role of national grandmother?

A: I guess I have to accept it now. I'd like to think of myself as "national teenager" but I don't believe I'm going to get away with that. I might even go for "national mother."

Q: Do you see Americans embracing a first lady who asserts herself in half the decisions that the president makes?

A: Some people share in their husband's work and some don't. That's going to depend upon the marriage or their wife's work. But you have to have influence. When you've been married forty-seven years, if you don't have any influence then I really think you're in deep trouble.

Q: It seems that everyone today, whether on Main Street or Pennsylvania Avenue, is talking about Ross Perot. He is a Texan. You spent a number of years in Texas. Are you old friends?

A: I knew him.

Q: Tell us your recollection of him.

A: I don't talk about Ross Perot. I don't think people know much about him right now. But I've never talked about the people George has run against.

Q: Well he's not running yet.

A: Oh, Ross is running. . . . Would I vote for him? *N-O!* . . . George Bush or no George Bush. That's about the strongest I'm ever going to get, and as succinct.[4]

Despite Barbara's disdain, Perot had captured the nation's attention, and much like her, he was quick, self-confident, and witty onstage, in contrast to the president. At a Texas state convention of Republicans in June, politicians and local press noted that both Barbara and Ross Perot put people at ease and conveyed a sense of warmth and caring.

"Everybody wants to feel good and Barbara makes everybody feel good," one said. "She has a better speech writer and delivers funny lines so well, when he can't at all," said another. And that was in Bush's home state.[5]

Not all of Barbara's press was positive. In midsummer *Vanity Fair* magazine quoted former staff members—none of them by name—as saying Barbara was demanding, difficult, tough as nails, and autocratic in her dealings with staff. "People always said Nancy Reagan would kill you if you said bad stuff about her but I always thought Mrs. Bush was the one who would kill you. . . . I think everyone was scared of her. It was just like when your mother said, 'I have eyes in the back of my head.' "

The article also zoomed in on Barbara's habit of making cutting remarks, which, while often witty, were nevertheless painful for those on the receiving end. Asked about the article, Barbara saw it as an attempt to hurt her husband's campaign. "How do you get George Bush?" she asked. "Clobber his wife." Later, she made light of the story and of her own reputation: "Nobody ever said I was a saint," she told reporters.

Although she had long declined to take stands on political issues, Barbara got involved in a number of high-profile controversies in 1992:

After it was reported that Ross Perot had investigated her sons, Barbara suggested that Perot might have been angered with George Bush for turning down a job offer from him twenty years earlier. "I'm not sure if I feel outraged or violated," she told ABC-TV. "I feel slightly violated. I don't think that sort of thing should happen in America." Perot denied that he had investigated the Bush boys, charging that the Bush campaign initiated the idea to embarrass him.

Barbara was furious at a *New York Post* story that George Bush had an affair with aide Jennifer Fitzgerald when he was vice president. "It is ugly and the press ought to be ashamed of themselves, printing something that is a lie," she said. "I felt the same way—I don't have a double standard—about printing the Bill Clinton story, from a woman who was paid" to tell her story. But she noted that Clinton had acknowledged having an affair: "He never denied he had a fling, did he?" and added, "That doesn't mean George Bush should be smeared with the same brush when he didn't."

In another interview, however, Barbara told a story that seemed to diffuse her anger and put a humorous twist on the issue. She said the morning after the story was published, granddaughter Noelle Bush, fifteen, asked what was going on. When Barbara told her the newspaper was reporting that her grandfather had had an affair eight years earlier, Noelle broke into giggles at the very thought. "That's sort of insulting to your grandfather," Barbara told her in mock anger, adding, "Well, I guess he looks ancient to her."

Barbara said she and Fitzgerald were friends but she hadn't spoken to her about the story because Fitzgerald was out of the country. "I haven't seen Jennifer but my heart goes out to her. This is just mean," she said.[6]

She criticized Republican party chairman Richard Bond for saying that Hillary Clinton had "likened marriage and the family to slavery."

"First, I don't like that kind of campaigning," Barbara said. "And secondly, when you have a superb candidate of your own, I don't think you need to knock other people. And if you're going to knock other people you ought to knock the person running . . . she's not running for office."

The most striking and controversial point she made was on abortion. The Republican party was getting ready to put into its political platform a statement saying there should be a constitutional amendment outlawing abortion. Democrats said in their party platform that a woman should have a right to an abortion.

Barbara told reporters that she didn't think abortion—or homosexuality for that matter—belonged in a political party's platform.

"I'm saying abortion should not be in there, pro or con," she said. "It's a personal choice. . . . The personal things should be left out of, in my opinion, out of platforms and conventions."

Conservative leaders pounced on her for this remark and were pretty condescending as well. "I'm not sure she understood the political ramifications," said Ralph Reed of the Christian Coalition. Thereafter Barbara refused to comment on abortion until after her husband left office. Then she acknowledged what had seemed apparent for many years: she is pro-choice.

But her comments were widely cited in the run-up to the 1992 Republican presidential convention and her motives questioned. Moderate Republicans were pleased that their point of view was getting a high-level airing since they didn't have the numbers among the deeply conservative delegates at the convention to defeat an abortion platform.

"It's clear that the president is feeling desperate about having to run on a platform that is so extreme," said Nancy Sternoff, executive director of the National Republican Coalition for Choice. "Obviously the campaign is panicked if they've given Barbara Bush permission to say this."[7]

Bill Clinton and other Democrats saw her comments as a cynical ploy by Republicans to have it both ways, with George Bush appealing to conservatives who demanded a strong antiabortion statement and Barbara softening the stance for moderates and independents.

"It makes you wonder about all their policies that they say one thing and do another on this," Bill Clinton said. "It appears that everybody involved in the Republican ticket is moving to the Democratic position on that issue."

By the time the Republican convention got under way in August 1992, Barbara had moved front and center into the campaign. What was different this year from previous campaigns was that Bush was woefully behind—20 points or more, with the unemployment rate at 7.6 percent—and her own popularity had never been higher. But even more important was what Barbara represented—just about everything that Hillary Clinton did not.

Both men and women of all ages were comfortable with Barbara's life approach—devoted wife and mother, helpmate, someone who would be proud to make cookies and had no desire for a career of her own. Hillary, a Yale graduate and successful lawyer who talked early in the campaign about an active role in her husband's administration and spoke knowledgeably on the issues of the day, was threatening to some. Republicans were betting in a showdown of potential first ladies that Barbara would win in a landslide. And indeed, polls showed Hillary Clinton far less popular than Barbara Bush and Hillary had much higher negatives. But Barbara acknowledged her rival's strength. When a reporter asked if she would be willing to debate Hillary, the first lady replied, "Are you crazy? She'd win hands down. A debater I am not. Wrestling, maybe."

"She's probably the most popular figure in America today," Bush campaign manager Fred Malek said of Barbara. "She speaks with great candor and credibility. It's a big plus to have her as a role model."

Barbara accepted and promoted this view of herself but occasionally couldn't resist noting that she did have a few accomplishments of her own. "Don't discount me," she said. "I've written two books. I've raised wonderful children. I've raised hundreds of thousands of dollars."

And, when one too many interviewers asked if she regretted being just a homemaker, she snapped, "Do you think you'd say that to Arthur Miller, who wrote two plays [he actually wrote more than a dozen]? Would you say, 'You chose to be a homemaker' to him? I've written two books. I've done a lot more than raise a wonderful family."

By the time she got to the convention, Barbara was even ready to join other Republicans in taking on Hillary. In an interview with Public Television, she suggested that Hillary would be a copresident if Bill Clinton were elected. "I mean, you vote for one, you get both—that's what they have said."

Bill Clinton was quick to notice Barbara's harder stance on Hillary. "They spent two months dumping on my wife; they even got Mrs. Bush to change her position," he said. He was even more angry at George Bush's attacks on Hillary: "You'd think he was running for first lady."

Daughter Doro acknowledged that her mother was much tougher than many people knew. "She is a pretty strong lady," Doro said. "She toughens when things get a little rough. I can't say she likes the campaign mode but she gets stronger at a time when other people, like myself, get weaker."[8]

In a tribute to her popularity, Barbara was given star billing at the Republican convention that summer. She gave a speech in prime time on the third night of the four-day gathering when more TV viewers are tuned in than earlier in the week. The talk was all about family, its problems, and its rewards.

"Both George and I believe that while the White House is important, the country's future is in your house, every house all over America," she said. "We've met heroic single mothers and fathers who have told us how hard it is to raise children when you're doing it all alone. We've talked to grandparents who thought their child-raising days were over but are raising their grandchildren because their children can't. We've visited literacy classes where courageous parents were learning to read and continuing their education so they could make a better life for their families. And we've held crack babies and babies with AIDS and comforted other victims . . .

"Now I would like to say a word to some special people . . . I would really like to talk for a moment to parents who have sacrificed for their children. You may be exhausted from working a job, or two jobs, and taking care of your children. Or you may have put your career on hold. Either way, you may wonder . . . am I really doing the right thing?

"Yes, from the bottom of my heart, I'm here to tell you that, yes, you're doing the right thing. God bless you for it."

At the end of the speech, Barbara invited her family—lots of family—to join her onstage. There were twenty-two in all including twelve grand-children.

It was a warm and friendly speech, devoid of the sharp attacks and harsh pronouncements many other speakers had made during the evening and Barbara got a rousing response just as the president did the next evening when he accepted the Republican party's nomination for a second term. But when the Bushes left the convention, they knew the next couple of months would be difficult. Polls still showed the president running far behind Bill Clinton.

At times, Barbara seemed to be preparing herself for a loss. She said she was "not going to be heartbroken" if she had to leave the White House.

However she really felt about a second term in the White House, she was a regular presence on the campaign trail in the months between the Republican convention and the November 3 election. She visited dozens of schools, libraries, and town squares, talking as usual about family values and literacy but also wading into issues, especially the troubling economic conditions that were largely responsible for Bush's poor showing in the polls.

"George's economic policies protect your paycheck," she said at a rally in Connecticut at the end of September. "In the next four years, George wants to do more and he will—if you just clean the House." By that she meant vote for Republicans for the U.S. House of Representatives, which at that time had been controlled by Democrats for decades.

At the end of that speech someone yelled, "We love you, Barbara." She replied, "I want you to love George."

At most stops where there were children, questions about Millie were among the first asked. By this time Barbara had learned how to turn the dog into a campaign asset. Noting that *Millie's Book* had been published in Japan and citing the trade imbalance between the United States and Japan, Barbara said of the dog, "She's not part of the problem. She's exporting."

But she also discussed health care, welfare, crime, the environment, and all the other points of contention between Democrats and Republicans, frequently comparing George Bush's record as president to Bill Clinton's performance as governor of Arkansas. "In Bill Clinton's Arkansas, in spite of what he says, the unemployment rate was higher than the national average eleven out of the twelve years he was governor," she said.

On Election Day, George and Barbara were in Houston, the city that was still their legal residence. The president started the day with a two-mile jog, accompanied by daughter Doro. He and Barbara voted together and later he went shopping, buying new tapes, a new fishing reel, and renewing his Texas hunting license. Then they settled back to wait for the vote to come in.

That night, it became clear early on that Bill Clinton was going to coast to victory. George Bush, with Barbara at his side in the Westin Galleria in Houston, made a concession speech early. "There is important work to be done and America must always come first," he said. "So we will get behind this new president and wish him well."

He didn't forget his campaign helpmate: "Finally, of course, I want to thank my entire family with a special emphasis on a woman named Barbara. She has inspired this entire nation and I think the country will always be grateful."

The crowd gave loud whoops and cheers at the mention of Barbara's name and she managed a weak smile. But for the most part, having to stand in public at a time when she obviously longed to be behind closed doors with her family, Barbara looked stricken. Her hard work on the campaign trail, her venture into the issue side of politicking, her soaring popularity in public opinion polls, hadn't been enough. The nation didn't want four more years of Republican rule. It was ready for a charismatic Democrat.

Yet once the family had retreated to a hotel suite with dispirited staff and friends, Barbara's steely side came to the fore and she was able to say briskly, "It's over. Let's move on."9

She kept this same stiff upper lip over the next two months that she remained in the White House, only lapsing into bitterness occasionally.

The day after the election, the Bushes were back in Washington where two thousand friends and supporters from the White House, Congress, the military, and other government agencies had gathered on the South Lawn to cheer their defeated leader.

It was such a heartfelt outpouring that Bush was clearly moved. "What a fantastic welcome back," he said. "Maybe you didn't read the election returns. It didn't work out quite the way we wanted."

Barbara wiped away tears as she stood with her husband before fifty state flags but she didn't speak. "It's been a wonderful four years and nobody can take that way from us," the President said. Slowly, the Bushes worked their way to the steps of the rear portico of the White House. Bush lingered briefly, putting one arm around Barbara's neck. Then they went inside.

On Thursday, two days after the election, they were able to escape to Camp David but not from Republican postmortems. There were reports that Barbara and George W. were seething at campaign chairman James Baker for only reluctantly leaving his post at the State Department to join the campaign and then not giving it his all. *The New York Times* said that Bush himself was deeply depressed and second-guessing his campaign, having convinced himself until a couple of days before the election that he would pull it out in the end.

In the days following the election, Bush "was, I would say, pretty devastated," Houston friend Robert Mosbacher said some years later. "He must have said to me, I don't know, more than half a dozen times, 'I'm so sorry I let you down.' He said that to a lot of people he's close to."[10]

George W., seeking to cheer up his dad, suggested a trip to Florida, and the family agreed. George and Barbara spent four days in Boca Raton golfing, fishing, and socializing.

But there were still duties to perform and endure. One of Barbara's was to show Hillary Clinton around the White House. The outgoing first lady was not in a good mood when the day arrived. With Millie and Ranger at her side—each wearing a little red rain hat—she awaited Hillary's arrival, all the while sniping at reporters. "Avoid this crowd like the plague," she told her visitor as they passed by the press. The two women made a show of affection for each other, patting shoulders and holding hands as they walked into the White House. But once inside they didn't spend a lot of time together. Barbara went on to a diplomatic reception and Hillary spent another two hours touring with Chief Usher Gary Walters.

Part of Barbara's pique may have been because of another family loss. George's mother, Dorothy Bush, died on November 19, a day after suffering a stroke. Barbara had been especially close to her mother-in-law and the death, coming right after the election, was hard for both her and George. A couple of years later, she said that her husband had been devastated by the death of his favorite dog, Ranger, in the spring of 1993. "I think he let Ranger be sort of the tunnel of mourning," she said. "You can't cry, if you're a man, over an election. You can't cry over your mother, I guess."[11]

Whatever Barbara thought of Hillary privately, she came to her defense in public a week after the White House tour. Cartoonists had already gone after the incoming first lady, showing her commandeering a Cabinet meeting. "The cartoons are ugly," Barbara said. "It's just not fair. She's going to be great, and let her do her own thing."

Barbara herself was making plans to move on. She announced that the Bushes would be building a house on a lot they owned in Houston. "We're building on the lot which you have all rudely said we cannot build on," she told reporters, referring to an odd-shaped parcel of land that totaled only 5,800 square feet. She said she and the president would rent until their new house was finished.

In late November, Barbara held a ceremony at the White House to announce a grant to her literacy foundation from the proceeds from *Millie's Book*. George Bush dropped in on the gathering, joking that he had "these marvelously responsible things left to do—walking the dogs and accepting this enormous turkey" for Thanksgiving.

The Bushes gave their usual Christmas parties at the White House that year and Barbara placed a star on the national Christmas tree one last time, taking her three-year-old grandson, Walker Bush, up with her. They spent the holiday itself at Camp David. Then, after for a quick trip to Moscow in early January for the signing of a weapons treaty, the last bittersweet days in the White House were upon them.

On the final night in the White House, they invited close friends in for a private party. On Inauguration Day, they took a final walk around the building and the grounds, stopping to talk with tourists at the fence. They hosted Bill and Hillary Clinton at a traditional coffee and farewell chat, then rode with them to Capitol Hill for the changing of the guard.

After Clinton was sworn in, George and Barbara went swiftly to Andrews Air Force Base where two thousand supporters were waiting to give them a ceremonial sendoff. They didn't linger long.

"I had a chance to wish our new president well," Bush said. "And now it's back to the real world for the Bushes."

And then, they were gone.

15

AFTER THE WHITE HOUSE

Being forced into retirement can be traumatic, especially when the ouster is performed on a public stage.

When George and Barbara Bush left Washington after twelve years of living in government housing, there were multiple adjustments. They settled into a rental house that would be their new home for nine months until a new house could be completed.

Barbara bought a navy blue station wagon and practiced driving on Houston's streets. It wasn't easy after a decade of chauffeurs. Her son Marvin told a reporter, "I got a call one day and it was Dad saying, 'You won't believe what I'm watching right now. Your mom is backing out of the driveway in the car.' My concern wasn't for her as much as it was for everyone else on the road."[1]

If George and Barbara felt angry or depressed or at odds, at least now they could nurse their wounds privately. They were no longer living in the public eye.

There were consolations. They had close contact with an extensive family, especially the children and grandchildren. Both had prodigious earning power so they wouldn't suffer financially. And they still had loads of friends and acquaintances around the world. They would be traveling more than ever.

The most public trip in the months after the Bushes left the White House was to Kuwait, the small oil-rich country that had been rescued from Saddam Hussein's grasp during the Gulf War. Bush, naturally enough, was a hero to the Kuwaitis and he and Barbara got an exuberant welcome. Children along the road to the airport chanted "Thank you, Bush" and held aloft signs with simple slogans: "A friend in need is a friend indeed." The Bushes also were greeted with flowers and whirling sword dancers.

The main event was a dinner honoring the former president, but Kuwait being the society that it is, the women all ate in another room, so Barbara was not present for the honors conferred. She dined with the other women.

During and after the visit, April 14 to April 16, 1993, the Kuwaiti government arrested sixteen people, eleven of them Iraqis, and confiscated a lot of explosives. They were charged with conspiring to kill Bush. But the would-be assassins never got close to the former president.[2]

In October that year, George and Barbara moved into their new three-floor brick house on the odd-shaped lot they had owned for many years. Barbara, confessing that being ousted from the White House "left a void in my life," put her energy into the house, unveiling a large needlepoint rug she had done for the living room featuring animals, flowers, and her grandchildren's initials. Much to her chagrin, she found that even though she was now a private citizen, hordes of people were still interested in her and rather intrusive in the way they approached.

"The worst shock I had was that I couldn't just meld into real life," she said. The Bushes were forced to put up a six-foot wall around their house to keep gawkers at bay.[3]

It probably was little consolation that in Gallup's "most admired" poll that year, Barbara was at the top of the women's list, outranking Mother Teresa, former British prime minister Margaret Thatcher, Hillary Clinton, and Queen Elizabeth. George Bush joked that when the two of them made appearances together, she got all the attention. "I've been here five minutes and everyone is saying, 'It's fine to see you, but where's Barbara?' "

Nine months after leaving the White House, Barbara returned to Washington for a speech at a charity event. "On January twentieth we woke up and we had a household staff of ninety-three," she said. "The very next morning we woke up and it was George, me, and two dogs—and that's not all that bad." She said she and her husband had rediscovered cooking and called him "the best little dishwasher in Texas." Still, she said, five hundred letters a day poured into the former president's office. A Mother's Day poll that year found that Barbara was the mother figure most Americans would like to phone on Mother's Day in addition to their own moms. It was just the kind of statistic that made Barbara grit her teeth.

Once they left the White House both Bushes made speeches for money. Barbara got between $40,000 and $60,000 for each with the former president bringing in even bigger bucks. They also made charity appearances, hers focusing largely on her literacy foundation but sometimes reaching farther afield. In December that year, Barbara made a one-day trip to Muslim refugee camps in war-torn Croatia in an attempt to call public attention to their plight. "It's extraordinary what these people are going through," she said. "There's a lot of depression in these camps and you can understand why."

At home, she was also working on her memoirs, writing each day on an IBM laptop without the help of a ghostwriter. Her book, *Barbara Bush: A Memoir*, came out in the fall of 1994 and she toured the country to promote it. Soon it was at the top of the national best-seller list and it remained in stores for years after publication.

As it happened, Barbara's book came out while her two oldest sons were running for governor—George W. in Texas and Jeb in Florida. In October of 1994, just weeks before the elections, she had two book events in Texas and two in Florida. In Florida, a reporter asked if she thought she would be able to give her son a boost. "If it weren't a boost I wouldn't have asked the book people to send me to Florida," Barbara replied, laughing.

Was she happy that two of her sons were running for public office?

"Somehow or other, it made George and me feel that the life we had chosen was not so bad after all for the children," she said. "All of our children have made a lot of sacrifices and we couldn't help but wonder if they felt they would have been much luckier if they hadn't been in politics."[4]

She said that her two oldest sons were very different, with Jeb "more like his father if the truth be known," and George W. more like his mother. "This is not a compliment to him," Barbara added.

She expanded on the subject at a rally in Tampa. "We are both of us so proud that our children have decided to serve their country," she said. "They're not children to you but they're our children to us. It was very ugly in 1992 for our family. Not the loss but the campaign was very ugly and yet these two young men weren't turned off because they want to serve their country."

Jeb lost that year in a close election to an incumbent. George W., in a particularly satisfying victory for the family, defeated Democratic governor Ann Richards in Texas who had gained the long-lasting enmity of the entire clan by her stinging remark in the 1988 presidential campaign when she made fun of Bush's odd syntax and his wealth. "Poor George," she said mockingly. "He can't help it. He was born with a silver foot in his mouth."

The proud parents were at the inauguration of their firstborn son January 17, 1995, but neither spoke. Jeb was at the ceremony, too, no doubt feeling a little blue.

George W. Bush said he has a photograph from that inauguration that shows him taking the oath of office with his father off to the side, wiping away a tear. "And there, on the other side, is Jeb," he said. "He's looking happy and proud, but also something else, maybe a little sad, too. It's a tough moment, tough for me to look at. I love my brother, you see."[5]

That same month, George and Barbara celebrated their fiftieth anniversary. The venue they chose was Nashville, Tennessee, where the Oak Ridge Boys and other country and western stars put on a special concert for the event. "If you knew how happy all these people have made us," Bush said. "Thank you so much for a special evening we'll never forget."

Another special evening that year occurred at the White House. George and Barbara were invited back by President Bill Clinton for the official unveiling of their portraits. "Welcome home," Clinton said to the Bushes. "We're glad to have you back." He added that the Bushes had set a good example for others by their public service.

"They have been guided by the basic American values and virtues of honesty, compassion, civility, responsibility, and optimism," Clinton said. "They have passed these values on to their family and on to our American family as well."

Indeed, Barbara was as active as ever in her efforts for a more literate population. "I've spoken to twenty-five groups since the first of the year and none of them have been spared my literacy sermon," she said in an April speech. "I've told them to turn off their TVs and read to their children, or to have quiet time where everyone reads his or her book."

By 1996, four years after they left the White House, George and Barbara were well out of politics. The presidential election that year would be a runaway victory for President Clinton but the Bushes stood by their old rival Bob Dole. "I'll do anything Senator Dole wants me to do. I'll campaign for him," Bush said. But no amount of help from the former presidential couple could have saved his campaign.

That year, Barbara was named "Biker Babe of the Year" by *Outlaw Biker* magazine. She gained another grandchild: daughter Doro gave birth to Georgia Grace in January. And George Bush, seventy-two, parachuted out of an airplane. During the year, he spent 143 nights on the road, with Barbara along much of the time.

Now they were spending the entire summer in Kennebunkport, entertaining both family and friends frequently. But during the winter months in Houston, Barbara said, it was usually early to bed. "We've never been night owls. We're always the first to leave a dinner party," she said. On the nights they watch television, she said, "we're crazy about A&E and the History Channel," although, "there's too much Hitler."[6]

Going out in Houston was often a problem, she said, because tourists followed her car, interrupted her in restaurants ("If I could give people one piece of advice it would be, 'Never go up to someone and say that you didn't vote for her husband.' ") and trained binoculars on her house.

In 1997 Millie died at age twelve. The Bush's English springer spaniel was so famous that both *People* magazine and the Associated Press ran her obituary.

The biggest event for the Bushes that year was the opening of George Bush's presidential library in College Station on the fringes of Texas A&M University. The ceremony on November 6 drew twenty thousand people including President Clinton, former presidents Carter and Ford and first ladies Barbara Bush, Hillary Clinton, Nancy Reagan, Rosalynn Carter, Betty Ford, and Lady Bird Johnson. The $83 million building includes Bush's presidential papers in the library and also has a museum, a school of government and public service, and a conference center. Barbara Bush's papers and her work on literacy are there, too. A&M was so eager to get the library that it built an apartment for George and Barbara to use when they are in town.

"Now that my political days are over, I can honestly say that the three most rewarding titles bestowed on me are the three that I've got left," Bush said, "a husband, a father, and a granddad."

A week later, another Bush was in the spotlight again. This time it was Jeb, announcing he would once again run for governor of Florida. And with George W. seeking a second term as governor of Texas, the campaign trail would prove irresistible for the senior Bushes.

In March 1998, Barbara made a two-day trip through Florida, headlining fund-raisers and campaigning for Jeb.

At the University of Miami a couple of months later both Barbara and George were given honorary degrees and she was the featured speaker. Nodding to her husband in the audience, she said, "He is the father of the governor of the great state of Texas and he may be . . ." and she glanced at Jeb. "Well, they told me I couldn't say that, but I am Jeb's mother. You knew I was going to work that in."

Jeb himself was a different candidate in 1998 than he had been four years earlier. He told reporters that the long, difficult campaign of 1994 had left him estranged from his wife, Columba, and that one of his children developed a drug problem and had to undergo treatment.

"It was painful to go through that," he said. "I had got so immersed that while I was still connected to my family on one level, I left them behind. So when I came back to the real world, there were some problems I began to see . . . that hardship was devastating."[7]

After that campaign, he said, he reconnected with his family and in 1995 he converted to Catholicism, the religion in which his wife was born and his children were raised.

In the 1998 campaign, he said, "I organize myself around my kids. They're involved in the campaign more. A day doesn't go by that I don't talk to them or e-mail them. The same with Columba."

Jeb also moved away from the hard-edged conservatism he had displayed in 1994, concentrating more on the compassionate conservatism that his brother would later make famous. And he began using more light touches and references to his extended family in his campaign speeches.

"I think about how blessed I was to be George and Barbara's son, growing up in my family," he said in a speech in Tampa in May of 1998. "Not for the reasons you might think, of having a wholesome family life, although I truly have been blessed in that regard. But after all, who else can say that they've been spanked by the president of the United States, had their ears boxed by the most popular first lady probably this country has ever had and been given a wedgie by the governor of the state of Texas?"[8]

As the campaign moved into the home stretch, Barbara spent much of her time in Florida. During an October debate she sat right in the front row listening and afterward told Jeb, "You were great."

"I've never been so proud of my son," she said. "I feel Jeb has a vision thing. I always wondered what all the vision thing was, but I think Jeb has a vision for Florida."

The next day at a campaign rally she expanded on the point, saying that her husband had had a vision for America "but he couldn't articulate it quite as well as Jeb can."

Columba Bush sometimes joined her mother-in-law on the campaign trail but generally kept a much lower profile. She said Jeb had learned a lesson from his father in his second statewide campaign—come home each night, even if it means a late-night flight. Over the years, she also has grown close to the senior Bushes. In 1996, she and George Bush went on a trip to South America, accompanied by secret service agents but no other family members.

While Jeb got most of the attention in 1998, George W. was doing all right in Texas all on his own and already was being mentioned as a potential presidential candidate in 2000. Talking with a reporter during the fall campaign that year about why he doesn't discuss his strong religious beliefs much in public, he cited a conversation he had with his mother on the subject some years earlier.

"Mother and I were arguing—not arguing, having a discussion—and discussing who goes to heaven," a subject that was on his mind at the time because he had recently sworn off alcohol and renewed his commitment to his faith. Bush said he pointed to the Bible and noted that it said only Christians had a place in heaven. "I said, 'Look, Mom, here's what the New Testament says.' And she said, okay, and she picks up the phone and calls Billy Graham. She says to the White House operator, 'Get me Billy

Graham.' I said, 'Mother, what are young doing? Seriously.' And about two minutes later, the phone rings and it's Billy Graham and Mother and I are on the phone with Billy. And Mother explains the circumstances and Billy says, 'From a personal perspective, I agree with what George is saying, the New Testament has been my guide. But I want to caution you both: Don't play God. Who are you two to be God?' "[9]

On election night, Barbara and George had planned to be at home in Houston rather than at the victory party—they hoped—of one son or another. But something, probably George W., persuaded them to change their minds and so there they were in Miami on November 4, one on either side of Jeb Bush as he told cheering supporters, "This is a victory for fresh ideas, for new ideas as we move into the next century."

With George's repeat victory in Texas, the two became the first brothers to be governors at the same since the 1970s when Nelson Rockefeller was governor of New York and Winthrop Rockefeller of West Virginia.

Nelson Rockefeller went on to higher office, serving briefly as vice president under Gerald Ford. But Rockefeller's liberal leanings were out of step with the Republican party and he wasn't on the ticket when Ford ran unsuccessfully for president in 1976. Barbara's boys, having also seen their father suffer at the hand's of the party's right wing, didn't make the same mistake. Their conservative credentials were impeccable and their political instincts just right for the times.

16

THE ELECTION OF 2000

During the early stages of George W. Bush's presidential campaign, he kept his popular parents under wraps, fearful that if they were active he would be overshadowed by questions of dynasty and charges of being a "daddy's boy." By the time he got to Philadelphia in August 2000 for the Republican National Convention, though, he was feeling confident enough to give George and Barbara a turn in the spotlight again.

The senior Bushes reveled in the fact that their firstborn was the man of the hour and thoroughly enjoyed the crowds of Republicans that surged around them wherever they went in what Barbara dubbed "The City of Motherly Love."

But they were careful to limit their time onstage, knowing how easy it would be to leave the impression that the old Bush presidency was back. "We don't do politics any more," the elder Bush told reporters shortly after he and Barbara arrived in Philadelphia. "We're staying out of the limelight. I don't miss it. It's just a question of the pride of a dad in his son."

Nevertheless, both George and Barbara were a steady presence in the convention audience, sitting in a VIP section through a number of mind-numbing speeches that other delegates skipped. Barbara often jumped up to hug family members and was generally first on her feet to applaud the speakers.

They were especially pleased when daughter-in-law Laura Bush made her debut on the convention stage Monday night, the first night of the convention, telling the delegates she was a "little bit overwhelmed to help open the convention that will nominate my husband for president of the United States."

Twin daughters Barbara and Jenna sat beside their grandparents as their mother spoke, along with their other grandmother, Jenna Welch, in a show of family unity that was on display throughout the convention.

George and Barbara have often described Laura as a "rock" in a complimentary way, and Laura told reporters that as first lady, she would follow the line that Barbara took, helping her husband behind the scenes. "Maybe she wasn't so out front in policy meetings but she's very strong," Laura said of Barbara. As it turned out, Laura was notably less visible than her mother-in-law during her first months in the White House, coming forcefully into public view only after the World Trade Center attack September 11, 2001.

Back at the convention, Laura was asked on CNN if Barbara had given her any advice before her big speech. "Her latest advice to me was to wear vivid colors," Laura said. "So I hope you think my wardrobe over the week is vivid."

On the second day of the convention, the senior Bushes got into the spotlight in ways they had hoped to avoid when the longtime hostility between them and President Clinton bubbled to the surface.

Just as George W. Bush kept his parents in the background for most of the campaign, Democratic presidential candidate Al Gore declined offers from President Clinton to get out and campaign, fearing that all of Clinton's weak points—the impeachment, Monica Lewinsky, fund-raising—would hurt rather than help his own campaign.

But Clinton, unable to resist jumping in occasionally, baited the Republicans on the Friday before the GOP convention opened, telling a Democratic fund-raiser in Rhode Island, "Nearest I can tell, the message of the Bush campaign is just that, 'How bad could I be? I've been governor of Texas. My daddy was president. I've owned a baseball team.' "

Clinton's comments made the senior Bushes so angry they could hardly contain themselves, especially Barbara: "George W. Bush is a great man.

He'll take care of it," she said. "He doesn't need his mother, although she's dying to do it."

And former president Bush told MSNBC: "I'm going to wait a month . . . and if he continues that, then I'm going to tell the nation what I think about him as a human being and a person."

The Gore campaign marveled at its good luck that the Bush family had struck back. "It tells you something about George Jr.," said Gore spokesman Chris Lehane. "He has to send his father out to defend him. People are starting to wonder, does he have what it takes."

There were more temperate moments as well. The Bushes joined former first lady Nancy Reagan during a nostalgic reception where George Bush said of Reagan "I think of him all the time" and Barbara called Reagan, "the kindest man, next to George Bush, I ever knew." That night they sat with Nancy at the convention hall during video salutes to former Republican presidents. It was a segment full of poignant moments. Nancy mouthed "Thank-you" almost tearfully as she was introduced as "the one true love" of the president now downed by Alzheimer's disease. Gerald Ford, eighty-seven looking frail and somewhat bewildered, watched as the video showcased the famous lines he spoke at the end of the Watergate years: "Our long national nightmare is over." Shortly afterward Ford was taken to a hospital with an acute sinus infection and kept overnight for observation.

The video of George Bush featured the high point of his presidency, the American triumph in the Persian Gulf War, recalling a time when it seemed he would be unbeatable for reelection. He was offered an opportunity to appear onstage, but declined.

Not so Barbara. Later in the evening, to the thumping sounds of "Devil in a Blue Dress," and a huge ovation, she was on the dais to introduce her son, who was speaking by satellite en route to Philadelphia. The proud son took a moment to rib his mom, recalling how someone once told him, "George W., you may have your daddy's eyes but you have your mother's mouth."

Sure enough, she was back into controversial territory Wednesday morning just hours before her son would be nominated for the presidency. Both George and Barbara were interviewed on *ABC News* and George Bush said he would not be getting into any more spats with Clinton. "It was slippage," Barbara added, referring to Bush's remarks that he would give Clinton just a month to straighten up.

"No, no, I did what I wanted to do," Bush said to Barbara, "but they're making a federal case about it. It's better just to say nothing about it, future, now, nothing, period."

Further along in the interview Barbara implied that Clinton had lowered the standards for White House conduct and that Gore would not be able to restore respect for the office. "It would be very difficult, I think, with some of the things he's done," she said. "It's the presidency that we hold to a very high standard. I think George respects the presidency, so if there's any disappointment, that's the disappointment."

ABC reporter Charles Gibson asked: "What do you mean?"

"You know what I mean," Barbara replied. "I know George held it up and the people that worked for him, and I think that's what's disappointing."

Had disrespect been visited on the presidency?

"By unnamed persons," Barbara replied.

George tried to intervene several times, saying, "You are on a roll," and "She went further today than she should have."

"I don't care," Barbara replied.

At a political convention pretty much devoid of drama, this public effort by the senior Bushes to control themselves—and each other—was much talked about and widely reported in newspapers. Later in the day, Barbara was somewhat contrite. "I'm not going to do any more interviews," she said, "because I cannot resist defending our men."

Father Bush also tried to make amends, telling reporters, "I made a mistake by even commenting. This is a race between George W. Bush and Gore and neither Clinton nor I are key players in this race." And in an interview on *Fox News*, he said his son "probably wished I kept my mouth shut, but I haven't heard from him yet."

The parents had a lot more fun at different events Wednesday—a visit to the Florida delegation, where they were introduced with a flourish as surprise guests by their second son, Florida governor Jeb Bush. Throughout the week, Jeb and his handsome young son, George P., had been making jokes about Barbara.

On Monday, George P., twenty-four, called his grandmother "the en-

forcer" and said he she had told him "not to be a showoff like my grandfather and keep my speech to a few minutes."

Jeb combined his fond mockery of Mom with an arrow aimed at Gore,
who some years ago claimed there was a "controlling legal authority" that
made his questionable fund-raising tactics okay. Said Jeb: "The number
one reason George W. Bush should be elected president: there definitely
will be a controlling legal authority—Barbara Bush."

Wednesday ended with a Bush family dinner—sixty people toasting and
triumphant. The final votes that night gave George W. Bush the Republican presidential nomination and that, too, was something of a family
affair. Jeb delivered the ballots for Florida, which would later figure largely
in the outcome of the election, and Doro, the only sister among four Bush
boys, offered Maryland's vote for her big brother.

The final day of the convention, when George W. accepted the nomination and gave a rousing speech, was an emotional one for the entire
family—George and Barbara, Jeb and Doro and brothers Marvin and Neil,
were all in attendance. Jeb said he had lunch with his father before the
big speech and Dad was worried that he might get teary as he watched his
oldest son. Jeb told him, "Let it rip."

During his speech, George W. singled out both his parents for praise,
more serious for his father, fondly ribbing his mother.

"Dad, I am proud to be your son."

Mom, "who gave me love and lots of advice. I gave her white hair."

Afterward, with "Signed, Sealed and Delivered" blaring through the
hall, the Bushes converged onstage under heavy confetti and balloons and
wild applause, although former president Bush made a point to stay seated
so as not to horn in on his son's turn in the spotlight. It was the end of
another convention, an event long familiar to this family but one that must
have been especially satisfying for George and Barbara after the bitter
outcome eight years earlier. They would be doing everything possible to
help their son get elected. And as they left the city, polls showed George
W. with an 11-point edge over Al Gore.

How different from the mood eight years earlier when the elder Bush
was the underdog coming out of the convention and stayed that way
through Election Day. George W. had run a far superior convention, showcasing the softer side of the Republican party and keeping the harsh rhet-

oric, the right wing, and the abortion issue off in the shadows. He emphasized that Republicans could be compassionate as well as conservative and the carefully arranged multicultural mix that appeared before the nation illustrated the point.

The outcome was sweet for Barbara, who had long decried the darker tactics of political campaigns, even though she partook of them herself when she felt her men were threatened.

"One out of every eight Americans is governed by a Bush," Barbara playfully told a campaign rally, referring to the fact that her sons governed two large states, "and with your help we'll make that all Americans."

It was a difficult campaign for her, though. At age seventy-five she wasn't on the road constantly as she had been for her husband. "When you're seventy-five, you're not running around town like you used to," she said, and back surgery in September slowed her down even further. But she helped out where the campaign felt she could do the most good. With polls persistently showing Al Gore capturing the women's vote, Barbara agreed to visit three states in the Midwest with Laura on a bus tour that the campaign called "W is for Women," a play on George's widely used middle initial. Laura would be the main speaker and hold the news conferences on the tour. Barbara would be the big draw.

The tour began in mid-October in Grand Rapids, Michigan, where Barbara was introduced to a partisan crowd as the "most admired woman in the United States" and got the most applause among a group that included not only her daughter-in-law but also a number of local and state female political leaders. She told the crowd she would not be discussing issues— "I might make a mistake or worse" but would talk about the virtues of her firstborn son. "I never thought I'd be on the campaign trail again," she said. "But there's no doubt in my mind that George W. Bush must be the next president of the United States."

The crowd, mostly women, many holding babies, waved pompons to the beat of a high school marching band and many said they had come especially to see Barbara. "I respect Barbara Bush more than any first lady," Deb Cheadle of Rockford, Michigan, said. "She stands for things that are real and familiar to American families, not something that is not attainable for the rest of us."[1]

Barbara said that the 2000 campaign was difficult for her because she couldn't stand seeing her son attacked. In defense, she said, she had mostly stopped reading newspapers and watching television. "I'm famously loyal to my son," she said. "When they say things that aren't true, I get really upset."

Barbara admitted that she had not watched the first of three debates between George W. and Al Gore, "not because I didn't think he would be wonderful but because I thought I might get sore." But she said she was shamed into watching the final two debates and was appalled at the way Gore behaved, especially in the last debate in St. Louis where Gore moved close to Bush while waiting his turn to answer, prompting Bush to give Gore a dubious look that made the studio audience laugh. "I thought he was going to hit George," Barbara said on *ABC News*. "It sort of scared me."

But, characteristically, Barbara entertained the crowd of women with humor as well as making her political pitch. She told a prowomen joke, speculating what would have happened if women rather than wise men had visited the Baby Jesus: "You know what would have happened if it had been three wise women? They would have asked for directions, arrived on time, they would have helped deliver the baby, cleaned the stable, made a casserole, and brought practical gifts."

Another joke: A new business owner is puzzled to receive flowers with a note that says, "Rest in peace." He calls the florist, who is embarrassed and also worried about what the funeral home must have thought when it received flowers with a card that said, "Give 'em hell, big fella."

"If I try to go into details, I might make a similar mistake," Barbara said.

Of her son, she said, he will have no trouble in foreign policy because he has raised "two wonderful, strong-willed teenage daughters. Thanks to them, there's absolutely no doubt in my mind he will be able to negotiate with any country in the world, regardless of how difficult, complicated, or stubborn the opposition is."

From there it was on to Lansing, where Barbara told a small crowd that she would be campaigning two or three days a week during the final lap of the campaign.

Later, at Brighton, Michigan, a picturesque town of sixty thousand about forty miles from Detroit, Laura had a bit of fun with Barbara while giving a speech about the concerns of women, including looking after elderly parents. "You know, people my mother-in-law's age." Barbara tried to look outraged at this, prompting Laura to add, "Only kidding. I don't think I'll be looking after my mother-in-law. She'll be looking after me."

The two women walked down the town's main street, followed by a crowd of one thousand, signing autographs and posing for photos. "I think the average woman can relate to them," Margaret Dunleavy said. "I think our concerns are the same as theirs: education, a stable economy and a peaceful country."[2]

A poll by the *Detroit News* showed that Michigan was a dead heat at the time of Barbara's tour, with Bush 10 points ahead among men and Gore 10 points ahead among women. Pollster John Zogby said the Bush campaign was smart to send Barbara and Laura Bush into the state to attract votes from undecided women. "Bush's wife is not Hillary and his mother is very popular," Zogby said. "Barbara Bush has always been a secret weapon because she is likable, honest, straightforward and a role model in a sort of white-haired, traditional way that is almost lost in most campaigns."[3]

Barbara was asked at most of the stops why her son was losing to Gore on the women's vote. She promptly turned the question around: Why was Gore behind among male voters? And she added, "It insults me as a woman a little bit that people believe we think differently than men about the important issues."

She also parried with reporters on the issue of abortion. George W. made plain during the campaign that he is against abortion while Barbara favors abortion rights. But rather than undercut her son's position, she said, "I agree with him on almost ninety-nine percent of things and shortly I'm going to agree with him on one hundred if people don't stop bringing up the subject." And she argued that the Republican party is more open on the question than Democrats: "George has made the Republicans more inclusive," she said. "We had prolife and prochoice people speak at our convention. How many prolife people spoke at the Democratic convention?"

Laura did not say how she felt on abortion during the campaign but after Bush won, she announced during a TV interview that she wouldn't want to overturn the Supreme Court ruling that made abortion legal, a stance different from her husband's.

The second and third days of the bus tour were in Pennsylvania, which like Michigan was a toss-up in the polls two weeks before the election. In Philadelphia, Laura and Barbara toured a cancer center and Laura told cancer survivors that her own mother had been successfully treated for breast cancer that was discovered through a routine mammogram. She and Barbara listened to the stories of women who were fighting cancer, and offered sympathy and encouragement. "You're a point of light," Barbara told one woman and gave many an "Atta girl" after hearing each tale.

One of the women told reporters later that she had been impressed enough by the Bush women to reconsider her vote. She had been leaning toward Gore but was now willing to take a new look at George W.

Later, at a rally in Blue Bell, Pennsylvania, Barbara told a rally that George W. has "always been surrounded by strong women. Sometimes by choice, sometimes by birth."

And while she generally avoided direct attacks on Gore, she told the audience in Blue Bell, "Al Gore is exaggerating again, this time on social security. He's trying to scare old people like me. But it's not going to work this time because we're smarter than that."

Barbara's campaign week ended in Pittsburgh on a down note. Reports had surfaced the previous day that George W. Bush had been convicted of drunken driving in Maine twenty-four years earlier. Barbara, at a brunch with hundreds of Republican women, called the charges "much ado about nothing." Instant polls showed that voters mostly agreed, irritated that charges lodged a quarter century earlier were sprung in the final days of the presidential campaign.

Barbara's Pittsburgh appearance focused heavily on social security and she excoriated the Democrats for implying that George W. would weaken social security or Medicare. "Do you think this white-haired old mother would allow him to wreck social security or Medicare?" she said. "Absolutely not."

Barbara also tape-recorded a message on social security for the Republican party in Florida, which distributed a letter from her as well. These missives weren't always well received.

"Without seeming cynical, I find it difficult to have confidence in someone who resorts to using a glowing letter ostensibly by his mother to garner votes," Alan Julian of Delray Beach, Florida, wrote to the *Sun-Sentinel* in Fort Lauderdale. "It reminds me of a parent writing a letter to her son's teacher not to punish her son because he really is a good little boy."[4]

Barbara's recorded message also asked voters to call an 800 number to show their support, which caused a problem for a limousine driver in Washington, D.C. Mohammed Hasanian told *The Washington Post* that a phone number he had for clients was the same as the one Barbara Bush was using and he was getting lots of calls from Republicans who wanted to show their support for Bush—and a few from people who didn't. "This morning one guy told me, 'Tell that . . . not to leave me any more messages or I'm going to sue.'"[5]

That didn't intimidate Barbara, of course. The phone messages continued though the campaign apologized to Hasanian for the mix-up in numbers.

In the midst of the "W is for Women" tour, Barbara got off the bus for a day and joined her husband in a heavily Republican Chicago suburb for a paid speaking event that had been arranged almost a year earlier by Illinois Benedictine University. The event, billed as part of a Great Issues Great Ideas lecture series, was said to be nonpolitical event, even though it was scheduled just days before the national election. So both Barbara and George tried to stay off campaign topics but couldn't resist a few segues into politics.

Barbara said she wouldn't be mentioning her son's campaign because "George W. is doing just fine without his mother trying to help." But, she joked, she had become hooked on the TV show *Survivor* because, "George and I know what it's like to be voted off the island."

When Barbara finished her fifteen-minute speech, George walked across the stage and gave her a long kiss—the *Chicago Sun-Times* said eight seconds, the *Chicago Tribune* said ten seconds—to good-naturedly make fun of the long kiss that Gore had planted on Tipper after her speech at the Democratic National Convention. The crowd howled. "Listen," Bush said, "after fifty-six years of marriage you learn how to do certain things."

In the final days of the campaign, Barbara spent most of her time in the Midwest, making appearances in Missouri, Minnesota, and stopping several times in Michigan and Wisconsin. Shaking hands with voters in

Green Bay, Wisconsin, two days before the election, she was asked whether the fact that George W. had once been arrested for drunken driving should matter to voters. "No," she said. "That was twenty-four years ago. He regrets it. It was a mistake."

The Bush campaign had given Barbara a difficult task—shore up support among women in states where the candidates were neck and neck going into the final days of the campaign. In the end, despite her best efforts, George W. lost Michigan, Pennsylvania, Illinois, and Minnesota. He won in Wisconsin and Missouri.

By Election Day, Barbara was back home in Houston. Her son called early Tuesday morning and found both his parents edgy, telling reporters later, "It's much harder to be the loved one than to be the candidate. I can understand why they're nervous. They're nervous for the vote. They're nervous for me personally."

Later in the day, the senior Bushes flew to Austin, the state capital, to be with their son as he awaited election results. They had a big family dinner in a restaurant and as the evening began, just about everyone was in a celebratory mood. The early exit polls looked good. The young campaign staff, in a nearby hotel, was ready to party. The senior aides were talking confidently of victory.

All that changed when the results began to roll in. At midevening, when the TV networks announced that Al Gore had won Florida, there was a complete turnabout in mood in Austin. The candidate, his wife, and his parents got up abruptly and left the restaurant.

It would be a very, very long night.

A LEGACY FULFILLED

The news wasn't good. The TV networks had announced that George W. Bush had lost Florida. They were wrong, of course. But the nation wouldn't know for sure for another thirty-six days.

George W. sat on a sofa in the Texas governor's mansion between his wife and his mother and joked with reporters about the TV projections. "The people who are actually counting the votes are coming up with a little different perspective," he said. "And so we're pretty darn upbeat about things."

Barbara said she had not been up so late in years. Former president Bush said the suspense was more difficult for him than it had been when his own presidency was on the line. He added that he was feeling "nervous and proud."

"Ditto," Barbara said.

After the TV networks reversed themselves and gave Florida to Bush, Democratic presidential candidate Al Gore called to concede. Then, very late in the evening, in an extraordinary first, the networks reversed themselves for the second time and said that Florida was too close to call. Gore telephoned to take back his concession.

It was becoming clear by this time that whoever won Florida would win the election.

An aide described the family's emotions when Florida was taken away from Bush: "The governor was pretty calm but it was frosty in that room. The boys [Jeb and George W.] avoided looking at each other too much. Jeb initially was dumbstruck and started to hit the phones and then reassured his brother that the television was just plain wrong. The old man [Bush senior], well, you could see the ghosts of 1992 coming back. And Barbara Bush. She just looked real pained.

"The only thing they could think of was to take the unprecedented step of calling in the press and flatly refusing to concede Florida while looking blissfully calm," the source said. "It took a lot for them to do that—especially for Laura and President Bush. Barbara Bush is just a trouper. I have no idea how she managed to crack jokes."[1]

The next day, with the election far from settled, Barbara and George flew home to Houston. George W. called his father's old campaign manager, James Baker, to help coordinate the battle for the presidency as it moved into Florida and the court system.

In the long weeks that followed, the nation became familiar with the term "hanging chads," and with Florida's woefully inadequate balloting system. A Democratic election official in Palm Beach County who had designed one of the worst ballots lost twenty pounds in her angst over the outcome. The Bush and Gore camps each spent millions of dollars to hire the best legal minds in America to try to sway the outcome on what was essentially a tie in Florida.

But even as they duked it out in a quest to triumph in both public opinion and the courtroom, there was no constitutional crisis as there might have been in many countries. For many Americans, life went on as usual. And even in Washington, there was civility between the warring parties.

A few days after it became clear that no winner was going to emerge from the election anytime soon, George and Barbara Bush spent an extraordinary evening with the enemy in Washington.

The occasion was the two hundredth anniversary of the White House itself and President Bill Clinton invited all the former presidents and first ladies to join in the celebration of two hundred years of democracy, including the senior Bushes. Topic A that evening among these seasoned politicians was another historic moment—the impasse between George W.

and Al Gore—and whether George Bush the elder would find himself in a face-to-face confrontation with Clinton after the recent unpleasantness between them.

Social grace prevailed, however. George Bush had had good manners drilled into him from the time he could sit up and they didn't fail him this evening. He was gracious and smiling all evening and even seen in benign conversation with an equally gracious Clinton. And Hillary Clinton said that the Bushes were "classy" for coming.

Barbara joked that, "I was the mother of a president for thirty minutes and I loved it."

It was quite a gathering. Besides the Clintons and Bushes, there were Jimmy and Rosalynn Carter, Gerald and Betty Ford, and Lady Bird Johnson, widow of President Lyndon Johnson. The only recent president missing was Ronald Reagan, felled by Alzheimer's disease, and Nancy Reagan wasn't there either.

At the head table, Lady Bird Johnson sat between George Bush and Bill Clinton, Barbara Bush was between Gerald Ford and Jimmy Carter, and Hillary Clinton was between her husband and Gerald Ford. In other words the Clintons had clearly designed the seating so that neither Clinton was forced to make dinner conversation with either Bush.

Barbara wore black satin pumps and a long black silk dress with white polka dots along with her usual three strings of pearls. The dress was by her longtime favorite designer, Arnold Scaasi. Over her shoulder was a black shawl.[2]

Rosalynn Carter was also in black—a silk crepe knee-length suit by Louis Feraud—and she wore pearls and black silk shoes as well.

Hillary Clinton, fresh from winning the New York Senate race where she was mostly in black pantsuits, chose a gold Oscar de la Renta floor-length gown with a button-down bodice and flared skirt.

Lady Bird Johnson wore a fur-cuffed brown dress by Victor Costa. Betty Ford chose a long sheath dress with a matching jacket in sapphire blue.

The two hundred guests enjoyed a five-course meal designed around foods served two hundred years ago—duck consommé, striped bass, smoked lamb, cheese, and a floating island dessert created by Abigail Adams.

The head table dined on a new set of presidential china with service plates that featured an engraving of the White House set within a wide gold border. The three hundred twelve-piece place settings cost $240,000, paid by the nonprofit White House Historical Association.[3]

"In the entire two hundred years of the White House's history, never before have this many former presidents and first ladies gathered in this great room," Clinton said.

Presidential historian Carl Sferrazza Anthony said the first time two presidents dined together at the White House was exactly two centuries earlier when John Adams invited Thomas Jefferson to dinner.

At the time, the two men were awaiting the outcome of the election of 1800 in which Jefferson was challenging the incumbent Adams. "The results were not in," Anthony said. "It was December when it was finally decided." Jefferson, in the Democratic party of his day, won.

Barbara didn't spend much time in public during the long weeks of court battles over the election but when she did appear, it was clear she was holding up well under the pressure.

"We sort of feel like the VCR is stuck on pause," she said during a speech in Cleveland, Ohio, in early December. "We are nervous but we're really doing just fine, taking each day and each court ruling as it comes."

She joked that her fifty-five-year marriage had included "fourteen grandchildren, four wars, three dress sizes, two parachute jumps, two governors and three recounts."[4]

A few days after that speech, the family suffered another blow. Former president Bush entered the Mayo Clinic in Rochester, Minesota, to have his left hip replaced, the same operation Barbara had gone through, at the same clinic, in 1997. Bush, like most of the tens of thousands who have the surgery done each year, recovered quickly.

Bush left the hospital and flew home to Houston on December 9. Four days later, on Wednesday, December 13, Al Gore conceded and George W. Bush became the president-elect. It was a sweet moment for the entire family even though the win ultimately came through a decision by the U.S. Supreme Court and despite the fact that Bush would be the first president since Benjamin Harrison in 1888 to win the election but lose the popular vote. Bush got just 271 votes in the electoral college, one more than the number needed to win. Gore finished with 267.

When the court made its decision late Tuesday evening, George W.

telephoned his parents with the news. They were already in bed, a clear sign that the days when election turmoil was at the center of their lives were over. George and Barbara had passed on the torch of worry to their oldest son.

The signs of relief were evident. In an interview with *Newsweek* a few days after the Supreme Court decision, Barbara took on the role of protective mother again. "We're very excited for [George and Laura]," she said. "You be nice to him, now. I want to start reading magazines and papers again ... I'm going to start reading again. But I'm giving you fair warning."

In an interview with ABC TV's *This Week*, Papa Bush took a more positive tone, saying that he and Barbara were "bursting with pride."

"It's hard to describe, to quantify," he said. "But it's strictly the pride of a father and, in Barbara's case, a mother, in a son."

George and Barbara spent Christmas that year in Houston with Neil and his family. The new president elect stayed at the state capital in Austin with Laura, their twin daughters, and Laura's mother, Jenna Welch. The holiday was interrupted when one of the twins, Jenna, was taken to the hospital for an emergency appendectomy.

During the week after Christmas, the extended Bush family did what many Americans do to escape the dull chill of winter—they went to Florida for a couple of days. Laura Bush stayed behind with her hospitalized daughter but George W., his parents, most of his siblings, and a spattering of nieces and nephews gathered in Gasparilla Island, which had been a favored Bush retreat ever since the elder Bush lost the presidency in 1992.

Their headquarters was the Gasparilla Inn, which since 1913 has been a popular retreat with old-money families, a place where the furniture is good but worn, and the fine wood floors creak charmingly. The family got a noisy welcome from well-wishers and George W. shook some hands before heading straight to the golf course with his brother Jeb and Jeb's son, George P. Mom and Dad rode along in a golf cart, but didn't play.

The next day much of the family went fishing but Barbara took her dog for a walk through the quiet streets of the five-block town. It would be one of the quietest times she had before the stress and excitement of the January inauguration.

Actually, the weeks heading up to the inauguration were full of fun for the senior Bushes. They saw old friends, attended fund-raisers, and hung out as a family. Barbara went to a charity ball that benefited the Chron's and Colitis Foundation of America, the disease that had struck her son Marvin. She also was on hand when Sharon Bush, wife of son Neil, was honored as one of thirteen Women of Distinction by ABC in Texas.

There was a stop in New York City where Barbara spent time getting fitted out for the ceremonies to come. After seeing the play *Contact* on Broadway and talking with star Deborah Yates about their common Texas heritage, she stopped in at the salon of Arnold Scaasi, who had designed seven outfits for her to wear during the high-profile weeks ahead. Among them were two long gowns, one in blue, of course, but another in black. There was also a coral coat and a blue coat with matching dress and a red coat dress with brass buttons.

"It's a much slimmer look for Barbara than before," Scaasi said. "She's in great shape. The black dress especially is a departure."[5]

Women's Wear Daily also reported that George Bush had finally replaced the Kenneth Jay Lane fake pearls that Barbara had long worn. She now had the real thing.

Barbara wore the black dress at a fund-raiser she and George dropped in on in Washington, along with their daughter Doro, a few days before the election.

But the harsh politics of the weeks between the election and the inauguration were not forgotten by either Barbara or George. The former president, standing next to Barbara and George P. at a party given by James Baker, gave vent to his frustrations.

"I think one of the things that troubled me most were the gratuitous attacks on this boy's father," George Bush said, referring to grandson George P. "The attacks on Jeb Bush, the governor, the most honorable, honest man in the world. It really burned me up, Barbara, too."

Then realizing how such bitter comments might sound during what was supposed to be a celebration, Bush added, "I don't know why I'm going off on this tangent but this seems like a friendly crowd." And so it was. The party was given in honor of the senior Bush by James Baker, the man who had led the recent fight to give George W. the presidency.[6]

The day before her husband was sworn in as president, Laura Bush stepped into the spotlight briefly, telling a national TV audience on ABC's

20/20 that she did not think abortion should be outlawed, a clear change from her position during the campaign. But she said she also supported efforts to limit the number of abortions "by teaching abstinence, having abstinence classes everywhere in schools, in churches, in Sunday schools." Barbara Bush, also in favor of abortion rights, had not revealed her own position on the controversial issue until her husband left office.

On the same day, Laura, a former school teacher and librarian, staged a celebration for books and authors, highlighting literacy in the same way Barbara—"my mother in law and friend" had during her term in the White House.

"Traditionally, inaugurations include a tribute to the first lady," Laura said. "I'd like to depart from that tradition by making this occasion a tribute to the thousands of people who have affected my life and all of our lives—our great American authors."

The event began with a short film introducing Laura to the nation. In it, Barbara said that after George W. became governor of Texas, "Laura sort of took charge in her own gentle, quiet way. She knew immediately what to do and how to do it."

The night before the inauguration, the Bush clan—twenty-four people in all—stayed at the elegant Blair House on Pennsylvania Avenue right across the street from the White House. But there were many, many more Bushes around town, an estimated five hundred all trying to get tickets to the many inaugural balls like everyone else. George and Barbara didn't attend the balls, though, having been through enough of them already. Far from being elegant and exclusive, most of the balls are uncomfortably reminiscent of cattle roundups with people stuffed in every corner of gargantuan spaces, little to eat or drink and a long wait for the new president and first lady to take a brief turn around a dance stage before moving on to the next overstuffed event.

The weather for the inauguration was miserably cold and rainy. Barbara wore her trademark blue to the ceremonies, but ever practical, covered up with a clear plastic rain poncho. Her eyes were red with emotion and both her husband and son had tears in their eyes.

George W. was sworn in as the forty-third president of the United States on the same Bible his father had used in 1989, a 234-year-old King James version, and his parents gave him a pair of silver cufflinks, first owned by

Prescott Bush, a U.S. senator and father of George Herbert Walker Bush, who wore them at his own inauguration in 1953.

After George W. took the oath of office at 12:03 P.M. January 20, he reached for his father's hand and hugged him. Barbara watched them both fondly.

"The look on their faces is hard to articulate: a beaming sense of pride and at the same time a sense of awe," said Rep. Mark Foley, a Florida Republican who sat near the family during the emotional ceremonies. "Mr. Bush was crying and Mrs. Bush's eyes were rimmed in red."[7]

Afterward, George W., his wife, and parents attended a traditional luncheon given by congressional leaders for new presidents in Statuary Hall. Among those sipping champagne and eating lobster pie was former President Jimmy Carter, the man whom Ronald Reagan and George Bush had defeated in 1988. The younger Bush recognized Carter, and also paid tribute to his parents: "Today is a testimony to two wonderful parents, people who instilled values and gave unconditional love," he said. Barbara got a standing ovation.

As the new president began his way along the inaugural parade, his parents went straight to the White House and later settled into the reviewing stand, cheering lustily for much of the afternoon. They spent the night in the Queen's Bedroom in the White House on the first night the new first family was in residence, the room that Barbara knew so well, along with all of its history. The next morning, the family went to the National Prayer Service at the sumptuous National Cathedral in Washington. The Rev. Billy Graham had led the service for years but is now too ill to do the job, so his son Franklin carried on the tradition, telling the Bushes, "You all have the opportunity to once again ignite the soul of America."

It was the beginning of a new era for the Bush family. As George and Barbara headed back to Houston to give their son his own time in the spotlight, George Sr. expressed the hope that both parents fervently felt.

"Be nice to my boy," he said.

When the Bushes left Washington this time, it was with a mission fulfilled. Though they strenuously denied they were seeking revenge for George Bush's devastating loss to Bill Clinton, there was no denying the satisfaction that came with having another Bush in the White House, with the possibility of more to come.

Barbara's place in history already is assured since she is only the second woman in history, along with Abigail Adams, to have both a husband and son as president. Perhaps she eventually will become the grand matriarch of a political dynasty, stretching all the way back to her grandfather, an Ohio state supreme court justice, all the way to her grandson, George P., and beyond. As long as her children and grandchildren still come home, she wouldn't mind this role at all.

CHAPTER NOTES

1

1. Megan Garvey, *Los Angeles Times*, Aug. 2, 2000, p. A18.
2. David Broder, *The Washington Post*, Jan. 20, 2001, p. P1
3. Glenn F. Bunting, *The Los Angeles Times*, May 31, 1992, p. M3.
4. Kati Marton, *Hidden Power: Presidential Marriages That Shaped Our Recent History*. Pantheon Books, 2001, p. 264.
5. Barbara Feinman, *The Washington Post*, Nov. 14, 1989, p. B6.
6. Paul Burka, *Texas Monthly*, Nov. 1997, p. 136.
7. Carolyn Barta, *Dallas Morning News*, Oct. 3, 1994, Viewpoint, p. 11A.

2

1. Donnie Radcliffe, *Simply Barbara Bush*. Warner Books, 1989, p. 73.
2. Myrna Blyth, *Ladies Home Journal*, Dec. 1991, p. 93.
3. Cory Servaas. *Saturday Evening Post*, Oct. 1988, p. 46–47.
4. Radcliffe, *Simply Barbara Bush*, p. 79.
5. Frank P. Jarrell, *The News and Courier*, Charleston, South Carolina, Feb. 10, 1980.

3

1. George Bush with Victor Gold, *Looking Forward*. Doubleday, 1987, p. 31.
2. Patricia McCarthy, *The News and Courier*, Charleston, South Carolina, June 4, 1984.
3. A&E cable channel, Barbara Bush biography, broadcast summer 2001.
4. Joe Hyams, *Flight of the Avenger*. Harcourt Brace Jovanovich, 1991, p. 55.
5. Smith College, *Associates News*, Nov. 5, 1943, p. 2.
6. Hyams, *Flight of the Avenger*, p. 68.
7. George Bush with Victor Gold, *Looking Forward*, p. 23.
8. Cathleen Decker, *Los Angeles Times*, Aug. 7, 1988, p. 1.

4

1. George Bush, *American West*, Jan.–Feb. 1986, p. 37.
2. Jean Libman Block, Good Housekeeping, Nov. 1989, p. 255.
3. A&E cable channel, Barbara Bush biography, broadcast summer 2001.
4. Donnie Radcliffe, *Simply Barbara Bush*. Warner Books, 1989, p. 111.
5. Jean Becker, *USA Today*, April 5, 1988, p. A8.
6. Kathy Lewis, *Houston Post*, June 29, 1986, p. A1.
7. Doug Wead, *George Bush, Man of Integrity*. Harvest House, 1988, p. 46–47.
8. Radcliffe, *Simply Barbara Bush*, p. 119.

5

1. Doug Wead, *George Bush, Man of Integrity*, p. 118.
2. Jean Libman Block, *Good Housekeeping*, Nov. 1989, p. 255.
3. A&E cable channel, Barbara Bush biography, broadcast summer 2001.
4. Betsy Cuniberti, *Los Angeles Times*, Nov. 20, 1988, View section, p. 1.
5. Mary Leonard, *Boston Globe*, Nov. 18, 1998, p. A1.
6. David Maraniss, *The Washington Post* magazine, Jan 22, 1989, p. 14.
7. Sam Howe Verhovek, *The New York Times Magazine*, Sept. 13, 1998, p. 52.
8. Rick Lyman and Mireya Navarro, *The New York Times*, Nov. 4, 1998, p. B1.
9. David Maraniss, *The Washington Post* magazine, Jan 22, 1989, p. 14.
10. Susan Schindehette, *People*, Jan. 30, 1989, p. 63.
11. Marvin Bush, *Ladies Home Journal*, Mar. 1989, p. 193.
12. Cory Servaas, *Saturday Evening Post*, Oct. 1988, p. 71–72.
13. *Good Housekeeping*, April 1989, p. 233.
14. Cindy Adams, *Ladies Home Journal*, Nov. 1990, p. 276.

6

1. Peter Wallstein, *St. Petersburg Times*, Oct. 18, 1998, p. A7.
2. Cindy Adams, *Ladies Home Journal*, Oct. 1988, p. 154.
3. A&E cable channel, Barbara Bush biography, broadcast summer 2001.
4. George Bush with Victor Gold, *Looking Forward*. Doubleday, 1987, p. 101.
5. Cindy Adams, *Ladies Home Journal*, Jul. 1986, p. 130.
6. Doug Wead, *George Bush, Man of Integrity*. Harvest House, 1988, p. 136.
7. Kenneth T. Walsh, *U.S. News & World Report*, May 28, 1990, p. 25–26.
8. Donnie Radcliffe, *Simply Barbara Bush*. Warner Books, 1989, p. 57.
9. Douglas Kneeland, *The New York Times*, Nov. 6, 1980, p. A25.
10. Joyce Purnick, *The New York Times*, Jul. 18, 1989, p. A10.
11. Betty Beale, *The Washington Star*, Oct. 19, 1980.
12. Donnie Radcliffe, *The Washington Post*, Oct. 18, 1980, p. B5.

7

1. Nina Hyde, Jura Koncius, *The Washington Post*, Jan. 21, 1981, Style section, p. E3.
2. Gloria Borger, *Savvy*, Aug. 1983, p. 43.
3. Joy Billington, *Washington Star*, Mar. 8, 1981, p. G2.
4. Gloria Borger, *Savvy*, Aug. 1983, p. 42–43.
5. John Robinson, *Boston Globe*, Dec. 21, 1988, p. 1.
6. Diane Casselberry Manuel, *Christian Science Monitor*, Jul. 10, 1984, p. 25.
7. Marjorie Hunter, *The New York Times*, Apr. 25, 1982.

8. Donnie Radcliffe, *The Washington Post*, June 5, 1988, p. F4.
9. Joan Nathan, *McCall's*, May 7, 1986, p. 129–132.
10. Kathy Lewis, *Houston Post*, March 17, 1985, p. A1.
11. Ibid.
12. Cindy Adams, *Ladies Home Journal*, Jul. 1986, p. 131.

8

1. Kathy Lewis, *Houston Post*, Oct. 11, 1987, p. A20.
2. Barbara Bush and Jean Becker, *USA Today*, Aug. 15, 1988, p. A4.
3. Barbara Bush and Jean Becker, *USA Today*, Aug. 16, 1988, p. A4.
4. Donnie Radcliffe, *The Washington Post*, Oct. 30, 1988, p. A13.
5. Barbara Bush and Jean Becker, *USA Today*, Oct. 17, 1988, p. A13.
6. Carol Horner, *Philadelphia Inquirer*, Oct. 23, 1988, p. K1.
7. David Kaplan, Houston Post, Oct. 16, 1988, p. G1.
8. Sue Reilly, *Los Angeles Daily News*, Oct. 19, 1988.
9. Barbara Bush and Jean Becker, *USA Today*, Oct. 31, 1988, p. A11.

9

1. Donnie Radcliffe, *The Washington Post*, Feb. 1, 1989, p. B8.
2. Thomas DeFrank and Ann McDaniels, *Newsweek*, Jan. 23, 1989, p. 25.
3. Kathy Lewis, *Houston Post*, May 17, 1989.
4. Dodie Kazanjians, *House & Garden*, June 1989, p. 141–144.
5. Kathy Lewis, *Houston Post*, June 4, 1989, p. F1.
6. Ann McFeatters, Scripps Howard News Service, June 2, 1989.
7. Donnie Radcliffe, *The Washington Post*, July 17, 1989, p. B1.
8. Donnie Radcliffe, *The Washington Post*, Jan. 21, 1990, p. F1.

10

1. Susan Baer, *Baltimore Sun*, April 27, 1990, p. 1F, 5F.
2. Ibid.
3. *The New York Times*, June 1, 1990, Editorial page.
4. Ellen Goodman, *Boston Globe*, April 22, 1990, p. A27.
5. Peggy Reid, *The New York Times*, May 16, 1990, p. A27.
6. David Stoughton, *Los Angeles Times*, May 21, 1990, p. 6.
7. Kenneth Walsh, *U.S. News & World Report*, May 28, 1990, p. 25–27.
8. Associated Press, *The New York Times*, May 20, 1990, p. 26.
9. Tom Shales, *The Washington Post*, June 2, 1990, p. C1.
10. Fox Butterfield *The New York Times*, June 2, 1990, p. 5.
11. Rania Nagulb, *Los Angeles Times*, June 8, 1990, p. B6.

11

1. Cory Servaas, *Saturday Evening Post*, October 1988, p. 48–49.
2. John Ensor Harr, *Saturday Evening Post*, December 1988, p. 43–44.
3. *The Washington Post*, April 11, 1981, p. A12.
4. Marian Christy, *Boston Globe*, Feb. 26, 1991.
5. Trude B. Feldman, *McCall's*, September 1988, p. 83.
6. Barbara Bush with Jean Becker, *USA Today*, Oct. 3, 1988, p. A9.
7. Donnie Radcliffe, *The Washington Post*, Feb. 15, 1989, p. C1.
8. Edward Klein, *Parade*, May 21, 1989, p. 4.

9. Lois Romano, *The Washington Post*, March 23, 1989, p. D5.

10. Art Harris, *The Washington Post*, May 15, 1989, p. C4.

11. Barbara Kantrowitz and Ann McDaniel, *Newsweek*, July 10, 1989, p. 44.

12. Jean Libman Block, *Good Housekeeping*, p. 254.

13. *Reader's Digest*, October 1990 as excerpted by Scripps Howard News Service, Sept. 5, 1990.

14. Jim Brosseau, *New Choices*, May 1990, p. 71.

12

1. Paula Chin, *People*, October 1990, p. 84.

2. Donnie Radcliffe, *The Washington Post*, Nov. 23, 1990, p. C4.

3. Landon Jones and Maria Wilhelm, *People*, Dec. 17, 1990, p. 49.

13

1. Karen Dewitt, *The New York Times*, May 14, p. A24.

2. Ann McFeatters, Scripps Howard News Service, published July 20, 1991, *St. Petersburg Times*, p. A21.

3. Carey Goldberg, *Los Angeles Times*, July 31, 1991, p. A9.

4. Susan Page, *Newsday*, Oct. 16, 1991, p. 19.

5. Myrna Blyth, *Ladies Home Journal*, December 1991, p. 93.

6. Ellen Warren, Knight-Ridder, published in the *Orlando-Sentinel Tribune*, June 23, 1991, p. A4.

14

1. Donnie Radcliffe, *The Washington Post*, Jan 9, 1992, Style section, p. D1.

2. Donnie Radcliffe, *The Washington Post*, Feb. 26, 1992, p. A30.

3. Marla Williams, *Seattle Times*, April 15, 1992, p. B6.

4. Glenn F. Bunting, *Los Angeles Times*, May 31, 1992, Opinion section, p. 3.

5. Jane Ely, *Houston Chronicle*, Jan. 21, 1992, Outlook section, p. 2.

6. Michael Duffy, *Time*, Aug. 24, 1992, p. 26.

7. E. J. Dionne, *The Washington Post*, Aug 14, 1992, p. A20.

8. Allesandra Stanley, *The New York Times*, Aug. 19, 1992, p. A15.

9. Anne Hull, *The Washington Post*, Jan. 20, 2001, p. P18.

10. Martin Kasindorf, *Los Angeles Times* magazine, July 23, 1995, p. 6.

11. Elizabeth Gleick, *People*, Oct. 3, 1994, p. 144.

15

1. Elizabeth Gleick, *People*, Oct. 3, 1994, p. 144.

2. Barton Gellman, Ann Devroy, *The Washington Post*, May 8, 1993, p. A1.

3. Elizabeth Gleick, *People*, Oct. 3, 1944, p. 144.

4. Margo Hammond, *St. Petersburg Times*, Oct. 10, 1994, p. A1.

5. Rick Lyman with Mireya Navarro, *The New York Times* News Service, published Nov. 9, 1998, *The Commercial Appeal* (Memphis), p. A2.

6. Paul Burka, *Texas Monthly*, November 1997, p. 136.

7. S. C. Gwynne, *Time*, June 8, 1998, p. 54.

8. Peter Wallsten, *St. Petersburg Times*, May 17, 1998, p. B1.

9. Sam Howe Verhovek, *The New York Times*, Sept. 13, 1998, sect. 6, p. 52.

16

1. Mary Leonard, *Boston Globe*, Oct. 19, 2000, p. A24.
2. Christy Hoppe, *Dallas Morning News*, Oct. 19, 2000, p. A1.
3. Mary Leonard, *Boston Globe*, Oct. 19, 2000, p. A24.
4. Alan Julian, *Sun-Sentinel*, Oct. 22, 2000, Op Ed page, p. H4.
5. Lloyd Grove, *The Washington Post*, Oct. 17, 2000, The Reliable Source, Style Section, p. C3.

17

1. Jamie Dettmer, *The Washington Times*, *Insight* magazine, Dec. 4, 2000, p. 19.
2. Candace Wedlan, *Los Angeles Times*, Nov. 16, 2000, p. E2.
3. Roxanne Roberts, Beth Berselli, *The Washington Post*, Nov. 10, 2000, Style Section, p. C1.
4. Sarah Treffinger, *Cleveland Plain Dealer*, Dec. 1, 2000, Metro Section, p. B3.
5. *Women's Wear Daily*, Jan. 18, 2001, p. 4.
6. Todd J. Gillman, *Dallas Morning News*, Jan. 20, 2001, p. 24.
7. William Gibson, *Sun-Sentinel* (Fort Lauderdale, Fla.,) Jan. 21, 2001, p. A1.

INDEX